OTHEA'S LETTER TO HECTOR

The Other Voice in Early Modern Europe:
The Toronto Series, 57

MEDIEVAL AND RENAISSANCE
TEXTS AND STUDIES

VOLUME 521

The Other Voice in
Early Modern Europe:
The Toronto Series

SERIES EDITORS Margaret L. King *and* Albert Rabil, Jr.
SERIES EDITOR, ENGLISH TEXTS Elizabeth H. Hageman

Previous Publications in the Series

The Other Voice in
Early Modern Europe:
The Toronto Series

SERIES EDITORS Margaret L. King *and* Albert Rabil, Jr.
SERIES EDITOR, ENGLISH TEXTS Elizabeth H. Hageman

Previous Publications in the Series

The Other Voice in Early Modern Europe: The Toronto Series

SERIES EDITORS Margaret L. King *and* Albert Rabil, Jr.
SERIES EDITOR, ENGLISH TEXTS Elizabeth H. Hageman

Previous Publications in the Series

The Other Voice in
Early Modern Europe:
The Toronto Series

SERIES EDITORS Margaret L. King *and* Albert Rabil, Jr.
SERIES EDITOR, ENGLISH TEXTS Elizabeth H. Hageman

Previous Publications in the Series

The Other Voice in
Early Modern Europe:
The Toronto Series

SERIES EDITORS Margaret L. King *and* Albert Rabil, Jr.
SERIES EDITOR, ENGLISH TEXTS Elizabeth H. Hageman

Previous Publications in the Series

The Other Voice in
Early Modern Europe:
The Toronto Series

SERIES EDITORS Margaret L. King *and* Albert Rabil, Jr.
SERIES EDITOR, ENGLISH TEXTS Elizabeth H. Hageman

Previous Publications in the Series

CHRISTINE DE PIZAN

Othea's Letter to Hector

≈

Edited and translated by

RENATE BLUMENFELD-KOSINSKI
and
EARL JEFFREY RICHARDS

Iter Press
Toronto, Ontario

Arizona Center for Medieval and Renaissance Studies
Tempe, Arizona

2017

Iter Press
Tel: 416/978–7074   Email: iter@utoronto.ca
Fax: 416/978–1668   Web: www.itergateway.org

Arizona Center for Medieval and Renaissance Studies
Tel: 480/965–5900   Email: mrts@acmrs.org
Fax: 480/965–1681   Web: acmrs.org

Library of Congress Cataloging-in-Publication Data

Names: Christine, de Pisan, approximately 1364-approximately 1431. | Blumenfeld-Kosinski, Renate,
    1952- editor, translator. | Richards, Earl Jeffrey, editor, translator.
Title: Othea's letter to Hector / Christine de Pizan ; edited and translated by Renate Blumenfeld-
    Kosinski and Earl Jeffrey Richards.
Other titles: Epître d'Othéa à Hector. English
Description: Toronto, Ontario : Iter Press ; Tempe, Arizona : Arizona Center for Medieval and
    Renaissance Studies, 2017. | Series: The other voice in early modern Europe: the Toronto series ;
    Volume 57 | Series: Medieval and renaissance texts and studies ; 521 | Includes bibliographical
    references and index.
Identifiers: LCCN 2017012842 | ISBN 9780866985772 (pbk. : alk. paper)
Classification: LCC PQ1575.E5 E55 2017 | DDC 841/.2--dc23
LC record available at https://lccn.loc.gov/2017012842

Cover illustration:
Frontispiece (fol. 1 v) of manuscript Paris, Bibliothèque nationale de France, fonds français 606, "The
Duke's Manuscript," containing only Christine de Pizan's *Othea's Letter to Hector*. The goddess Othea
presents her letter to Hector. Reproduced courtesy of the Bibliothèque nationale de France.

Cover design:
Maureen Morin, Information Technology Services, University of Toronto Libraries.

Typesetting and production:
Todd Halvorsen.

Contents

Introduction

The Other Voice

No other late medieval woman writer has received the attention that Christine de Pizan has garnered over the last thirty years or so. When we were in graduate school in the late 1970s, no modern English translations of her works existed, and many of her works did not yet exist in critical editions.[1] All this has changed today with numerous new editions and translations of her texts. It would perhaps not be quite accurate today to call Christine de Pizan's voice "The Other Voice," since she has become the subject of countless studies, is taught in a variety of college courses, and, as one of Judy Chicago's dinner party plates, even resides at the Brooklyn Museum of Art. But how "other" was her voice in the Middle Ages? Christine, in fact, had many voices that she brilliantly varied from genre to genre. In her early lyric poetry she spoke as a woman in love but also as a man in love; and she spoke as a bereaved woman who tragically lost her husband and missed him profoundly. It is that voice that many modern readers take to be her most "authentic" one. "Je, Christine," is a formula that appears again and again in her works, but that name, and the persona "Christine," are not always staged in the same way. Christine inhabits and deploys the name "Christine" in many different ways, creating different kinds of authority for herself. By turns, her voice is that of a widow, a historian, a preceptor, a philosopher, or a prophetess.[2]

One of the key moments in Christine's development as a writer, and—in somewhat anachronistic terms—as a "public intellectual," was her participation

---

1. Earl Jeffrey Richards's translation of *The Book of the City of Ladies* (1405) in 1982 (New York: Persea) brought Christine de Pizan into the mainstream of American university curricula. Richards's French edition, with facing Italian translation by Patrizia Caraffi followed in 1997: *Le livre de la cité des dames= La città delle dame* (Milan: Luni). For bibliographical guides up to 2004, see Angus J. Kennedy, *Christine de Pizan: A Bibliographical Guide* (London: Grant and Cutler, 1984); Kennedy, *Christine de Pizan: A Bibliographical Guide: Supplement 1* (London: Grant and Cutler, 1994); and Kennedy, *Christine de Pizan: A Bibliographical Guide: Supplement 2* (Rochester, NY: Tamesis, 2004).

2. Jacqueline Cerquiglini-Toulet brilliantly explored the many ways in which Christine deploys her name in her lecture "Christine de Pizan et le pouvoir du nom," *Le Moyen Français* 75 (2017): 3–17. For the establishment of these different kinds of authoritative voices see Claire Le Ninan, *Le sage roi et la clergesse: L'écriture du politique dans l'œuvre de Christine de Pizan* (Paris: Honoré Champion, 2013), Part 1.

1

in the Debate on the *Romance of the Rose* in 1401–1402.[3] David F. Hult has translated the relevant documents of this quarrel for this series, and has shown that by voicing her strong objections to the perceived misogyny and obscenity of the *Romance of the Rose* Christine launched "an active counterassault against an entire intellectual establishment to which women were solely the object of discussion, and which greatly limited their ability to take up the subject position of speech."[4] Christine also made herself a speaking subject in her later allegorical works, where her voice was not so different from those of many male writers of her time, such as Guillaume de Deguileville (1295–before 1358) or Philippe de Mézières (1327–1405), who invented personas, often bearing their own names, that traveled through allegorical landscapes in order to reveal political and spiritual truths.[5] Nonetheless, what marks Christine's voice as "other" is her insistent evocation of women's historical experiences and her positioning of women as full participants in the political events and the intellectual life of this world.

At the time that Christine composed the *Epistre d'Othea* (Othea's Letter) in 1399–1400, her vast allegorical compositions still lay ahead of her.[6] Her voice in that text is literally that of another, since, apart from the Prologue, the person who speaks is an ingenious invention of Christine, Othea, the Goddess of Prudence, representing the "wisdom of women." The "Christine" persona, by contrast, claims to be "a poor creature / An ignorant woman of low stature, / ... a woman unworthy / Of written learning,"[7] deploying an almost excessive humility topos. Othea's voice is didactic and at times ponderous, presenting extracts of mythological tales in the form of an imperative, followed by an explanatory gloss punctuated by a quote from a philosopher, and a spiritual allegory ending with a biblical quotation. The letter is addressed to the Trojan hero Hector when he was fifteen years old. The reinforcement of Christine's own voice with so many layers of authorities—the voice of Othea, classical myth, sayings of ancient pagan philosophers and the Church Fathers, and quotations from the scriptures—creates a kind of polyphony, joining her own voice with those of a whole chorus

---

3. For an argument in favor of using this term in a medieval context, see Daniel Hobbins, "The Schoolman as Public Intellectual: Jean Gerson and the Late Medieval Tract," *American Historical Review* 108 (2003): 1308–1337.

4. Christine de Pizan, *Debate of the* Romance of the Rose, ed. and trans. David F. Hult (Chicago: University of Chicago Press, 2010), 1. See also Kevin Brownlee, "Discourses of the Self: Christine de Pizan and the *Rose*," *Romanic Review* 79 (1988): 199–221.

5. See Philippe Maupeu, *Pèlerins de vie humaine: Autobiographie et allégorie narrative de Guillaume de Deguileville à Octavien de Saint-Gelais* (Paris: Honoré Champion, 2009).

6. *Epistre d'Othea*, ed. Gabriella Parussa (Geneva: Droz, 1999).

7. Prologue, vv. 52–53. The French phrase here, "*femme indigne / de sens acquis*," uses the rare expression "*sens acquis*" for written learning. References here and henceforth are to the translation presented in this volume.

of authorities in order to fashion a figure of female authority capable of advising a prince, her recipient Duke Louis of Orléans (1372–1407). Christine thus creates a genealogy of wise counsel: Just as her father had advised King Charles V, Louis's father, so now Othea/Christine offers her own lessons for a prince in a troubled kingdom. The *Othea* thus marks an important moment in Christine's career and the development of her voice, the moment she herself sees as a point of transition: when in the *Advision Cristine* (Christine's Vision, 1405) she sums up her prodigious literary production of fifteen major works between the years 1399 and 1405, she says: "Thus I began to forge pretty things, at the beginning of a lighter nature," but then "improving my style by more subtleness and nobler subject matter."[8]

The *Othea* is indeed a "subtle and noble" text that offers us a multi-layered and extremely complicated didactic work with a challenging vocabulary and syntax. This is undoubtedly why a rigorous and accurate modern English translation of the *Othea* is still lacking.[9] The *Othea* is a crucial text not only for an understanding of Christine's career and the mission she set for herself but also for that of late medieval mythographic and didactic literature, topics we will explore below. Still extant in some fifty manuscripts, the *Othea* was vastly more popular in the Middle Ages than her *Livre de la cité des dames* (Book of the City of Ladies) of 1405, the work that is taught most often in colleges and universities. We hope that with this new translation of the *Othea*, this intriguing text and its challenges will appeal to a new audience of students and scholars.

Life and Works of Christine de Pizan

Christine de Pizan was born in Venice in 1365 and as a small child moved to Paris when her father, Thomas of Pizan, was appointed the court physician and astrologer of King Charles V of France (r. 1364–1380). The family, landed rural nobles, hailed from Pizzano, a small town near Bologna, and Christine therefore always wrote her name as "Pizan," although earlier generations of scholars often referred

---

8. "Adonc me pris a forgier choses jolies, a mon commencement plus legieres …, amendant mon stille en plus grant soubtillité et plus haulte matiere." *Le livre de l'advision Cristine,* ed. Christine Reno and Liliane Dulac (Paris: Honoré Champion, 2001), 111. Translation in *The Selected Writings of Christine de Pizan,* ed. Renate Blumenfeld-Kosinski, trans. Blumenfeld-Kosinski and Kevin Brownlee (New York: W. W. Norton, 1997), 194.

9. Parussa's excellent critical edition appeared in 1999. The 1990 translation by Jane Chance contains much good information but is inadequate as a translation: *Christine de Pizan's Letter of Othea to Hector,* ed. and trans. Jane Chance (Newburyport, MA: Focus Information Group, 1990). See also the 2008 modern French translation and adaptation by Hélène Basso: *Lettre d'Othéa, déesse de prudence, à un jeune chevalier, Hector,* preface by Jacqueline Cerquiglini-Toulet, 2 vols. (Paris: Presses universitaires de France, 2008).

to her as "de Pisan," believing her family to be from Pisa.[10] In 1379 Christine married Etienne de Castel, a notary and secretary at Charles V's court. By all accounts her marriage was a happy one, and within a few years the young couple had three children, of whom two, a son and a daughter, survived into adulthood. Life for the de Pizan family was prosperous as long as Charles V was alive, but after his death in 1380 their fortunes changed, for Charles VI was less generous and in 1392 fell into a state of madness that destabilized the kingdom. Thomas de Pizan died some time between 1384 and 1389, leaving no inheritance to speak of. Then, in 1389, Etienne de Castel perished in an epidemic and left the young mother of three to fend for herself. Christine, confronted by numerous debts she had been unaware of, now had to provide for her children, her mother, and a niece. Unlike most widowed women who remarried or entered religious institutions, Christine decided to become a professional writer. She probably began her career as a scribe, but soon managed to acquire patrons for her works. How unusual and daring this step was becomes clear when we think of male writers of this time period. Her contemporaries, prolific writers such as Eustache Deschamps (ca. 1340–1406/07), Honorat Bovet (1340/45–1410), or Philippe de Mézières lived from court or ecclesiastical appointments; they wrote many influential works but they did not earn their living from their writing. That Christine succeeded in her enterprise and managed to live from her literary activities, and also to become an important political voice in her troubled period, is a testament to her intellectual vigor and moral force.

Christine's earliest works were a collection of one hundred ballads, love poetry desired by her patrons, as she herself stated. Several poems dealt with widowhood, a new topic for lyric poetry,[11] and it is these verses that have often been considered to be her most autobiographical. In her *Epistre au dieu d'amours* (The God of Love's Letter, 1399) she began to think about the status of women and how they were maligned and subjugated in medieval society.[12] The years 1399–1400, when she composed the *Othea*, signaled the beginning of an extremely fertile period, which saw the creation of her long allegorical works, both in prose and verse, as well as several devotional texts. In her *Advision*, as we saw above, she describes how she composed fifteen major works in the span of five years. These include the *Livre du chemin de long estude* (The Book of the Path of Long Learning, 1402),[13] where, inspired by the late antique philosopher Boethius and by the

10. And this in spite of such excellent early biographies as that of Philipp August Becker: "Christine de Pizan," *Zeitschrift für französische Sprache und Literatur* 54 (1931): 129–64.

11. See Kevin Brownlee, "Widowhood, Sexuality, and Gender in Christine de Pizan," *Romanic Review* 86 (1995): 339–53.

12. Translated by Kevin Brownlee in Blumenfeld-Kosinski and Brownlee, *Selected Writings*, 15–29.

13. *Le chemin de longue étude,* ed. Andrea Tarnowski, with modern French translation (Paris : Librairie générale française, 2000).

great Italian poet Dante, a figure named Christine, guided by the Sibyl of Cumae, embarks on a voyage around the known world and toward the heavens; there, a tribunal of allegorical ladies tries to determine who would be the best ruler for the troubled world. Next, Christine composed the very long *Livre de la mutacion de Fortune* (The Book of Fortune's Transformation, 1403),[14] a universal history that features, in its first part, a veiled autobiography where she describes how, after her husband's death, she was transformed into a man. In both of these allegories political troubles throughout history play a major role. The troubles of her own times—the Hundred Years' War, the Great Schism of the Western Church, and the incipient civil war between different factions of powerful French dukes—begin to shape her writings more frequently.[15] During the Great Schism, a division of the Catholic Church that lasted from 1378 until its resolution at the Council of Constance in 1417, two, and at one point three, popes struggled for power and divided Europe in the process. This crisis of spiritual and political authority caused widespread anxiety, an emotion that found its expression in many poetic and prophetic writings, including those of Christine.[16] The Great Schism surfaces in several of Christine's works, beginning with the *Chemin de long estude* and the *Mutacion de Fortune*, where she indicts the Church leaders as wolves that devour their flocks. In her biography of the late King Charles V (1404), commissioned by his brother, Duke Philip of Burgundy, Christine devotes ten chapters to the Schism and demonstrates that she is familiar with the political wrangling that led to France's adherence to the Avignon faction of the papacy. Here she accuses the devil of having planted "this painful schism and poisonous, contagious plant into the bosom of Holy Church."[17] In the 1405 *Advision* (which also contains a detailed autobiographical section in Part 3), Christine devotes many chapters to contemporary politics, especially the Schism, the war against the English, and the

14. *Le livre de la mutacion de Fortune,* ed. Suzanne Solente, 4 vols. (Paris: Picard, 1959–1966). The new translation of the abridged text that was published in 2017 (Toronto: Iter Press; Tempe, AZ: Arizona Center for Medieval and Renaissance Studies) is entitled *The Book of the Mutability of Fortune,* ed. and trans. Geri L. Smith.

15. See Sandra Hindman, *Christine de Pizan's "Epistre Othea": Painting and Politics at the Court of Charles VI* (Toronto: Pontifical Institute of Mediaeval Studies, 1986); Renate Blumenfeld-Kosinski, "Christine de Pizan and the Political Life in Late Medieval France," in *Christine de Pizan: A Casebook,* ed. Barbara K. Altmann and Deborah L. McGrady (New York and London: Routledge, 2003), 9–24; Le Ninan, *Le sage roi et la clergesse*; and Tracy Adams, *Christine de Pizan and the Fight for France* (University Park: Pennsylvania State University Press, 2014).

16. Renate Blumenfeld-Kosinski, *Poets, Saints, and Visionaries of the Great Schism, 1378–1417* (University Park: Pennsylvania State University Press, 2006), chap. 5.

17. *Livre des faits et bonnes moeurs du sage roi Charles V,* trans. Joël Blanchard and Michel Quereuil (Paris: Pocket, 2013), Part 3, chap. 61. Blanchard and Quereuil translate the work previously edited by Suzanne Solente: *Le livre des fais et bonnes meurs du sage roy Charles V,* 2 vols. (Paris: Honoré Champion, 1936–1940; reprint, Geneva: Slatkine, 1977).

internal French conflicts, whose culmination as a full-blown civil war was still in the future at the time she composed the *Othea*.

Several specific political events may have inspired Christine to undertake the composition of a major didactic work for a prince in 1399: the defeat of a European alliance, led by Jean de Nevers, the son of the Burgundian Duke Philip the Bold, in the fateful battle of Nicopolis (in today's Bulgaria) against the Ottoman Turks in 1396; the French withdrawal of obedience from the Avignon pope Benedict XIII in July 1398; and the deposition of the English King Richard II and his subsequent death in 1399.

In 1393 ambassadors from Hungary had arrived in Paris to ask for help against the Turks' advance in the Balkans. Although Charles VI promised them aid, in the end only the Duke of Burgundy committed himself—or rather his son—to the military campaign to assist King Sigismund of Hungary. The complete defeat of the European forces, countless deaths, and the imprisonment of scores of knights led to soul searching among the survivors and to laments and reproaches by those who had counseled against the expedition. Philippe de Mézières, with whom Christine was acquainted, offered a searing indictment of the French forces in his *Epistre lamentable and consolatoire* (A woeful and consoling letter) addressed to the Duke of Burgundy in 1397.[18] He believed that only a complete moral and spiritual reform of French chivalry could save it from extinction. The *Othea*, with its moral glosses and spiritual allegories addressed to "the good knight" and "the good spirit," could be seen as a response to Philippe's exhortations.

In the year before Christine began to compose the *Othea*, one of the major crises caused by the Great Schism erupted in Paris. When Clement VII, the pope supported by the French, died in 1394, the French king insisted that peace should be made in the Church and that no new pope should be elected for the Avignon faction until negotiations with the Roman pope, Boniface IX, could lead to his abdication and an election of a new pope. However, through various machinations, the Spanish cardinal Pedro de Luna had himself quickly elected as Benedict XIII, and all hopes for a resolution of the Schism were dashed. Louis of Orléans, the dedicatee of the *Othea*, was much involved in the negotiations to get Benedict XIII to step down. After a few years the stalemate between the French monarchy and the tenacious pope came to a head, when several ambassadors departed for Avignon in order to persuade the pope once more to abdicate. These ambassadors were two uncles of Charles VI, the dukes of Berry and Burgundy, and the king's brother, the much younger duke Louis of Orléans. Despite being confronted by such an illustrious group, Benedict XIII remained deaf to the French entreaties.

18. Philippe de Mézières, *Une epistre lamentable et consolatoire adressée en 1397 à Philippe le Hardi, duc de Bourgogne, sur la défaite de Nicopolis, 1396,* ed. Philippe Contamine and Jacques Paviot (Paris: Société de l'histoire de France, 2008).

The pope's stubborn refusal led the French to withdraw obedience from Benedict XIII through an elaborate edict published on July 27, 1398.[19] This withdrawal, which had serious financial and political repercussions for the Avignon papacy, was a huge event in Paris and, given Christine's close relations with the court, she surely must have known that Louis of Orléans was one of the frustrated ambassadors. The advice that Othea gives to Hector in the areas of diplomacy would have come in handy in the critical years before 1399.

The Hundred Years' War began in 1337 because the English King Edward III, as a grandson of the French King Philippe le Bel, wanted to claim the French throne.[20] The English still possessed a fief on the continent, the duchy of Guienne in southwestern France, and when Philippe occupied that area, the conflict that was to last until 1453 began. The French lost a number of major battles, notably at Crécy in 1346 and at Poitiers in 1356, when King Jean le Bon was taken prisoner and was liberated only through payment of a huge ransom. In 1360 the French surrendered the large region of Aquitaine to the English in the Treaty of Brétigny. When Christine and her family arrived in France, hostilities were at a low ebb. Indeed, almost the entire period between 1364, when Charles V, Jean le Bon's son, assumed the throne, and 1399, had been relatively peaceful. The Truce of Leulinghem, concluded between the French and the English in 1389, was still holding. But 1399 brought a series of calamitous events: King Richard II, who in 1396 had married Charles VI's seven-year-old daughter Isabelle,[21] was brutally deposed by the Lancastrians, and Henry IV took his place. Richard died under mysterious circumstances a few months after his deposition. Henry IV, for his part, was determined to resume the war with France.

This particular crisis touched Christine personally, as her son was in England at the time. In 1398 the Earl of Salisbury had met Christine on one of his

19. For details see Howard Kaminsky, "The Politics of France's Subtraction of Obedience from Pope Benedict XIII, 27 July 1398," *Proceedings of the American Philosophical Society* 115, no. 5 (1971): 366–97. The withdrawal of obedience came to an end in 1403, but not before Benedict was imprisoned in his palace in Avignon. Louis tried to act as a mediator, and at that time the conflict with the House of Burgundy grew until it reached the tragic outcome of Louis's assassination on the order of the Duke of Burgundy in 1407. For details on the events of this period see Noël Valois, *La France et le Grand Schisme d'Occident,* vol. 3 (Paris: Picard, 1901), chap. 3.

20. There are hundreds of studies of this conflict. See, for example, Anne Curry, *The Hundred Years War,* 2nd ed. (New York: Palgrave Macmillan, 2003).

21. Such a marriage would not be consummated until the bride was at least twelve years old. Philippe de Mézières was a strong advocate of this marriage, which he hoped would bring lasting peace to France and England. See his *Epistre au roi Richart II,* in *Letter to King Richard II: A Plea Made in 1395 for Peace between England and France,* ed. and trans. G. W. Coopland (Liverpool: Liverpool University Press, 1975).

embassies to Paris in connection with the marriage of Richard II and Isabelle.[22] He had taken Christine's son Jean with him as a companion to one of his own sons. About a year later, the Earl of Salisbury was executed by the citizens of Chichester for leading an uprising in support of the deposed Richard II, and King Henry IV took charge of Christine's son. Christine despaired of seeing him again but managed to negotiate his return, a strategy which cost her several manuscripts, as she put it in the *Advision*.[23] One of these works was the *Epistre au dieu d'amours* (adapted in 1402 by Thomas Hoccleve as *Cupid's Letter*); another one was the version of the *Othea* that features a dedication to "a king" and which was translated into English by Stephen Scrope around 1440. James L. Laidlaw argues persuasively that this king was Henry IV, whom, in the *Advision* (in 1405, once her son was safely back in France!) she labels a usurper, but to whom she gives some praise in the dedication—or, as Laidlaw puts it, "she used a minimum of fulsome phrases, just enough to secure Henry IV's good will."[24] Christine's plan succeeded, and her son returned to France in 1402. Thus the *Othea* had a critical function in Christine's own life and in that of her son. But its wider function was to provide expert chivalric, moral, and spiritual leadership to a country confronted by multiple crises.

Thus, in the years after 1398 Christine's engagement with public life progressed on several fronts. Just when she had finished the *Othea* she became a player in the acerbic intellectual debate on the *Romance of the Rose*. Composed by Guillaume de Lorris and Jean de Meun between 1228 and 1270, this text was one of the most popular of the Middle Ages, featuring an allegorical quest for the love of a rosebud. It was the second part by Jean de Meun that gave rise to the debate between, on one side, Jean de Montreuil (1354–1418), provost of the city of Lille, and the brothers Pierre and Gontier Col, and, on the other, Christine and Jean Gerson (1363–1429), the powerful chancellor of the University of Paris. At stake was the morality of the work, since Jean de Meun had created a number of fictional characters, such as the Jealous Husband or the Old Woman, into whose mouths he put discourses that could be interpreted as immoral and misogynistic.

---

22. For details of these events see James L. Laidlaw, "Christine de Pizan, the Earl of Salisbury, and Henry IV," *French Studies* 36, no. 2 (1982): 129–43.

23. This is how Christine speaks of her anguish about her son's situation and her strategy to get him back in the *Advision Cristine*: "Le roy Henri, qui encores est, qui s'atribua la couronne, vid desditz livres et dictiez que j'avoie ja plusieurs envoiez comme desireuse de lui faire plaisir, audit conte." The king invites Christine to come to England but she is not "tempted" to go, and instead sends some of her books: "Et a brief parler, tant fis a grant peine et par le moien de mes livres que congié ot mon dit filz de me venir querir par de ça pour mener la, qui encore n'y vois" (112–13). This return is also the subject of Autres Balades XXII, in *Œuvres poétiques de Christine de Pisan*, ed. Maurice Roy, 3 vols. (Paris: Firmin Didot, 1886–1896; reprint, New York: Johnson, 1965), 1:232–33.

24. Laidlaw, "Christine de Pizan," 140. This version exists in the British Library manuscript Harley 219, a mid-fifteenth-century copy of the original Christine sent to Henry IV.

At one point during the debate Christine collected a selection of the letters that had flown back and forth between the debate participants in a dossier that she presented to Charles VI's wife, Queen Isabeau of Bavaria, an act that made her known and also promoted the anti-misogyny stance that came to full fruition in her *Book of the City of Ladies*.[25] Here, in a by now famous pro-woman move, Christine assembled hundreds of women from the past and from her own age to show how much they had contributed to the achievements of civilization and to the spread of the Christian faith. Inspired by Boccaccio's *Concerning Famous Women,* a book she could read in the original Latin as well as in the translations by Laurent de Premierfait,[26] Christine did not hesitate to reinterpret existing stories and chronicles in order to highlight women's intellectual and political power. Boccaccio had not dealt with Christian women, so Christine turned to the thirteenth-century chronicler Vincent of Beauvais and combed his vast histories of the early Church to find examples of saintly women who, through their piety and constancy, would support the arguments she used in her fight against misogyny.[27] Right after the *City of Ladies*, Christine composed a kind of continuation to it, a didactic treatise addressed to all classes of women, *Le livre des trois vertus* (The Book of the Three Virtues).[28] During this time Christine also became a publisher of her own works by copying and assembling her works into beautiful volumes for specific patrons, such as Louis of Orléans, Duke Jean of Berry, and the queen, whose splendid manuscript found its way to England late in the Hundred Years' War and is now known as British Library Harley 4431.[29]

Christine's literary activity became more and more overtly political as the crises in France deepened. In 1407 she composed another didactic work, the *Livre du corps de policie* (The Book of the Body Politic),[30] addressed to the French dauphin Louis of Guienne (d. 1415), which drew on ancient history for exemplary tales, but did not return to the abundant use of classical mythology of the

25. See Rosalind Brown-Grant, *Christine de Pizan and the Moral Defence of Women: Reading Beyond Gender* (Cambridge: Cambridge University Press, 1999), for Christine's defense of women across most of her œuvre.

26. Giovanni Boccaccio, *Famous Women,* trans. Virginia Brown (Cambridge, MA: Harvard University Press, 2001). Christine also used Boccaccio's *Decameron,* not yet translated into French in 1399; Laurent de Premierfait's translations, both done for Jean de Berry, date from 1401 to 1409.

27. See Renate Blumenfeld-Kosinski, "'Femme de corps et femme par sens': Christine de Pizan's Saintly Women," *Romanic Review* 87 (1996): 157–75.

28. *Le livre des trois vertus,* ed. Eric Hicks, introduction and notes by Charity Cannon Willard (Paris: Honoré Champion, 1989).

29. On this manuscript, see *Christine de Pizan: The Making of the Queen's Manuscript*, <http://www.pizan.lib.ed.ac.uk>. See also Gilbert Ouy, Christine Reno, and Inès Villela-Petit, *Album Christine de Pizan* (Turnhout: Brepols, 2012), 316–43.

30. *Le livre du corps de policie,* ed. Angus J. Kennedy (Paris: Champion, 1998).

Othea. As the French factional strife escalated after the assassination of Louis of Orléans,[31] Christine's voice turned more urgent and even desperate. In 1410 she tried to persuade the warring dukes to make peace in her *Lamentacion sur les maux de la France* (Lamentation on the evils that have befallen France),[32] and the 1412–1413 *Livre de paix* (Book of Peace)[33] is a further plea for peace in France. Finally, after the French defeat at Agincourt in October 1415 and the English invasion of France, Christine seems to have retired to the convent of Poissy not far from Paris, where her daughter was a nun. In her 1418 *Epistre de la prison de vie humaine* (Letter on the Prison of Human Life), Christine turned her back on the strife of this world by offering consolation to those women who had lost loved ones at Agincourt. They should seek hope in the afterlife and no longer count on any blessings in this earthly prison of human life.[34] Only in 1429 a ray of hope appeared: Joan of Arc burst on the scene, trying to crown the French King Charles VII, disinherited in 1420 through the Treaty of Troyes, which assured that the English king Henry V would succeed as monarch of France. When Charles VI and Henry V both died in 1422, Henry VI became king of France, leaving the French king Charles VII to wander around France, dispossessed. On July 27, 1429, Joan succeeded in having Charles VII crowned, and just two weeks later Christine wrote a celebratory poem in her honor, the *Ditié de Jehanne d'Arc* (The Poem about Joan of Arc). In Joan, Christine saw the fulfillment of her twinned dreams: a woman with a divine mission whose intervention in a hundred-year old conflict brought about peace—or so she thought, for Christine did not live to see Joan's brutal execution at the stake on May 30, 1431.[35] The English did not completely leave French territories for another twenty years.

31. For a lively account of this event see Eric Jager, *Blood Royal: A True Tale of Crime and Detection in Medieval Paris* (New York: Little, Brown, 2014); see also Bernard Guenée, *Un meurtre, une société: L'assassinat du duc d'Orléans, 23 novembre 1407* (Paris: Gallimard, 1992).

32. Translated in Blumenfeld-Kosinski and Brownlee, *Selected Writings*, 224–29. Also included in the edition and translation by Josette A. Wisman of Christine de Pizan, *The Epistle of the Prison of Human Life with an Epistle to the Queen of France and Lament on the Evils of Civil War* (New York: Garland, 1984).

33. *The "Livre de la paix" of Christine de Pisan: A Critical Edition,* ed. Charity Cannon Willard (The Hague: Mouton, 1958); *The Book of Peace by Christine de Pizan,* ed. and trans. Karen Green, Constant J. Mews, and Janice Pinder (University Park: Pennsylvania State University Press, 2008).

34. See Renate Blumenfeld-Kosinski, "Two Responses to Agincourt: Alain Chartier's *Livre des Quatre Dames* and Christine de Pizan's *Epistre de la Prison de la Vie Humaine,*" in *Contexts and Continuities: Proceedings of the IVth International Colloquium on Christine de Pizan, Glasgow 21–27 July 2000, Published in Honour of Liliane Dulac,* ed. Angus J. Kennedy et al., 3 vols. (Glasgow: University of Glasgow Press, 2002), 1:75–85. See also *The Epistle of the Prison of Human Life,* ed. Wisman.

35. Kevin Brownlee, "Structures of Authority in Christine de Pizan's *Ditié de Jehanne d'Arc*" in Blumenfeld-Kosinski and Brownlee, *Selected Writings of Christine de Pizan,* 371–90. See also *Le ditié de*

Christine de Pizan and Classical Mythology

No medieval writer encountered classical mythology in its pure or "naked" form, that is, without commentaries or interpretations that often crowded the margins of the manuscript pages that transmitted Ovidian tales, or the epics of Virgil or Statius. These explanatory textual accompaniments usually offered several different layers of possible interpretations for mythical tales: the historical, which saw ancient kings and queens in the pagan gods and goddesses; the physical, in which the sun, wind, and other natural phenomena were represented by divine figures such as Helios or Aeolus; the astrological, which saw the pagan gods figured in the starry constellations; and finally the moral, which looked for lessons on good and evil in the deeds of mythological characters.[36] All of these interpretive possibilities surface in the *Othea*.

Throughout late antiquity and the Middle Ages a further strand of interpretations transformed ancient myths: many commentators grafted Christian meanings onto the tales of pagan antiquity, using images such as the "gold of the Egyptians," which, for Saint Augustine, meant that Christian writers were allowed to use pagan materials as long as they employed them in the service of Christian truths.[37] One of the most influential late antique writers who dealt with classical mythology was Fulgentius (d. ca. 533), who wrote in his *Mythologies*: "once the fictional invention of lying Greeks has been disposed of, I may infer what allegorical significance we should understand in such matters."[38] In the twelfth century, the preferred images for the interpretation of ancient myths in medieval Latin sources were those of the covering or the veil, items that needed to be removed in order for the true meaning of the myth to emerge. Images of trees whose bark had to be stripped away, or fruit whose peel had to be removed to allow access to the true inner meaning, were also popular; in fact, Christine invokes the image of the fruit and its peel in the gloss to chapter 82 of the *Othea*.[39]

Jehanne d'Arc, ed. and trans. Angus J. Kennedy and Kenneth Varty (Oxford: Society for the Study of Mediaeval Languages and Literature, 1977).

36. Jean Seznec, *The Survival of the Pagan Gods: The Mythological Tradition and its Place in Renaissance Humanism and Art,* trans. Barbara F. Sessions (New York: Pantheon, 1953; reprint, Princeton, NJ: Princeton University Press, 1972), chaps. 1–4.

37. Paule Demats, *Fabula: Trois études de mythographie antique et médiévale* (Geneva: Droz, 1973), 39–40. See also below, 26.

38. Fabius Planciades Fulgentius, *The Mythologies,* in *Fulgentius the Mythographer,* edited and translated by Leslie G. Whitbread (Columbus: Ohio State University Press, 1971), 13–102, at 45.

39. See Marie-Dominique Chenu, "'Involucrum': Le mythe selon les théologiens médiévaux," *Archives d'histoire doctrinale et littéraire du moyen âge* 22 (1955): 75–79; and Winthrop Wetherbee, *Platonism and Poetry in the Twelfth Century: The Literary Influence of the School of Chartres* (Princeton, NJ: Princeton University Press, 1972).

In addition to commentaries and annotated manuscripts, a medieval writer could also use collections of mythological tales and interpretations. Handbooks such as those of Arnulf of Orléans, who wrote around 1180, or John of Garland, active in Paris in the early thirteenth century, attempted "through allegory to uncover the hidden truths of the Ovidian fables."[40] In the vernacular tradition the most important work for the transmission of ancient Ovidian fables was the vast translation and interpretation of Ovid's *Metamorphoses,* the *Ovide moralisé* (The Moralized Ovid)*,* composed in verse between 1316 and 1328 by a Franciscan friar.[41] This poem of 72,000 lines featured not only translations of the many tales of the *Metamorphoses* but also of parts of Ovid's *Heroides,* a collection of fictional letters, supposedly written by mythological heroines to the lovers who abandoned and mistreated them. Through the *Ovide moralisé* their stories became part of the vernacular canon. The many thousands of verses devoted to the different levels of historical, moral, and spiritual interpretations provided a huge storehouse for future writers such as Guillaume de Machaut (1300–1377), Jean Froissart (ca. 1337–1410), and Christine, who drew freely on the materials offered by the anonymous fourteenth-century poet. She did not slavishly follow the interpretations offered by the *Ovide moralisé,* but used its materials in creative ways, rewriting and reorganizing as she saw fit in the new context of the *Othea.* Another author who moralized ancient myths was Évrart de Conty, with his glosses in the *Eschecs amoureux moralisés* (The moralized chess game of love; ca. 1390–1400). This work is a massive encyclopedia/mirror for princes, which presents itself as a commentary on an allegorical poem itself inspired by the *Romance of the Rose.* Conty had been the court physician of Charles V and was certainly acquainted with both Christine's father, Thomas de Pizan, the court astrologer, and Christine herself. His extremely involved interpretive strategies may have

---

40. Frank T. Coulson, "Ovid's *Metamorphoses* in the School Tradition of France, 1180–1400: Texts, Manuscript Tradition, Manuscript Settings," in *Ovid in the Middle Ages,* ed. James C. Clark, Frank T. Coulson, and Kathryn L. McKinley (Cambridge: Cambridge University Press, 2011), 59. See also Arnulf of Orléans, *Allegorie super Ovidii Metamorphosin,* ed. Fausto Ghisalberti, in "Arnolfo d'Orléans: Un cultore d'Ovidio nel secolo XII," *Memorie del reale istituto lombardo di scienze e lettere* 24 (1932): 157–234.

41.*Ovide moralisé,* ed. Cornelis de Boer, *Verhandelingen der Koninklijke Akademie van Wetenschappen te Amsterdam: Afdeeling Letterkunde,* vols. 15, 21, 30, 36–37, 43 (Amsterdam, 1915–1938); for which see Renate Blumenfeld-Kosinski, *Reading Myth: Classical Mythology and Its Interpretations in Medieval French Literature* (Stanford, CA: Stanford University Press, 1997), chap. 3; Ana Pairet, *Les mutacions des fables: Figures de la métamorphose dans la littérature française du Moyen Age* (Paris: Champion, 2002); and Marylène Possamaï-Pérez, *L'Ovide moralisé: Essai d'interprétation* (Paris: Champion, 2006).

shaped some of the *Othea*'s interpretations, and he and Christine frequently share similar expressions.[42]

The *Ovide moralisé* offers many different interpretations of each Ovidian story, and does not follow a consistent pattern that would be repeated from section to section. In the *Othea*, by contrast, Christine consistently adopts a tripartite division that seems more reminiscent of Biblical exegesis, a technique she describes herself in her biography of Charles V when she praises the king for the many translations from Latin into French he commissioned, including the Bible "that he had translated in three manners or styles, to wit: the text, then the text together with glosses, and then allegorized in another manner."[43] This description sounds very much like the compositional technique she followed in her own *Othea* four years earlier. A further text that may have suggested this pattern to Christine was Pierre Bersuire's *Ovidius moralizatus*, composed around 1340,[44] which unlike the *Ovide moralisé* segmented the text into interpretable portions, not unlike Christine's *textes*. However, Christine's *textes* are not mere narrative excerpts but her own compositions, written deliberately as imperatives. That is, Christine draws a lesson from a given myth even before she interprets it explicitly: thus she offers an exegesis of texts she herself had created. In her earlier lyric poetry she had already frequently used myths in a very personal way, as an analogy or parallel to the experiences of the lyrical "I" that enunciates the poem. But now, in a moralizing mode, she draws lessons on chivalric and spiritual virtues and vices from these stories: it is important to note that she has Othea speak as an authoritative moralist already in her *textes*. The "conative" or advisory function of the imperative has been described by the linguist Roman Jakobson, who

42. Jane Chance, *Medieval Mythography,* vol. 3, *The Emergence of Italian Humanism, 1321–1475* (Gainesville: University Press of Florida, 2015), vol. 3, 228–44. The date of this text has not been established with certainty. De Conty died in 1405, and he must have been very old since he was already teaching at the Faculty of Medicine in Paris in 1353. For details of his life, see Françoise Guichard-Tesson, "Évrart de Conty, auteur de la *Glose des echecs amoureux*," *Le Moyen Français*, 8–9 (1982): 111–48. See also the edition of Évrart de Conty's work by Guichard-Tesson and Bruno Roy: *Le livre des eschez amoureux moralisés* (Montreal: CERES, 1993).

43. Solente, ed., *Livre des fais et bonnes meurs*, 2:43: "[*Charles V*] *fist* [...] *translater de latin en françois tous les plus notables livres, si comme la Bible en .iii. manieres, c'est assavoir: le texte, et puis le texte et les gloses ensemble, et puis d'une autre maniere alegorisée.*" Christine repeats this same account in her *Livre de de la paix* from 1412–1413: "*fist translater par tres souffisans clercs maistres en theologie tous les plus notables livres, tant de la sainte escripture comme autres. Si comme la bible en .iii. volumes, c'est assavoir le texte, et puis le texte et les gloses ensemble, et puis d'une autre maniere alegorisee*" (Christine de Pizan, *The Book of Peace*, 283.) See also *Le Livre des faits et bonnes moeurs*, trans. Blanchard and Quereuil, 245. We will return to this point below.

44. Petrus Bersuire [Berchorius], "The 'Ovidius moralizatus' of Petrus Berchorius: An Introduction and Translation," trans. William Donald Reynolds (PhD diss., University of Illinois at Urbana-Champaign, 1971).

states that an imperative, unlike other verb forms, is not subjected to verification because its value derives from the authority of the speaker.[45] Christine further buttresses this authority through the citations from philosophical and scriptural authorities.

Christine skillfully interweaves Ovidian myths of metamorphoses, a major component of the *Othea's* content, with the myth of the Trojan origin of the French monarchy: as she reminds Louis of Orléans in the Prologue, he comes from ancient Trojan stock. The Trojan War itself was popularized by two widely read Latin texts, ostensibly written by Dares and Dictys, claiming to be eyewitnesses to the Trojan War, but in fact dating from late antiquity.[46] In medieval French culture the Trojans became part of a myth of national origins. The concept of *translatio imperii*, or the transfer of empires, was a bedrock of medieval political thought. Beginning in Latin chronicles in the seventh century, the story of the Trojan origins of the French was transmitted in a variety of texts, including such vernacular romances as Benoît de Sainte-Maure's twelfth-century *Roman de Troie* (Romance of Troy).[47] In the mid-fourteenth century, a prose version of this romance was included in the second redaction of the early thirteenth-century *Histoire ancienne jusqu'à Cesar* (Ancient History up to Julius Caesar),[48] a compilation, mostly in prose, of stories drawn from ancient history and one of Christine's major sources for ancient historical events. The story appears as well in the *Grandes Chroniques de France* (Great Chronicles of France).[49] It was here that Christine found the version she adopted in her own works: that after the fall of Troy, when the Trojans were dispersed all over Europe, Hector's son Francio founded France. In other versions, Francio was the Trojan King Priam's nephew and not his grandson, as he is for Christine. In making Hector the father of Francio and thus of the French nation, Christine showed that she had a specific political agenda in the *Othea*: to make a plea for national unity founded upon the noble Trojan origins of the French. In the *Chemin de long estude* Christine recounts that

---

45. Roman Jakobson, *Essais de linguistique générale* (Paris: Éditions de Minuit, 1963), 214–20.

46. *The Trojan War: The Chronicles of Dictys of Crete and Dares the Phrygian*, trans. R. M. Frazer (Bloomington: Indiana University Press, 1966).

47. Benoît de Sainte-Maure, *Le roman de Troie,* ed. Léopold Constans, 6 vols. (Paris: Société des anciens textes français, 1904–1912).

48. *Histoire ancienne jusqu'à César*, édition partielle by Marijke de Visser-van Terwiga, 2 vols. (Orléans: Paradigme, 1995 and 1999). This edition, however, does not include the Troy material.

49. *Les grandes chroniques de France*, ed. Jules Viard, 9 vols. (Paris: Société de l'histoire de France, 1920–1937). See Jacques Krynen, *Idéal du prince et pouvoir royal en France à la fin du Moyen Age, 1380–1440: Étude de la littérature politique du temps* (Paris: Picard, 1981), 245–51; Colette Beaune, *The Birth of an Ideology: Myths and Symbols of Nation in Late-Medieval France,* trans. Susan Ross Huston, ed. Fredric L. Cheyette (Berkeley and Los Angeles: University of California Press, 1991), chap. 8; and Hindman, *Painting and Politics*, 34–38.

Francio was the noblest of the Trojan princes, and that he settled in Gaul, a region that subsequently changed its name to France in his honor (ll. 3576–80).[50] The story also appears in the *Mutacion de Fortune* and in her biography of Charles V, where Christine makes it clear that France as a nation was founded with the coronation of Francio's direct descendant, the legendary King Pharamond (Part 1, chap. 5). In the *Advision* Christine offers an original interpretation of the Trojan War when she attributes its cause to Lady Opinion, the allegorical character that dominates Part 2. Lady Opinion claims that "I was the cause of the death of Hector, for I made him believe that he should not beware of Achilles who was constantly lying in wait for him, and who in the end killed him" (79). Here we find one of Christine's famous auto-citations, for what Lady Opinion says here is precisely what Othea had said in chapter 85 to warn Hector: "Beware of Achilles!"

The *Othea* represents the first articulation of the Trojan myth in Christine's œuvre, a myth a she will exploit for its political value in many subsequent works that deal with questions of national origin and national unity. It is thus in the context of the *translatio imperii* that we have to understand the Trojan stories and their moral and spiritual interpretations in the *Othea*.

Genre, Allegory, and Textuality in the Othea

In order to consider the *Othea*'s genre, its use of allegory, and its incorporation of sources, it is useful to begin with a description of the manuscripts and their idiosyncratic format. As rigorous and as repetitive as is the organization of individual chapters in the *Othea*, this very rigor and repetition mark a disconcerting and disorienting phenomenon that Liliane Dulac accurately described as "breaks or fissures in meaning" (*ruptures de sens*). The three textual sections of each of the one hundred chapters represent three very different, very disparate literary traditions, which Christine successfully welds together into a single work. This fusion of different textual traditions is as astounding and complicated as it is provocative. By the same token, the text's editor, Gabriella Parussa, called the work a "hybrid, composite text that always changes course" (*texte hybride, composite, déroutant*, 16)—and here lies the challenge of the *Othea*. Its textually hybrid or composite nature—arguably its essential feature, and one that might perhaps be called, more neutrally, its textual heterogeneity—is seen in the strict divisions among the individual sections explicitly devoted to text, gloss, and allegory, a division complicated by the addition of illuminations (expanded from six in the earliest manuscript to one hundred and one in subsequent versions). These later copies, executed under Christine's direct supervision, enrich each chapter with

50. In the *Advision*, Christine allows for a second explanation of the name "France": she plays on the meaning of the word "franc" (=free) by stating that the country was called France "pour la grant liberté" (the great freedom) that its founders established there (8).

its own highly detailed colored illumination, which suggests that Christine from the outset deliberately and consciously exploited the textual heterogeneity of the *Othea* through the contrast with a fourth visual level. Whether the illuminations of the manuscripts illustrated under Christine's supervision offer a political program remains an open and much debated question, but the *Othea* also survives in many other manuscripts copied and illuminated after Christine's death, with different iconographic programs from the manuscripts done under her control, a phenomenon which implies that later scribes and readers took their cue from Christine's intention to play off the different sections of the text against each other. With this physical description in mind, let us first turn to the question of genre.

The *Othea* survived in some fifty manuscripts, some no longer extant, according to the list published by Gabriella Parussa in 1999.[51] Many of these manuscripts have since been digitized by the British Library and by Gallica, the digital library of the Bibliothèque Nationale de France, making it easy to consult and compare them. When one lists the dedicatees of manuscripts executed under Christine's control (some now lost), one is confronted with an original, closely knit readership drawn from the highest echelons of France and England, and this during a lull in hostilities during the Hundred Years' War. These first readers included:

- Louis, Duke of Orléans (the younger brother of Charles VI and sometime regent during his periods of mental illness that began in 1392). BnF, f. fr. 848, with only six illustrations, represents the earliest manuscript of the text and is dedicated to him.

- Philip the Bold, Duke of Burgundy (Charles VI's uncle and sometime regent, and founder of the Burgundian branch of the House of Valois). Only copies of this manuscript survive, and all of these present a dedication, not to Louis of Orléans, but to Philip himself.

- Henry IV, King of England.[52] Only copies of this manuscript survive, the earliest of which dates from the mid-fifteenth century, British Library, Harley 219.

- John of Berry (also Charles VI's uncle, and after Louis of Orléans's murder in 1407, the head of the Armagnac or Orléanist faction). The version dedicated to John is preserved in a copy in Oxford's Bodleian Library, ms. Laud misc. 570, which probably served as

---

51. Besides Parussa's discussion of the manuscripts, it is helpful to consult the recent exhaustive codicological study of Christine: Ouy, Reno, and Villela-Petit, *Album Christine de Pizan*.

52. See above, 8, for details on how the dedication to Henry IV came to be.

the basis for the Middle English translation done around 1440 by Stephen Scrope. John also acquired Paris BnF f. fr. 606 shortly after the assassination of Louis of Orléans.

- The French queen Isabeau of Bavaria (Charles VI's wife, who repeatedly attempted to mediate between the rival Armagnac and Burgundian factions, particularly after Louis of Orléans's murder). The utterly stunning luxury manuscript dedicated to her, British Library Harley 4431, called "The Queen's Manuscript," and dating from 1410–1412, is the basis for the critical edition by Gabriella Parussa used for the translation here.

In view of these readers and of the political rivalries between them, it would seem logical to identify the genre of the *Othea* as a "mirror for princes." In fact, the work is about an ideal of knighthood based on lessons from classical sources, the Church Fathers, and the Bible. Indeed, in one later manuscript, BnF, fr. 1186, dated 1482, the *Othea* is followed by a treatise entitled *The Duties of Kings and Princes* (*Devoirs des rois et des princes*). In one other early manuscript, BnF f. fr. 1187, the *Othea* is followed by the Middle French translation of Cicero's *On Old Age* (*De senectute*) done by the early French humanist Laurent de Premierfait, Christine's contemporary and also active at the royal court; it is entitled *Tully's Book on Old Age* (*Le Livre de Tulle de vieillese*), since Cicero was commonly referred to as Tully until the end of the Renaissance. These scattered indications, like pieces of a jigsaw puzzle, suggest that the *Othea* was composed with an intention to reconcile the competing political factions of the day under an ideal of enlightened Christian knighthood. Gabriella Parussa argues in the same vein that the *Othea* was written in the sincere hope of convincing this first circle of readers to restore peace and justice and to stop the internecine bickering for the sake of the common good.[53] Her insights suggest that the *Othea's* political dimensions went beyond any one single event, but addressed a general crisis in the wake of events in the 1390s such as "The Ball of the Burning Men" (*Le bal des ardents*) on January 18, 1393, or the catastrophic defeat of a Crusader army at Nicopolis between September 25 and 28, 1396.

"The Ball of the Burning Men," also sometimes called "The Ball of the Wild Men" (*Bal des sauvages*), speaks volumes about the young Louis of Orléans (born in 1372) to whom the *Othea* is dedicated. Held at the royal court, it was a masquerade ball—or, more precisely, a *charivari* (a French folk custom with deep pagan roots in which invited guests make a lot of noise on the eve of a wedding to scare off evil spirits)—that went terribly wrong. The King and several noblemen dressed up as wild men in highly flammable costumes made of linen, soaked in

---

53. On this point see Parussa, *Epistre d'Othea*, 85.

pitch covered with feathers and stalks of flax, in order to create the impression of their being shaggy savages. Some accounts, such as that of the chronicler Jean Froissart, relate that Louis of Orléans held up a torch to identify one of the revelers and that a spark fell—igniting several of the dancers, who died in misery from their burns. Louis of Orléans was blamed for the disaster and ultimately forced to do public penance: he ended up donating money to build a memorial chapel for the victims at the Celestine monastery on the banks of the Seine across from Notre-Dame (whose only modern trace is found in the name of a street there, *Le Quai des Célestins*). And it is this Louis of Orléans, a highly literate and cultivated, if also perhaps impetuous young man, whom Christine seeks to counsel in the *Othea*. He would later, in December of 1405, become the political ally of the Queen—an alliance concluded virtually at the same time that the *Book of the City of Ladies* was written.

The fact that the advice given to the ideal knight Hector comes from a woman should also not be overlooked, for it anticipates and corresponds to a predominant current running through Christine's subsequent prose writings: enhancing the position of Isabeau of Bavaria as one of the three regents governing France during her husband's mental illness. When Christine "feminizes" her writings, her intentions are profoundly and directly political, specifically creating a rationale for female regency.[54] The third part of *The Book of the City of Ladies* begins with an illumination showing how the Virgin Mary is ushered into the nearly completed City: this scene is schematically based on the entry of the queen into Paris, specifically the entrée of Isabeau of Bavaria to Paris on August 22, 1389, which Christine, living in Paris at the time, must certainly have personally witnessed and which Jean Froissart describes in his *Chroniques* (magnificently illustrated in a manuscript from 1470–1472 in BL Harley 4379).[55] The implicit analogy between the Virgin Mary and the Queen of France is anything but gratuitous: just as Christ shares his kingdom with his Spouse, so too does the King of France, the possessor of Christ's Crown of Thorns sometimes used in coronation rituals, share his kingdom with his Spouse. For this reason Christine also invokes early queens of France who had served as regents: Fredegund, the queen

---

54. See Earl Jeffrey Richards, "Political Thought as Improvisation: Female Regency and Mariology in Late Medieval French Thought," in *Virtue, Liberty, and Toleration: Political Ideas of European Women, 1400–1800*, ed. Jacqueline Broad and Karen Green (Dordrecht: Springer, 2007), 1–22; and Richards, "À la recherche du contexte perdu d'une ellipse chez Christine de Pizan: La 'coagulence regulee' et le pouvoir politique de la reine," in *Christine de Pizan, La scrittrice et la città / L'écrivaine et la ville / The Woman Writer and the City: Atti del VII Convegno Internazionale Christine de Pizan, Bologna, 22–26 settembre 2009*, ed. Patrizia Caraffi (Florence: Alinea, 2013), 93–112. See also Tracy Adams, "Christine de Pizan, Isabeau of Bavaria," *French Historical Studies* 32:1 (2009): 1–32; and Adams, *The Fight for France*.

55. Reproduced at <https://commons.wikimedia.org/wiki/File:Entr%C3%A9e_d%27Isabeau_de_Bavi%C3%A8re_dans_Paris.jpeg>.

of Chilperic, and Blanche de Castille, the queen of Louis IX. In her biography of Charles V, *Les fais et bonnes meurs du sage roy Charles V* (*The Deeds and Good Conduct of the Wise King Charles V*), commissioned by Philip the Bold before his death in 1404, Christine twice uses a neologism, *coagulence* ("gestation, fertility; harmony"), first to describe the dormant fertility of a seed in winter waiting to sprout in spring, which she compares to a child waiting to emerge from the mother's womb, and second to describe the order and "regulated harmony" governing all business in the court of Jeanne of Bourbon, Charles V's queen.[56] When Christine speaks of "regulated harmony" emanating from Queen Jeanne's court, she has a very specific fact in mind: Jeanne was the granddaughter of the Capetian monarch Philip III, the Bold (d. 1285), and her marriage to Charles V represented the physical reunion of the Capetian and Valois dynasties. In a similar move in the next generation, the marriage of Charles VI to Isabeau of Bavaria, a princess of the House of Wittelsbach-Ingolstadt, represented a renewed reunion between the French monarchy and the Holy Roman Emperor, for the mother of Charles V himself, Bonne de Luxembourg (born as Jutta von Luxemburg) was an Imperial princess and the sister of the Emperor Charles IV. Politically, the Queen's Court played a vital strategic role in late medieval Europe: for Christine's first noble and royal readers, Minerva advises Hector in the *Othea* much as Isabeau of Bavaria sought to advise Louis of Orléans as co-regent.

The entire *Othea* is structured according to the rhetorical topos of *sapientia et fortitudo*: wisdom and military valor, incarnated by the classical goddess Pallas/Minerva, who, despite her two different names in the *Othea*, is one and the same,[57] with "Pallas" being associated with wisdom and "Minerva" (whom Othea also calls "Hector's mother") with *chevalerie*, that is, military strength and valor.[58] In his classic study of the influence of medieval Latin literature on the

---

56. "We see in the nature of trees during different seasons strange operations, just as in winter the production and fertility is taken from the fruit to come, engendered by the sun's strength in the earth's womb, nourished in the root moistened by the necessary wetness, a time which can be compared to the infant in the womb of the mother" ("*nous veons en la nature des arbres en diverses saisons operacions estranges, si comme en yver est prise leur pregnacïon et coagulence du fruit à venir engendré des vertus du soleil ou ventre de la terre, nourri en la racine attrempée par moisteur couvenable, lequel temps se peut comparer à l'enfent ou ventre de sa mere*" (*Les fais et bonnes meurs du sage roy Charles V*, ed. Solente, 1:32 [chap. xii]); "In what order, in what regulated harmony in all things was governed the court of that most noble lady, the Queen Jeanne de Bourbon" ("*En quelle ordre, en quel coagulence regulée en toutes choses estoit gouvernée la court de la tres noble dame, la royne Jehanne de Bourbon*"), Ibid., 1:54–56 [chap. xx].

57. "[U]ne mesmes chose": Gloss 14; ed. Parussa.

58. See Andrea Tarnowski, "Pallas Athena, la science et la chevalerie," in *Sur le chemin de longue étude…. Actes du colloque d'Orléans, juillet 1995*, ed. Bernard Ribémont (Paris: Honoré Champion, 1998), 150. Christine plays with the goddess's twofold nature—represented by her Greek and Latin names (Pallas and Minerva, respectively)—in many subsequent works.

vernacular literatures of Europe, Ernst Robert Curtius identified a wide range of rhetorical commonplaces which attest to a continuity between medieval Latin and vernacular cultures. [59] In fact, the commonplace of *fortitudo et sapientia* is also biblical. It is found in Job and Ecclesiastes, texts frequently commented upon by the Church Fathers and as a result widely disseminated in sermons for the next millennium.[60] At the same time, as Barbara Newman has demonstrated, there was a long-standing Christian veneration of the divine wisdom as a feminine aspect of God.[61] In the entry on *fortitudo* ("strength, valor") in the *Manipulus florum* ("A Handful of Flowers," an early fourteenth-century thematically organized—actually indexed—Latin florilegium made up of over six thousand citations from the Church Fathers, essentially designed as a shortcut to help preachers in search of "quotable quotes"), Christine would have found a frequently cited comment by Saint Ambrose: "For where there is wisdom, there is virtue, there is constancy and strength" (*Ubi enim sapiencia, ibi uirtus, ibi constancia et fortitudo*).[62] For these reasons, the advice given by Othea, spokeswoman for wisdom, to Hector, representative of valor and Trojan ancestor of Louis of Orléans, would have been understood by the original public for the text within the context of the symbiosis of wisdom and strength. Othea herself is the voice of wisdom, of *sapientia*, speaking to Hector as the representative of military valor, and in the allegory of the entire work, *mutatis mutandis*, Christine takes on the role of the spokeswoman

---

59. See Ernst Robert Curtius, *European Literature and the Latin Middle Ages*, trans. Willard R. Trask (New York: Pantheon, 1953; reprint, Princeton, NJ: Princeton University Press, 2013), 167–76. Among these commonplaces, Curtius identified the importance of "fortitudo et sapientia" ("strength [or valor] and wisdom"—a cliché which survives in the saying that the pen is mightier than the sword). Curtius argued that this commonplace originated with Virgil, and that it was enshrined in medieval culture in a remark by Isidore of Seville in his *Etymologiae* ("Etymologies," the standard encyclopedia in Europe for over a millennium): "For men are called heroes as though worthy of the skies and of heaven because of their wisdom and strength" ("*Nam heroes appellantur viri quasi aerii et caelo digni propter sapientiam et fortitudinem*"). See Isidore of Seville, *Etymologiarum sive Originum Libri XX*, ed. W.M. Lindsay (Oxford: Clarendon Press, 1911), I.39.9.

60. Job 12:12–13: "In the ancient is wisdom, and in length of days prudence. With him is wisdom and strength" ("*in antiquis est sapientia et in multo tempore prudentia, apud ipsum est fortitudo et sapientia*"). Ecclesiastes 9:16: "And I said that wisdom is better than strength: how then is the wisdom of the poor man slighted, and his words not heard?" ("*et dicebam ego meliorem esse sapientiam fortitudine quomodo ergo sapientia pauperis contempta est et verba eius non sunt audita*").

61. Barbara Newman, *God and the Goddesses: Vision, Poetry, and Belief in the Middle Ages* (Philadelphia: University of Pennsylvania Press, 2003), chap. 5: "Sapientia: The Goddess Incarnate," 190–244.

62. Ambrose, *Epistulae et acta*, ed. Otto Faller (Vienna: Hoelder-Pinchler-Tempsky, 1968), 1:45, ll. 34–41. We have consistently consulted the original Latin of Thomas Hibernicus, *Manipulus florum* at Chris L. Nighman's website, *Digital Medievalist* <http://web.wlu.ca/history/cnighman/>. We have also repeatedly consulted the online Brepols Library of Latin Texts at <http://www.brepols.net/Pages/BrowseBySeries.aspx?TreeSeries=LLT-O > in order to verify Christine's Latin quotations.

for wisdom, and Louis of Orléans the representative of military valor. The political allegory could not have been plainer.

Later, in 1410, in writing her second, but very practically rather than spiritually oriented chivalric manual, the *Fais d'armes et de chevalerie* (*Deeds of Arms and Chivalry*),[63] Christine turns another female figure, Minerva, into the spokeswoman and authority of the work, and she tells Minerva that the two are both Italian women—again hinting at Isabeau of Bavaria who, while a German princess, had an Italian mother: Taddea Visconti, the daughter of Bernabò Visconti, Lord of Milan. In other words, Christine's allusion to her "Italian connection" applied to Isabeau as well—all in the name of enhancing the Queen's power.

The celebrated frontispiece of the Queen's Manuscript, showing Christine presenting the work to the Queen surrounded by her ladies in waiting, is itself a political statement. The walls of the Queen's chambers are covered by the impaled arms of Bavaria and France: white and blue oblique fusils, adopted by the House of Wittelsbach in 1242, are still used to this day in the Bavarian coat of arms, and hang next to the royal *fleurs de lys* in gold on a blue field (technically: *azure, semé-de-lys or*). When the manuscript was finished, the white fusils were done in silver, which has unfortunately tarnished over the centuries: all the same, with this in mind, one must imagine, when this manuscript was first opened, that the shiny silver of the Bavarian arms and the radiant gold of the French royal arms presented an overwhelming image of the *coagulence regulée*, of the regulated harmony emanating from Isabeau's court.[64] And it is in this luxury manuscript that Christine presented to the Queen this, her final version of the *Othea*, in which she retains her original dedication to the dead Louis of Orléans almost as a monument not only to his efforts as regent, but also to Christine's original advice to him and to Christine's attempts to represent Isabeau allegorically as Othea.

One final generic component of the *Othea* must, however, be mentioned before discussing the thorny question of Christine's use of allegory. In analyzing the format or arrangement of text (*mise en page*) of the many *Othea* manuscripts, Parussa observes that the tripartite presentation reproduces a specific format found in translations of the Bible and other "notable works" commissioned by

63. A bilingual Middle French-Middle High German edition is forthcoming: *Le Livre des fais d'armes et de chevalerie/Das Buoch von dem vechten und der ritterschaft*, ed. Danielle Buschinger, Earl Jeffrey Richards and Phillip Jeserich (Berlin: Berlin/Brandenburg Academy of Sciences). For a modern English translation, see: *The Book of the Deeds of Arms and of Chivalry*, ed. Charity Cannon Willard, trans. Sumner Willard (University Park: Pennsylvania State University Press, 1999).

64. Representing the Queen surrounded by her ladies in waiting was also not a gratuitous gesture. Thanks to the careful archival research of Yann Grandeau in "De quelques dames qui ont servi la reine Isabeau de Bavière," *Bulletin philologique et historique* (1975): 129–238, it is almost possible to identify the noblewomen surrounding Isabeau; more importantly, it is clear that Isabeau dynamically used her Court to arrange strategic marriages among noble families in order to preserve the stability of the kingdom.

Charles V.[65] In other words, Christine chose in the *Othea* to present her mirror for princes in a format originally used for translations with commentaries of the Bible. The crux of the difficulty in understanding Christine's use of allegory in the *Othea* is that she follows a threefold rather than the more traditional fourfold exegesis of Scripture. In her *Advision Cristine* (1405), Christine explicitly says that "the fiction of this book can be allegorized in a threefold way, first with regard to the world in general, which is the earth, then to the individual man, and then to the kingdom of France."[66] The word used here for "threefold," *triblement* (from the very common Scholastic Latin term *tripliciter*, which also frequently occurs in prayers asking for a threefold intercession), is extremely rare in medieval French.[67] The rarity of the word should on the one hand alert us to the fact that when Christine decided to use allegory in the *Othea*, she did not feel bound by traditional genres, and on the other hand make us search for Christine's possible inspiration or source, a search made easy by the online Brepols Library of Latin Texts. The answer emerges quickly: Thomas Aquinas speaks of threefold allegory in explaining a passage in the Psalms.[68] Christine often seems to take her cue from the Angelic Doctor in matters allegorical: on four occasions she speaks of the "theologizing poets" or *poetes theologisans*, which translates a concept used by Aquinas at least seventeen times (his terms are *poetae theologi, poetae theologizantes*, or *theologi poetae*), particularly in discussing how ancient poets, especially Ovid, spoke of Chaos. The reason that Christine must have had Aquinas in mind is that one of the times when she uses *poetes theologisans* is at the beginning of the *Advision* when she herself speaks of Chaos—again, a rare term,[69]

---

65. See above, 13, and note 43.

66. "Nous avons ja dit comment la fiction de cestui livre se puet alegorisier triblement, c'est assavoir assimiller au monde general, qui est la terre, aussi a homme simgulier et puis au royaume to France": *Advision Cristine*, 6.

67. The first example is found in the late twelfth-century Anglo-Norman Cambridge Psalter, which translates the alternate Latin translation of Psalms 79:5 "*et potabis nos in lacrymis tripliciter*" ("Thou giveth us to drink three times in tears") as "*e abrevas nus en lermes treblement*." A second Anglo-Norman attribution, from the first quarter of the thirteenth century, shows up in the *Miroir ou Les Évangiles des domnées* (an anthology of the Gospel readings for Sundays), translated by Robert de Gretham: "*treblement pecchum par curage / E treblementes par charnage*" ("We sin threefold in thought, / And threefold in the flesh," ed. Aitken, p. 49). A century and a half later, Nicole Oresme uses *treblement* in his translation of Aristotle's *De caelo, Le livre du ciel et du monde* (1377). Christine uses *triblement* in the *Advision*, in the *Book of the Body Politic* (*Livre du corps de policie*), and in her account of the Passion ("The Hours of Contemplation of the Passion of Our Lord," *Heures de la contemplation de la Passion de Nostre Seigneur*).

68. Thomas Aquinas, *In Psalmos reportatio*, Psalmus: 26, sectio: 12, ed. Parmensis, pag.: 240, col.: 2, linea: 43: "*Haec verba exponuntur tripliciter: historice, allegorice et moraliter.*"

69. Prior to Oresme, there are only two earlier attributions of the word "chaos" in medieval French: in *Les faits des Romains* (1214) and in *L'Ovide moralisé* (1317–1328).

which like *treblement/triblement*, is also found before her in Oresme's translation of Aristotle's *De caelo*.[70] Yet even when Aquinas speaks of threefold allegory, he is essentially recycling an extremely common Scholastic formula (particularly popular among Franciscans) on how a question "can be understood in a threefold manner" (*tripliciter intelligi potest*). Christine Reno and Liliane Dulac, the editors of the *Advision*, rightly stress the elasticity of allegory and permeability of its categories for Christine. The allegorical procedure of the *Advision*, while different from the threefold format of the *Othea's texte, glose, allegorie*, shares the same creativity and unconventionality—and the allegorical figures of *The Book of the City of Ladies* follow a different allegorical pattern all together. For this reason, we would conclude that the *Othea's* genre is an unconventional mirror for princes couched in the format of recent Bible translations with commentary, which in turn opens up the complicated question of the *Othea's* much misunderstood use of allegory.

Christine's threefold allegory undoubtedly represents a departure from the more traditional fourfold allegory, summarized around 1260 by Thomas Aquinas's colleague at the Sorbonne, Augustinus de Dacia, probably for the benefit of his students, in what has often been taken as the unchangeable and monolithic formulation of fourfold allegory: "the letter teaches what happened, allegory teaches what you should believe, the moral sense what you should do, and the anagogical sense teaches where you should hope (or tend)" ("*littera gesta docet, quid credas allegoria, / moralis quid agas, quo speres* [var. *tendas*] *anagogia*").[71] Christine's threefold allegory forgoes the anagogical sense, and reverses the order of the moral sense (which she calls the gloss) and the allegorical sense.

In her posthumously published (1966) and highly influential *Allegorical Imagery: Some Mediaeval Books and Their Posterity*, the medievalist Rosemund Tuve[72] defined the *Othea's* genre as being a treatise on Christian morality modeled after Laurent d'Orléans's *Somme le roi* (*The King's Encyclopedia*, a treatise on the

---

70. While there is no consensus regarding Aquinas' influence on Christine, there does seem to be a direct connection between Aquinas' reflections on the role of theology and poetry and Christine's use of allegory. In his commentaries on Aristotle's *Metaphysics* and *Physics*, Thomas revives the concept of poet-theologians attested in Augustine (*theologi poetae* in the *City of God*), and used by Isidore in his *Etymologies* (a search at the online Brepols Library of Latin texts documents the relative rarity of the term). Thomas also uses the parallel term *poeti theologizantes*, or "poets speaking theologically," (a term otherwise only found in scholastic Latin translations of Dionysius Areopagita). Here the present participle of the rare verb *theologizare* stands out in particular. Christine has followed Aquinas closely in her use, not only of the phrase *thelogiens pouetes* (used twice in *Advision*), but also of the phrase *poetes theologisans* (used five times in *Advision*).

71. Augustine of Dacia, *Augustini de Dacia O. P. "Rotulus pugillaris" examinatus atque editus,* ed. Angelus Walz (Rome: Angelicum, 1929), 30.

72. Rosemond Tuve, *Allegorical Imagery: Some Mediaeval Books and Their Posterity* (Princeton, NJ: Princeton University Press, 1966).

virtues and vices finished in 1280 for King Philip III, the Bold), a work composed toward the end of a period that saw the composition of similar encyclopedic works such as Gautier de Metz's *Image of the World* (*Image du monde*) and Brunetto Latini's *Book of Treasure* (*Livres dou tresor*).[73] Tuve, a pioneer in studies on the *Othea* with whom one still needs to engage, calls the work "an ingenious little classical *Somme le roi* with adornments."[74] This generic identification is simply wrong. She goes on to level a series of sharp but also deeply flawed criticisms of Christine's use of allegory in the *Othea*, criticisms which, until the publication of Armand Strubel's 2002 study, "*Grant senefiance a*": *Allégorie et littérature au Moyen Âge*,[75] dominated the reception of the *Othea* for fifty years (we have added underlined italics to problematic phrases):

> Many explanations of Christine's method have been given; even the best students of the *Othea* do not make the connection between it and the ancient distinctions of religious exegesis. Accordingly, and as always, *much criticism at her expense derives from expecting her to do what she is not doing*. She glosses her *texte*, not the full ancient story: she is providing ways to read, not substitutions, and they are sketches of illuminating extensions, *not ways to get rid of the pagan story* […]. One reason for Christine's lesser success in obtaining *our sympathetic concurrence* as to where lie moral beauty and ugliness, is in *her ineptitudes touching a literary quality* which we extolled in Jean de Meun: careful government of the decorum of details.[76] (emphasis added.)

Tuve summarizes precisely the problem: much criticism of Christine stems "from expecting her to do what she is not doing." Tuve's criticism boils down essentially to the fact that she does not think Christine's *Othea* is as good as Jean de Meun's part of the *Romance of the Rose* or Edmund Spenser's *The Fairie Queene*. However, since we know from the Quarrel over the *Rose*, which took place at virtually the same time Christine was writing the *Othea*, that Christine objected to Jean's use of allegory and contrasted it with that of Dante, it is unfair to criticize her for not following Jean de Meun—which in fact amounts to expecting her to do what she is most certainly not doing. Moreover, her application of allegory in the *Othea*, given the contemporaneity of the Quarrel, may in part be seen as claims made for

73. Edith Brayer, "Contenu, structure et combinaisons du *Miroir du monde* et de la *Somme le roi*," *Romania* 79 (1958): 1–38.

74. Tuve, *Allegorical Imagery*, 286.

75. Armand Strubel, "*Grant senefiance a*": *Allégorie et littérature au Moyen Âge* (Paris: Honoré Champion, 2002).

76. Tuve, *Allegorical Imagery*, 290–91.

Jean de Meun's personification allegory, which continuously, as a kind of running joke, promises a gloss that is never given.[77] If anything, the rigor and clarity of the *Othea*'s allegorical structure contrast markedly with the teasing playfulness of Jean de Meun's allegory, which always demurs from glossing his text, whereas Christine resolutely, almost obsessively, supplies gloss and allegory to hers. During the Quarrel over the *Rose*, Christine compared Jean de Meun's use of allegory to the "glosses of Orléans that destroy the text"—an allusion to a famous debate between legal scholars from the Universities of Orléans and Bologna, in which the jurists from Orléans used commentaries or glosses on a text from Roman law to undermine the arguments put forth by the jurists from Bologna, to subvert the very referentiality of the legal text itself.[78]

How does allegory function in the *Othea*? She begins with an illumination for the short text in verse dedicated to a mythological figure that immediately follows. These text sections in each chapter are often the most difficult passages in the work to translate because they combine in a very dense manner both a mythological tale and a moral lesson, which are then explicated in the gloss and allegory sections. The gloss sections explain the original mythological tale, citing first a pagan authority drawn from sapiential literature. The allegorical section presents the moral lesson of the story, and regularly quotes a Church Father or patristic author. As Christine herself explains in the gloss of Chapter One, "We at present, Christians by the grace of God illumined by the true faith, can deduce the moral sense in the opinions of the ancients. And on these matters many beautiful allegories can be constructed." A few lines later she continues in her brief "Prologue to the Allegory," placed before the allegory section of Chapter 1: "In order to break down the argument of our subject matter into its underlying allegory, let us apply Holy Scripture to our writings for the edification of the soul

---

77. See Renate Blumenfeld-Kosinski, "Overt and Covert: Amorous and Interpretive Strategies in the *Roman de la Rose*," *Romania* 111 (1990): 432–53.

78. See Earl Jeffrey Richards, "*Glossa Aurelianensis est quae destruit textum*: Medieval Rhetoric, Thomism and Humanism in Christine de Pizan's Critique of the *Roman de la Rose*," *Cahiers de recherches médiévales, XIIIe-XVe siècles* 5 (1998): 247–63, at 247: "The continuous and systematic subversion of referentiality in Jean's work ultimately, at least in Christine's view, destroys the text's meaning in the name of the text's form. Christine's claim captures *in nuce* her entire philosophy of literature itself, for she was combatting the rhetorization of literature for its own sake, divorced from a concern for society's morals." See also Richards, "*Les contraires choses*: Irony in Jean de Meun's Part of the *Roman de la Rose* and the Problem of Truth and Intelligibility in Thomas Aquinas," in *Nouvelles de la Rose: Actualité et perspectives du* Roman de la Rose, edited by Dulce María González Doreste and Maria del Pilar Mendoza-Ramos (La Laguna: Servicio de Publicaciones, Universidad de La Laguna, 2011), 375–90; and Richards, "Introduction: Returning to a 'Gracious Debate': The Intellectual Context of the Epistolary Exchange of the Debate about the *Roman de la Rose*," in *Debating the* Roman de la Rose: *A Critical Anthology*, ed. Christine McWebb, with introduction and Latin translations by Richards (New York: Routledge, 2007; reprint, 2011), xxi–xxxvi.

abiding in this wretched world." Why did Christine feel this particular need to explain allegory to her readers?

The simple and somewhat stupefying answer is that the term *allegorie/alegorie* was relatively rare in French before Christine. The first attribution is found in an Anglo-Norman work by Philippe de Thaon, *Li compuz* (The book of calculation), written between 1113 and 1119. Around 1225, the word is used once in the saints' lives of Barlaam and Josaphat.[79] The *Ovide moralisé*, written about a century later, and which is 72,000 lines long, uses the term *alegorie* only eight times. Some fifty years later, Eustache Deschamps and Philippe de Mézières, both of whom Christine personally knew, use the word a few times in their works as well, but it is not until the *Othea* that the word *allegorie* is used frequently in any French text. Christine apparently could also not rely on her readers, some of whom like Louis of Orléans spoke Latin well, to understand the word *allegorie* as a Latinism, so she added her prologue. Hitherto critics of the *Othea* have overlooked the fact that, despite the prevalence of personification allegory in medieval French texts, explicitly allegorical exegesis, following Patristic and scholastic models, only begins with the *Othea*. As early as 1979, Mary Ann Ignatius argued that the *Othea* was in fact an experiment in literary form whose textual non-linearity combined with illuminations sets up an open metaphorical game.[80] In effect, Ignatius has identified how the Othea produces in readers a kind of open-ended meditation that was in fact traditionally long associated with allegory, namely a process of rumination or *ruminatio*, which entails almost a kind of free association. This process underscores the kind of hermeneutic dynamism—perhaps volatility—central to the *Othea*. Christine intentionally challenges her readers, especially when these readers were princes of the blood, to reflect, to ruminate on the exempla she assembles and comments upon—for rumination was the basis of all allegorical commentary in the first place.[81]

How legitimate is it to fault Christine for "not getting rid of the pagan story," as Rosemund Tuve did in the quote discussed above? Traditionally, the metaphor of "Egyptian gold" introduced by Augustine in *On Christian Doctrine* in invoked here: the Israelites fleeing Egypt absconded with the ("borrowed") golden idols and treasures of their neighbors, which they later melted down for their own purposes (but not for the Golden Calf, as the Church Fathers hastened

79. Gui de Cambrai (attributed), *Balaham und Josaphas*, ed. Carl Appel (Halle: M. Niemeyer, 1907), 228, v. 7718, dated ca. 1220–1225.

80. Mary Ann Ignatius, "Christine de Pizan's *Epistre Othea*: An Experiment in Literary Form," *Medievalia et Humanistica*, n.s. 9 (1979): 127–42.

81. Gabriella Parussa, "Christine de Pizan: Une lectrice avide et une vulgarisatrice fidèle des *rumigacions du latin et des parleures des belles sciences*," in *Traduction et adaptation en France à la fin du Moyen Âge et à la Renaissance: Actes du colloque organisé par l'Université de Nancy II, 23–25 mars 1995*, ed. Charles Brucker (Paris: Champion, 1997), 161–75.

to explain). However, getting rid of the pagan story would contradict Christine's purpose in celebrating French political legitimacy based on a continuity flowing from the pagan Trojan origins of the French monarchy. Her appeal to the Trojan origins of Louis of Orléans are emblematic when, in her dedication, she calls him the "lofty flower (…) Ancient nobility of Trojan stock." And briefly, to speak of Christine's "ineptitudes touching a literary quality" is an objection that has been put to rest in the last thirty years. We now recognize a profoundly creative and original—and provocative—quality in Christine's works that was routinely denied to them before the publication of the first modern English translation of *The Book of the City of Ladies* in 1982.

In his analysis of late medieval allegory, Armand Strubel draws a careful comparison between Christine's practice and that found in the *Ovide moralisé*. His brief, precise observations allow us to move from Christine's use of allegory to the question of her sources, for he begins by contrasting the coherence of *Othea*'s allegorical organization with the more erratic approach of the *Ovide moralisé*. He finds fault with earlier scholars who criticized Christine for not conforming to early traditions of allegory: he aptly points out "the singularity of her approach" ("*la singularité de sa démarche*").[82] That the text section of chapters affords counsel wins his approval as well: this conative function proves close to the explicit didactic impulse of the Othea, a departure from the opinion of Tuve, for whom "*good allegory never tells* in so many words."[83]

Recent scholarship, particularly the edition of Gabriella Parussa and studies by Mary A. and Richard H. Rouse[84] and by Jane Chance,[85] has carefully identified the sources used by Christine in the *Othea*. These include the above-mentioned *Ovide moralisé* and *Histoire ancienne jusqu'à César* as well as *Le Chapelet des vertus* (The Garland of Virtues, a late fourteenth-century collection of quotations drawn from sapiential literature: the Church Fathers and the Bible); the *Manipulus florum*; the *Dits moraulx des philosophes* (The Moral Sayings of the Philosophers), a collection of sapiential literature, originally composed in Arabic, and translated from a Latin version into Middle French by Guillaume de Tignonville,[86] to whom

---

82. Strubel, "*Grant senefiance a,*" 248.

83. Tuve, *Allegorical Imagery*, 290 (italics in the original).

84. Mary A. Rouse and Richard H. Rouse, "Prudence, Mother of Virtues: The *Chapelet des vertus* and Christine de Pizan," *Viator* 39 (2008): 185–228.

85. Jane Chance, "Franco-Italian Christine de Pizan's *Epistre Othea,* 1399–1401: A Feminized Commentary on Ovid," in Chance, *Medieval Mythography*, 3:206–71.

86. See David J. Wrisley, "Modeling the Transmission of al-Mubashshir Ibn Fātik's *Mukhtār al-Ḥikam* in Medieval Europe: Some Initial Data-Driven Explorations," in "Digital Humanities in Jewish, Christian and Arabic/Islamic Ancient Traditions," Special issue, *Journal of Religion, Media, and Digital Culture* 5:1 (2016): 228–57.

Christine sent her first collection of letters from the Quarrel over the *Rose* in 1402; and the *Eschecs amoureux moralisés*.

Another interesting facet of Christine's sources is provided by a passing reference in Gloss 6, "as one sees in the works of Geber [Jabir ibn Hayyan] or Nicolas [Flamel] and other authorities in this science."[87] At first glance this reference seems like just another obscure and learned reference that the attentive editor needs to explain and then basically file away. Clearly Christine expected her readers, especially Louis of Orléans, to recognize the names. The difference in this case is that this passing reference is one of the earliest, if not the earliest, reference to two major alchemist authors in a vernacular text: Jabir ibn Hayyan or Geber (d. 815) and Nicolas Flamel (ca. 1340–1418), who claimed to have found the Philosopher's Stone, and who reappears in 1997 in J. K. Rowling's first *Harry Potter* novel. Geber, which transliterates Jabir ibn Hayyan, was the Latin name associated with a huge body of alchemist works. Besides this allusion in the *Othea*, Christine also mentions him in her later biography of Charles V, "as Geber says at the beginning of his alchemist work" (*"comme dit Geber au commencement de son livre albrimiste"*).[88] Christine's father Thomas was considered one of the greatest alchemist authorities of his time. Although Christine voiced clear reserves about alchemy in *Advision*, she clearly was abreast of alchemist topics, as the second allusion to Nicolas Flamel here confirms. Nicolas Flamel became—but only at the end, not the beginning, of the fifteenth century—the epitome of the alchemist.[89] Christine's remark, however, is one of the earliest, if not the earliest reference to him as an alchemist, and she could have known him personally for two reasons: first, he began his career as a scribe, and Christine, during her early widowhood, is assumed to have earned her living as a scribe in a legal chancery; and second, he was interested in alchemy, and Christine's father was the major alchemist authority of late fourteenth-century France. The salient point here is that this passing casual remark suddenly revives a lost courtly audience by whom this reference would have been immediately understood.

The same applies to another passing remark made by Christine in the prologue to the still unpublished *Livre de la prod'hommie de l'homme* (*The Book of Man's Probity*). Here, Christine portrays what was apparently a daily scene at the royal court, where, speaking of Louis of Orléans holding court, she notes that

---

87. For the reasons explained below, we believe that Christine meant Nicolas Flamel when she wrote *Nicolas*. Parussa, *Epistre d'Othea*, 394, offers two other conjectures: Nicholas Comes or Nicholaus de Paganica.

88. Ed. Solente, 2:164 and 165n1. The work in question has since been identified as the Pseudo-Geber's *Summa perfectionis magistri*, "The Master's Handbook of Perfection."

89. See Didier Kahn, "Recherches sur l'alchimie française des XVe, XVIe et XVIIe siècles," *Chrysopœia* 5 (1992–1996): 321–452, especially the part "Un témoin précoce de la naissance du mythe de Flamel alchimiste: *Le Livre Flamel* (fin du XVe siècle)," at 387–429 of the "Recherches."

he regularly cited Latin and French authors to characterize *prodommie* (probity, prudence, honesty, integrity): "And I used to hear you describe [probity] so well and so nobly, citing intentionally holy authorities, both in Latin and in French, in cogent proofs on this subject, as the legislator of the noble and virtuous man's integrity" ("*Et je vous ouioe descrire tant bien et tant notablement, allegant a propos auctoritez sainctes, tant en latin comme en françois, par preuves vraies, comme legiste de la prodommie du noble et vertueux homme …*")[90] The allusions to alchemy and to a bilingual Latin-French court should make us, so many centuries later, sensitive to the original public of the *Othea*.

The most obvious conclusion to be drawn from this list of sources is that the *Othea* was written within the erudite environment of the French royal court, and that Christine's careful combination of these sources, which might appear perplexing to contemporary readers, was immediately comprehensible and coherent to her medieval audience.

Afterlife of the Othea

The *Othea* continued to be copied in richly illuminated manuscripts for the rest of the fifteenth century. Sometime around 1460, Jean Miélot, a cleric and secretary of Philip the Good, Duke of Burgundy, produced a simplified, but slightly expanded rewriting of the entire text,[91] adding an extra chapter where he explained that Christine's laconic verses had obscured the work's content for its readers ("*briefveté rend les materes obscures aux liseurs*"), and that although she had taken much material from Boccaccio's *Genealogy of the Gods*, Virgil's *Aeneid*, and Ovid's *Metamorphoses*, among other poets and philosophers, it was still necessary to expand her allegorical explanations. In other words, the expectations of a mid-fifteenth century public had clearly and subtly shifted from those of the original readers. This phenomenon needs to be studied in much detail, because it goes hand in hand with the survival of some of Christine's works in print.

The introduction of printing in the mid-fifteenth century dramatically changed the afterlife of Christine's work in both France and England. Early printers, like Antoine Vérard in France or William Caxton in England, were keenly sensitive to the demands of the new market for printed books. Vérard published two works by Christine, the *Fais d'Armes et de Chevalerie* in 1488 and *the Livre des Trois Vertus* in 1497. Caxton published translations of *The morale proverbes of Cristyne* (Christine's Moral Proverbs) in 1478 and, commissioned by the King, *The Book of Fayttes of Armes and Chyvalrye* in 1489. The *Othea*, however, was not printed until 1499, by Philippe Pigouchet. While the *Othea* was translated twice

---

90. *Livre de la prod'hommie de l'homme,* MS Vatican, Reg. lat. 1238, fol. 2r–2v.

91. This version is in manuscript Fondation Martin Bodmer 49, the basis of the modern French translation by Basso in her 2008 *Lettre d'Othéa* (2008), reproduced as a beautiful facsimile.

into English in the fifteenth century, first around 1440, by Stephen Scrope (*The Epistle of Othea to Hector or the Boke of Knyghthode*), and dedicated to his father-in-law John Fastolf,[92] and then again in the second half of the fifteenth century by Anthony Babyngton *(Lytil bibell of knyghthod, The epistle of Othea to Hector)*, it was only first printed in a third English translation in 1549 by Robert Wyer (*Here foloweth the. C. hystoryes of Troye. Lepistre de Othea deesse de Prudence, enuoyee a lesperit cheualereny [sic] Hector de Troye, auec cent histoires*).

Whether Edmund Spenser, in his allegorical depiction of Elizabeth I in *The Fairie Queene* (1590), had Christine's *Othea* in mind (and perhaps also her *City of Ladies*, which appeared in an English translation, *The boke of the cyte of ladyes,* done by Brian Anslay in 1521 for the court of Catharine of Aragon when her position as Henry VIII's queen had become tenuous) is still an open question that has fascinated scholars for decades. Elizabeth I herself possessed six sets of tapestries depicting scenes for the *City of Ladies*,[93] so it is clear that Christine's thoughts on chivalry and women enjoyed significant influence among aristocratic women of the Elizabethan age. As the saying goes, *habent sua fata libri*: books have their own individual fates, and the *Othea* is no exception. What remains striking, though, is how dynamic the memory of her works has remained through the centuries, and it is hoped that this translation will continue this dynamism.

92. Fastolf was a distinguished knight who became a member of the Order of the Garter in 1426, and, of course, later served as the prototype for Shakespeare's Falstaff in *Henry VI, Part 1*.

93. See Susan Groag Bell, *The Lost Tapestries of the* City of Ladies: *Christine de Pizan's Renaissance Legacy* (Berkeley and Los Angeles: University of California Press, 2004).

Othea's Letter to Hector

O most lofty flower, praised throughout the world,
Pleasant to all, and approved by God,
O flower of the lily,[1] o fleur de lys, sweet, fragrant, delightful
Whose powerful worth and high value are well-known above all,
First of all, praise be to God,
And then to you, noble flower
Who were transplanted from heaven to ennoble the world.
A legitimate and pure dominion,
Ancient nobility of Trojan stock,[2]
Pillar of faith unsullied by the least error,
Whose high renown no place could conceal.
And praise to you, most noble excellent prince,
Louis, duke of Orléans, of great fame,
Son of Charles, the fifth of this name,
You, who, besides the King, know no greater,
My most acclaimed and revered lord.
I, with humble intention, a poor creature
—An ignorant woman of low stature,
Daughter of a late philosopher and doctor
Who was the counselor and humble servant[3]
Of your father, whom God may spare,
And by whose command long ago
Came from Bologna the Fat,
Where he had been born,
Master Tommaso da Pizzano, otherwise

1. The translation here attempts to reproduce a recurrent rhetorical feature of the verse passages of the *Othea*, namely *hyperbaton*: the separation of grammatical elements or reversal of normal grammatical order in an individual phrase (such as in Shakespeare's *Hamlet,* I.v.27–28: *Murder most foul*). Here, between lines one and three, Christine separates "fleur," or flower, from "de lys," or of the lily (the *fleur de lys* was the heraldic symbol of the French monarchy), in her description of Louis of Orléans, in order to insert the phrase "praised throughout the world, / Pleasant to all, and approved by God" between "flower" and "of the lily."

2. This reference to the Trojan origin of the French monarchy in the midst of the Hundred Years' War was anything but a gratuitous gesture. Christine's intention is to enhance Louis of Orléans as a co-regent during the episodes of madness suffered by his brother, King Charles VI.

3. Here Christine skillfully links her own genealogy to that of Louis of Orléans: just as her father Tommaso da Pizzano was the adviser to Louis's father, Charles V, she, Tommaso's daughter, will assume the role of adviser to Charles V's son.

Known as da Bologna,
Famous everywhere as a celebrated scholar—
But I desire, as best as I know how,
To create something pleasant
Which would put you on the path
To some pleasure, which would be great glory for me.
And for this reason I, of unworthy memory,
Have now undertaken to put this work to verse,
My revered lord, and to send it to you
On the first day when the year begins anew,
For its subject is quite new
Though envisaged with a coarse intelligence—
For I do not have an intellect based on a perception of the physical world,
Nor in this case do I resemble my good father, except as one gathers
Ears of wheat while gleaning at harvest
In the middle of these fields, near the bushes,
Or the crumbs falling from the high table
Which one gathers when fine dishes are served up—
I gathered nothing else from his great knowledge of the physical world
Which he had long cultivated.
So please do not disparage my work,
My revered lord, humane and wise,
Out of scorn for my ignorant person,
For a small bell often rings out loud enough
To wake the most wise,
And counsel them to labor in study.
For this reason, most honorable and kind prince,
I, Christine, a woman unworthy
Of written learning[4] in order to undertake a work conceived this way,
Wish to begin to put to rhyme and prose
An epistle which was sent to Hector of Troy,
Just as the story admits.

---

4. Christine's original phrase *une femme indigne / de sens acquis* seems to echo a phrase used by Eustache Deschamps in a poem composed after 1403 praising Christine: *Nompareille que je saiche au jour d'ui / En sens acquis et en toute dotrine* ("incomparable, as best as I know, nowadays, in book-learning and doctrine"): Deschamps, *Œuvres complètes*, ed. Auguste Queux de Saint-Hilaire and Gaston Raynaud (Paris: Firmin-Didot), vol. 6 (1889):251. The term *sens acquis* is first attested in the prologue to *Les enseignements de Théodore Paléologue*, ed. Christine Knowles (London: Modern Humanities Research Association, 1983), where Jean de Vignay, the French translator of the Latin version, writes of *.iij. choses bien droiturieres et justes* ("three most right and just things") needed to understand a text, and the second right and just thing is called *sens accidentel, c'est a dire sens acquis comme est escripture* ("that incidental knowledge, that is, that acquired knowledge which is like book learning").

Were this not so, it still could be probable,
And in this epistle there would still be
Many verses and notable sayings
Worth hearing and even more worth understanding.
Starting now I want to turn to the beginning,
May God grant me in His praise to write
The deeds and sayings and events which might please
You, my revered lord, for whom I accept this task
And, should I commit any error, I humbly beseech
The generosity of your great nobility
To pardon me if, by writing to you, such a worthy person,
I, in unworthy wisdom, undertake something too audacious.

In order that those who are not learned poets might understand concisely the meaning of the stories in this book, it should be understood that wherever images are shown in clouds, these are figures of gods and goddesses about whom the letter which follows in this book speaks,[5] following the manner of speech used by the ancient poets. And because deity is a spiritual matter, and elevated above the earth, these images are represented in clouds, and the first image is that of the goddess of wisdom.

Here begins the epistle of Othea the goddess, which she sent to Hector of Troy when he was fifteen years old.[6]

5. Here Christine explains one of her iconographic strategies. The running commentaries later on in the text at the end of several Allegories may have been designed to give illuminators directions on illustrating the text. We have few other examples in medieval literature of similar personal commentaries by authors on the illuminations of their works, but it suggests that Christine's works need to be interpreted closely with the help of iconography.

6. The first forty-four chapters are organized according to the Four Cardinal Virtues, the moral influences of the planets, the Seven Deadly Sins, the Articles of Faith, and the Ten Commandments, an original format within the genre of a mirror for princes. The remaining chapters present distinct moralizing tableaux, each with its own lesson. While Christine invokes traditional associations between pagan traditions and Christianity (such as Apollo as a figure of Christ), the larger associations that she creates by weaving together mythology, pagan sapiential literature, Biblical lore, and Patristic sources are all strikingly original. After this point in the work, the thematic organization is less rigid. See the Introduction for more details.

Text 1

Othea, goddess of prudence,[7]
Who addresses brave hearts in courage,
First sent greetings with true love
And without deception to you, Hector,
Noble and powerful prince,
Successor of the noble Trojans,
The heir of Troy and its citizens,
Ever distinguished in arms,
Son of Mars, the god of battle,
Who exhibits and perfects feats of arms,
And of Minerva,[8] the powerful goddess,
Herself the mistress of arms.[9]
And since I desire that your worthiness,
Which I seek here,
Be preserved and increased,
And that your valor and great courage,
Now in the prime of youth,
Be observed at all times,
I want to admonish you with this letter,
And to express and exhort
Those things which are necessary
For great valor, and contrary
And opposed to bravery—
So that your good heart will direct itself
To acquire through good schooling
The horse which flies through the air—
The famed Pegasus
Beloved of all brave men.
Because I know your condition
By its direct inclination

7. Throughout all of her works, Christine uses the term "prudence" some 218 times, particularly in the *Othea*, in her biography of Charles V, in the *City of Ladies*, and in the *Livre de la Paix*—all works whose political didactic purpose is obvious.

8. Christine here prepares the reader for the two very important chapters, 13 and 14, dedicated to the synthesis of wisdom and military valor in the mythical Greek deity Pallas Athena, called Minerva in Latin.

9. Here Christine sets up the fundamental dialogic structure underlying the entire *Othea*, a dialogue between wisdom and military valor, between Othea and Hector, which corresponds to the rhetoric topos of *sapientia et fortitudo* and, by extension, to the double nature of Pallas Athena/Minerva.

Is more skilled at knightly deeds
Than five hundred thousand others.
And since as goddess I know
With certainty and not by trial
The things which will come about,
I must commemorate you,
For I know that you will always be
The bravest of the brave, and will have
Fame above all others,
Provided that I am loved by you—
Loved, and why shouldn't I be loved?—
For I am the one who arranges everything.
From my chair[10] I give lectures
To those who love me and hold me dear,
Lectures which will lift them to heaven,
And so I ask you that you also be in heaven
And that you are willing to believe in me devoutly.
Now commit firmly to your memory
The sayings which I want to write to you,
And if you dare to recount or to say to me
Something which is to come,
I will tell you that you must remember it,
As though it were something past:
Know that these things are in my thoughts
In the spirit of prophecy.
And understand, and do not be distressed,
For I will say nothing which will not happen,
And if it has not already happened, then try to remember it.

10. The term "chair" here refers to a professorial chair and is highly provocative, given the prohibition against women teaching men expressed by Saint Paul in 1 Timothy 2:12 ("I do not permit a woman to teach"), a prohibition embraced throughout the Middle Ages. Two illuminations of Christine in the Queen's Manuscript show her lecturing from a professor's chair to a group of men and to her son.

Gloss 1

In Greek "Othea"[11] may be taken for the "wisdom of women."[12] And, whereas the ancients, still lacking the light of the true faith, worshipped many gods, under which religion the mightiest empires arose ever to have existed in the world, such as the kingdoms of Assyria, Persia, of the Greeks and Trojans, Alexander, of the Romans and many others, and likewise the greatest philosophers flourished, although God had not yet opened the door of His mercy, we at present, Christians by the grace of God illumined by the true faith, can deduce the moral sense in the opinions of the ancients. And on these matters many beautiful allegories can be constructed. And as the ancients were accustomed to worship all things which had the privilege of some grace beyond the common course of events, they called several wise women who lived in their time goddesses. And it is true, according to history, that at the time when great Troy flourished in such high renown, a very wise woman named Othea, reflecting on the fair youth of Hector of Troy, who flourished in virtues which could demonstrate future divine bounties in him, sent him fair and remarkable gifts, even including the beautiful war-horse called

11. The origins of the name "Othea" have been widely commented upon, but all explanations remain speculative; some commentators argue, apparently with little regard for grammar, for a Greek etymology, since "thea" (θέα) is the Greek word for goddess. The problem is that the correct definite article in Greek for "thea" would be "he" (ἡ) and not "ho" (ὁ)—unless "o" (and not "ho") here is taken as a kind of vocative, but here the argumentation starts to become contortionist. Christine will of course later speak of Minerva explicitly as goddess of both wisdom and of arms (uniting the two elements of the topos of *sapientia et fortitudo*), but Christine knew no Greek. When she plays on the etymology of a Greek word such as philosophy, and speaks in the *City of Ladies* of some supposedly wise but misogynist men as being adherents of "philosofolly" rather than philosophy, it is clear that she puns on Greek words using Latin etyma.

12. There is a very modest body of Patristic and scholastic commentary on the most influential biblical sources for the wisdom of women (*sagece de femme*): Proverbs 14:1, "Every wise woman buildeth her house" (*Sapiens mulier aedificat domum suam*) and the so-called *versio antiqua* reading of Job 38:36, "Who gave women the wisdom to weave?" (*Quis dedit mulieribus texturae sapientiam*, follows exactly the Septuagint reading, τίς δὲ ἔδωκε γυναιξὶν ὑφάσματος σοφίαν;—translated by Jerome as *Quis posuit in visceribus hominis sapientiam*? "Who hath put wisdom in the inward parts?"). The influential Marian encyclopedia from the mid-twelfth century composed by Richard de Saint-Laurent, *De laudibus Beatae Mariae Virginis* ("On the praises of the Blessed Virgin Mary") marks a turning point in speaking of women's wisdom. It repeatedly references the Virgin's wisdom, and this, in turn, sparked the rise in Franciscan devotion to the Virgin as a sapiential figure (already present of course in the Orthodox tradition of Hagia Sophia) in the late thirteenth-century writings of Bonaventure. Here the theme of how Mary's wisdom redeemed Eve's folly is prominent, and was connected to the Parable of the Wise and Foolish Virgins (Matthew 25:1–13). In this sense, Christine's figure of Othea, by constantly alluding to pagan sapiential literature and Patristic and scholastic authors, acts as a kind of pagan allegorical anticipation of the Virgin. The use of iconographic details in *Othea* illuminations supervised by Christine, such as the traditional blue mantle of the Madonna of Mercy, underscores this association.

Galathea, without equal in the world. And because all worldly bounties which a good knight must have were in Hector, we can say that the moral sense here signifies that he took them from the admonishment of Othea who has sent him this epistle. We understand by "Othea" the virtue of prudence and wisdom[13] with which he was himself adorned. And as the four cardinal virtues[14] are necessary for good government, we shall speak of them later. And we have given a name to this first virtue and assumed a way of speaking somewhat poetically, harmonizing with the true story in order to follow better what our subject teaches, and we will take several authoritative texts from the ancient philosophers for our argument. For this reason we will say that this present epistle was given or sent by this lady to the good Hector, and similarly could be given to all others desiring goodness and wisdom. And Aristotle, the prince of philosophers, said that wisdom as the virtue of prudence is very much to be recommended: "Because wisdom is the noblest of all things, it must be presented by the best argument in the most fitting way."

Prologue to the Allegory

In order to break down the argument of our subject matter into its underlying allegory, let us apply Holy Scripture to our writings for the edification of the soul abiding in this wretched world. As all things were created by the supreme wisdom and in utmost power of God, all things must logically seek their end in Him. And because our spirit, created by God in His image, is the noblest of created things after the angels, it is fitting and necessary that it be adorned with the virtues by which it can be conveyed to the end for which it was made; and because it can be obstructed by the traps and assaults of its enemy in hell, its mortal enemy which often diverts it from reaching its blessedness, we may call human life "true chivalry," as Scripture says in many places. And as all earthly things are fallible, we must constantly remember the future which is without end. And because it is the supreme and perfect chivalry, and all others nothing by comparison, and whose victors will be crowned in glory, we will assume a manner of speaking, and this shall be principally to the glory of God and the benefit of those who will read this present work.

13. The combination of prudence and wisdom was common in late medieval devotion to the Virgin Mary, where the phrases "most wise Virgin" (*virgo sapientissima*) and "most prudent Virgin" (*virgo prudentissima*) recur with some frequency.

14. The four cardinal virtues are prudence, temperance, fortitude, and justice, and these supply the topics of the next four chapters.

Allegory 1[15]

As prudence and wisdom are the mother and director of all virtues, without which the others cannot be governed well, it is necessary for the chivalrous spirit to be adorned with prudence, as Saint Augustine says in *The Singularity of Clerics* [*De singularitate clericorum*][16] that wherever prudence is found, one can easily stop or destroy all things contrary, but where prudence is scorned, all things contrary hold sway. Temperance[17] is also called a goddess, and because our human body is composed of different things and must be tempered or regulated according to reason, it can be represented by a clock with many wheels and weights.[18] Yet just as a clock is worth nothing if it is not properly regulated, so too our human body is worth nothing if temperance does not regulate it.

Text 2

And in order that you know
What you must do, you must first know
The virtues most beneficial to you
In order to arrive better at the basis
Of knightly valor—
And although she is subject to chance,
I still will tell you who leads me—
I have a very close sister,
Overflowing with every beauty,
But above any other special trait
She is sweet, tranquil and well-tempered,
And at no time has ever been touched by anger,
She thinks of nothing but balance:
She is the goddess of temperance.

15. For the sources of the allegory section of, and notes on each chapter, please see the table of "Authors and Works Cited in the Allegories" assembled by Cheryl Lemmens as an Appendix to this translation.

16. *On the Singularity of Clerics* is by an uncertain author. Christine's source is the *Manipulus florum*, and the text there is is found in the Patrologia Latina, v. 4, col. 945 B, "*ubicunque fuerit providentia, frustrantur universa contraria, ubi autem providentia egligitur, monia contraria dominantur.*" Providence was frequently associated with the Virgin Mary as well. Othea thus emerges as an allegory of the Virgin Mary herself.

17. Temperance was frequently termed one of the prerogatives of the Virgin Mary.

18. The kind of clock described here is a verge and foliot escapement clock, invented in the fourteenth century, which in fact requires carefully regulated motion between wheels and weights in its mechanism. A surviving example of this kind of clock is found in Salisbury Cathedral, which dates from around 1386. The regular ticking sound produced by the mechanism suggested balance and temperance, particularly because the gyrating foliot with its weights resembled a balance.

I cannot have the name of great grace
Except for her
Because if she does not weigh in,
Nothing is worth a fig.
For this reason I want her to be your friend
Alongside of me, and do not forget this,
For she is a well-informed goddess
Who is wise: love and esteem her well!

Gloss 2

Othea says that temperance is her sister. The virtue of temperance can truly be called her sister and similar to prudence, for temperance is a demonstration of prudence, and temperance results from prudence. For this reason she says that Hector should consider her his friend, something which every good knight must do who desires the reward due to the good, just as the philosopher called Democritus says, "Temperance modifies vices and perfects virtues."

Allegory 2

The good spirit must possess the virtue of temperance, whose property is to limit things. And Saint Augustine says in *On the Church's Mores* [*De moribus ecclesiae catholicae*][19] that the office of temperance is to refrain and appease lustful behavior which is contrary to us and which diverts us from God's law, and also to scorn carnal pleasures and worldly praise. St Peter in his First Epistle speaks to this point: "I beseech you as aliens and exiles to abstain from the passions of the flesh that wage war against your soul." [1 Peter 2:11: *Obsecro vos tanquam advenas et peregrinos abstinere vos a carnalibus desideriis quae militant adversus animam.*]

Text 3

With us you need strength
And if you are concerned about great virtue
You must turn to Hercules[20]
And contemplate his courageous deeds
In which he showed too much bravura

---

19. Saint Augustine, *De moribus ecclesiae catholicae et de moribus Manichaeorum*, ed. J. B. Bauer (Vienna: Hoelder-Pinchler-Tempsky, 1992), 39–40, ll. 2–8.

20. Hercules was frequently viewed as a traditional allegorical "type" of Christ. For an author like Dante, his labors anticipated in pagan terms Christ's victory over sin. The subtext of this chapter is essentially that the good knight needs to be a *miles Christi*, a soldier of Christ.

And, although he was opposed
To his lineage and quarreled with them,
Do not feel hate for this reason
Toward his noble strong virtues
Which opened the doors of bravery,
But if you wish to emulate them,
In order to follow his valiant deeds,
It is not necessary for you to wage war
Against the infernal gods
Nor to contend with the god Pluto
To seek to rescue Proserpine,
The daughter of the goddess Ceres
Whom Pluto abducted on the sea off Greece,
Nor is there need for you to break the chains
Of Cerberus, gatekeeper of hell,
Nor pick quarrels with those in hell
Who are disloyal dogs—
As Hercules did for his companions
Pirithous and Theseus,[21]
Who were almost deceived
Into venturing to that valley
Where many a soul is greatly tortured—
You will find enough war on earth
Without having to go look for it in hell.
Nor is it necessary at all
In pursuing or performing deeds of arms
To go fight vicious snakes
Or lions and bears on the prowl—
I do not know whether you imagine it like this—
Or even other serpents,
In order to achieve fame for bravery,
Unless it be in distress
To defend your own body.
If beasts like this were to attack you
To hurt you, then your defense
Certainly does you honor,
And if you are victorious over them,
Yours will be the honor and glory.

---

21. Christine will mention Hercules, Pirithous, and Theseus again in Chapter 27.

Gloss 3

The virtue of fortitude should be understood as meaning not only bodily strength, but constancy and endurance that the good knight must show in all his deeds, judiciously planned, and strength to resist adversities that might befall him, whether misfortunes or tribulations, where a strong and mighty heart can be useful in enhancing valor. And to give a concrete example of force, useful in two ways, in other words, insofar as it concerns both this virtue itself and the deeds of knighthood as well, look at Hercules, for he greatly excelled in these feats. And bearing in mind Hector's nobility, it was fitting to give him a noble example. Hercules was a knight of Greece, with spectacular strength, and he accomplished many feats of knightly valor. He travelled widely throughout the world and, because of the great and marvelous acts of bravery, voyages, and deeds of great strength that he achieved, poets, who speak with dissimulation and in fictions, said that he went to the underworld to fight with the princes of hell, and that he fought with serpents and wild animals, which should be understood to mean the mighty exploits that he accomplished. And for this reason Othea tells the good knight that he should reflect on these things, that is, on his deeds of bravery and feats of valor, according to the means at his disposal. And just as the clarity of the sun is profitable to all, it can be a good example, as a philosopher once said that when a grain of wheat falls onto good soil, it is beneficial to all.[22] Similarly it can be a good example, useful for all those who wish for courage. And for this reason a wise man noted, "The virtue of strength makes man steadfast to conquer all things."

Allegory 3

Just as the good knight, lacking strength and vigor, could not win the prize in feats of arms, so too the good spirit, lacking fortitude, could not earn the reward due to the good. And in the first book of *On the Duties of the Clergy* [*De officiis*], Saint Ambrose says that the true force of the human heart is that it is never broken in adversity and that it never boasts in prosperity, that it tries to save and defend the adornments of virtue and to uphold justice, that it is courageous in the midst of peril and firm against carnal lust.[23] And on the topic Saint John the Evangelist wrote in his first epistle: "I write to you, young men, because you are strong, and the word of God abides in you, and you have overcome the evil one."

22. Christine has combined two parables, that of the sower (Matthew 13:1–8) and that of the grain of wheat (John 12:24).

23. The contrast between the duties of the clergy in the allegory section (the clergy were seen as the representatives of wisdom, of *sapientia*) and the duties of the good knight in the gloss section (the knights symbolized valor or *fortitudo*) is striking here, but completely consistent with the synthesis of *sapientia et fortitudo* in the entire work.

[1 John 2:14: *Scribo vobis juvenes quoniam fortes estis et verbum Dei manet in vobis; vicistis malignum.*]

Text 4

Again, if you wish to be one of us,
You must resemble Minos
Even though he was the judge and master
Of hell and all its places,
For if you want to advance yourself,
You must be a judge,
Otherwise you are not worthy to wear a helmet
Or to hold sway over a kingdom.

Gloss 4

Prudence tells the good knight that if he wants to be among the ranks of the good, he must have the virtue of justice, that is, he must uphold equitable justice.[24] And Aristotle notes that "[h]e who would be an equitable judge must first be able to judge himself, for the person who fails to judge himself would not be worthy of judging someone else." This should be understood to mean that he must correct his own faults so that they are completely expunged, and so, as a man who has corrected himself, he may, indeed must, be the corrector of other men. And to speak of the moral sense we could cite a fable on this topic, following the dissimulation of the poets. Minos, as the poets said, was the judge of hell, just as one would speak of a law officer or magistrate, and all the souls which had descended into this valley were brought before him, and, depending on what punishment they deserved, he would wrap his tail around his body as many times as he wanted to indicate the degree to which they should be confined in the depths of hell. And because hell represents the equitable justice or punishment of God, let us now take somewhat this direction in the way we speak about our argument. And the truth was that long ago in Crete there was a king named Minos, extremely

24. This passage in the *Othea* marks the beginning of a career-long meditation on the nature of justice in Christine's work. Christine's connection to medieval jurisprudence has been well established: her paternal grandfather and great-grandfather were professors of jurisprudence in Bologna. In all of Christine's subsequent works her reflections on the nature of justice are challenging and provocative: "equity," for example, refers to the judge's (or the prince's) exercise of judgment in applying written law—justice in action. In the *Othea*, her recommendation of equitable justice to Louis of Orléans would have been taken quite literally. The quotation from Saint Bernard in the allegory section is actually a paraphrase of the opening of Justinian's codification of Roman law, in which a fundamental principle of justice is "to give to each his own." Here one sees how Christine strives to condense enormous learning in very concise terms.

ruthless, and particularly scrupulous in matters of justice. And for this reason the poets claimed that after his death he was charged to be the judge of hell. And Aristotle says, "Justice is a measure which God instituted on earth to limit all things."

Allegory 4

And as God is the head of justice and all order, so it is necessary for the spirit of knighthood to have this virtue in order to achieve a glorious victory. And Saint Bernard says in a sermon that justice is nothing besides rendering to each his own; thus he says, "Give to three groups of people what is theirs: to you sovereign, reverence and obedience, reverence of the heart and obedience of the body; to you peer, you should render counsel and aid, counsel in instructing his ignorance and aid in comforting his incapacities: to your subject, you must give protection and discipline, protection by preventing him from doing evil, and discipline by chastising him when he does wrong." And on this topic Solomon says in Proverbs: "The righteous observes the house of the wicked so that he may withdraw the wicked from evil.… When justice is done, it is a joy to the righteous." [Proverbs 21:12, 15: *Excogitat iustus de domo impii ut detrahat impios a malo … gaudium est iusto facere iusticiam.*][25]

Text 5

Afterwards reflect on Perseus[26]
Whose noble name is known
Throughout the world, in all parts.
He rode Pegasus, the agile horse,
Flying through the air,
And delivered Andromeda from the sea-monster,
Tearing her away from him by force
And as a brave knight errant
Took her back to her parents.
Remember this deed,
For a good knight should follow
This path if he desires to achieve
Honor, which is worth more than any material goods.
So contemplate yourself in his shining shield,
Which has vanquished many,

25. The Revised Standard Version (RSV) translation has been modified here by using the Douay-Rheims translation for the second part of Proverbs 21:12.

26. For the medieval context of Christine's invocation of Perseus, see John M. Steadman, "'Perseus upon Pegasus' and *Ovid Moralized*," *Review of English Studies* n.s. 9 (1958): 407–10.

And be armed with his saber,
So that you will strong and robust.

Gloss 5

And because it is something necessary that honor and reverence are due to a good knight, we will speak figuratively, following the manner of the poets. Perseus was a very courageous knight and he had conquered many kingdoms, and the great land of Persia was named after him. And the poets said that he rode a horse which flew through the sky that they called Pegasus, which should be understood as fame which flies through the air. He carried in his hand a curved sword or sickle, which was said because of the large harvest of people who had been defeated by him in many battles. He delivered Andromeda from the sea-monster; she was a maiden and daughter of the king whom he saved from a sea-monster who was supposed to devour her according to the will of the gods, by which is understood that all knights must aid women who might need their help. Therefore, Perseus and the horse who flies should be taken for the good reputation which a good knight must possess and acquire by his good merits, and the good knight must ride this reputation, that is, his name must be carried to all lands. And Aristotle says, "A good reputation makes a man resplendent in the world and outstanding in the presence of princes."

Allegory 5

The spirit of knighthood should desire fame, acquired by his good merits, among the company of the saints in Paradise. Pegasus, the horse which carries him, will be his guardian angel who will give a good report about him on the Day of Judgment. Andromeda, who will be delivered, is his soul which he will deliver from the infernal enemy by overcoming sin. And that one should wish as well to have a good reputation in this world desirous of God, and not because of vainglory, Saint Augustine said in *Concerning the common words of the clergy* [*De communi sermone clericorum*] that two things are necessary to live well, to wit, a clear conscience and good reputation—conscience for one's own sake, and reputation for the sake of one's neighbor—and whoever puts his trust only in having a clear conscience and despises good reputation is cruel, for the sign of a noble heart is to love having a good reputation. And on this topic the wise man said, "Have regard for your name, since it will remain for you longer than a thousand great stores of gold." [Ecclesiasticus/Sirach[27] 41:12: *Curam habe de bono nomine, hoc enim magis permanebit tibi quam mille thesauri preciosi.*]

27. Ecclesiasticus (not to be confused with Ecclesiastes, quoted in Gloss 80) is a non-canonical book of the Bible, also known as the Book of Sirach.

And it should be understood that because the seven planets in heaven rotate in what are called the zodiac circles, the images of the seven planets depicted here are sitting on a sphere, and because they are established in the firmament and above the clouds, they are portrayed here in a starry heaven above the clouds, and they were called long ago the great gods. And because Jupiter is the planet in the sky which exercises influence over sweet favor and friendship, as a sign of love, the image extends its hand to the men on earth; and because the dew of heaven is the cause of fertility and abundance, and sweet humid air comes from this planet, it is portrayed here hurling down dew.[28]

Text 6

With your inclinations
Strive to have the conditions
Of Jove: you will show your strength better
When you uphold them precisely.

Gloss 6

As has been said, the ancient poets who worshipped many gods considered the planets in the heavens to be special gods, and they named the seven days of the week after the seven planets. They revered Jupiter or Jove and deemed him their greatest god because he is seated in the highest sphere of the planets below Saturn. Thursday was named after Jove, and even the alchemists attributed and compared the seven metals to the seven planets, as one sees in the works of Geber [Jabir ibn Hayyan] or Nicolas [Flamel] and other authorities in this science.[29] They assigned to Jove copper or brass. Jove or Jupiter is the planet of a sweet condition, friendly and joyful, and is portrayed with a sanguine complexion. For this reason Othea, that is Prudence, says that the good knight must have the conditions of Jove, and all noblemen pursuing chivalry should have the same. On this topic Pythagoras says that a king must converse graciously with his people and show them a joyful

---

28. This textual "interlude" is important because Christine is now signaling how she will structure the next section of the *Othea*. The first five chapters focus on the four cardinal virtues, with a double emphasis on justice, and the next seven chapters, based on the seven planets, discuss their positive and negative influences, and the respective virtues or vices associated with them. For the chapters devoted to the planets, it is important to remember that Christine's father was, among other things, an astrologer, so that the first five chapters of the *Othea* seem to reflect her family heritage in jurisprudence and the next seven chapters her family tradition in astronomy. In the section of the *Othea* devoted to the planets, Christine often first describes the values associated with the individual planet before she begins her verse text.

29. See the Introduction (28) for information on these authors.

countenance, and by this it should be understood by all courageous men seeking honor.

Allegory 6

Now let us break down our argument into its allegory, the properties of the seven planets. Jupiter, which is a sweet and human planet whose qualities the good knight should have, may signify for us the mercy and compassion that the good knight, Jesus Christ, that is the spirit, must have in himself, for Saint Jerome says in his Letter to Nepotian: "I do not remember," he says, "to have read or heard that anyone has died a bad death who freely did works of mercy, for mercy has many intercessors and it is impossible that the prayers of many not be granted." On the subject Our Lord says in the Gospel, "Blessed are the merciful, for they shall obtain mercy." [Matthew 5:7: *Beati misericordes quoniam ipsi misericordiam consequentur.*]

Venus is the planet in the heavens that the pagans in the past called the goddess of love because she exercises influence over being in love, and for this reason lovers are depicted here who present their hearts to her.

Text 7

Do not make a goddess out of Venus,
And do not care about her promises;
The pursuit of this is laborious,
Dishonorable, and dangerous.

Gloss 7

Venus is the planet of the heavens after whom the day Friday has been named, and the metal which we call tin or pewter has been assigned to it. Venus influences love and inconstancy, and there was a lady so named who was Queen of Cyprus. And because she exceeded all other women in her outstanding beauty and gaiety, and because she was very passionate and not faithful to one love, but abandoned herself to many, they called her the goddess of love. And because she influences lust, Othea tells the good knight not to make her his goddess, that is, he must abandon neither his body nor his mind to whatever causes vice. And Hermes says, "The vice of lust extinguishes all the virtues."

Allegory 7

The reason that the good knight must not make Venus his goddess is that the good spirit must harbor no vanity. And Cassiodorus says about Psalms, "Vanity made the angel turn into a devil, and he gave death to the first man and stripped him of the happiness that had been granted to him. Vanity is the fountain of all vices, the source of all iniquity which removes man from God's grace and places him in His hate." For this reason, in speaking to God, David says in his Psalms: "Thou hatest those who pay regard to vain idols." [Psalm 30:7 (31:6): *Odisti observantes vanitates supervacue.*]

Saturn is a sluggish and heavy planet and can signify in any case wisdom and a moderate and measured state of mind. And for this reason he is portrayed as an old man; and because he sits in the firmament above all the other planets, he is depicted here sitting above the seven spheres, and, on earth, below him, are depicted lawyers and wise men who speak together about wisdom. He holds a sickle because this planet was named after a wise king whose name was Saturn who invented cutting wheat with sickles.

Text 8

If you collect yourself for a long time in reflection,
Mind that you resemble Saturn,
Before you pronounce your sentence,
Mind that you do not deliver it in uncertainty.

Gloss 8

The day Saturday has been named after Saturn, and the metal we call lead is assigned to it, for it is a planet with a slow, weighty, and wise nature. And there was a king in Crete so named who was very wise, about whom the poets spoke under the dissimulation of fiction, and claimed that his son Jupiter cut off his genitals, which should be taken to mean that he stripped him of the power he had and dethroned and chased him off. And because Saturn is weighty and wise, Othea would say that the good knight must weigh a matter carefully before he delivers his sentence, whether it be in taking up arms or in some other affair; and all wise men who hold offices handing down verdicts might take note of this. And on this topic, Hermes said, "Think well in all your affairs, and especially in judging others."

Allegory 8

Just as the good knight must be slow to judge others, that is, to reflect at length on a verdict before giving it, by the same token must the good spirit be slow to judge what applies to him, for judgment belongs to God who alone knows how to discern with equity matters in dispute. And Saint Gregory says in the *Morals* [*Moralia*] that since our weakness does not know how to understand the judgments of God, we must discuss them not in self-assured arguments, but must honor them in respectful silence, and as astonishing as they may seem to us, we must deem them just. And on the subject David says in the Psalter, "The fear of the Lord is clean, enduring forever; the ordinances of the Lord are true, and righteous altogether." [Psalm 18:10 (19:9): *Timor Domini sanctus permanens in saeculum saeculi iudicia Domini vera iustificata in semet ipsa.*]

The sun, which they called in ancient days Phoebus or Apollo, is the planet which illuminates or lights up all dark and shadowy objects, and it signifies the truth which enlightens all things obscure and hidden; and for this reason there are people shown below who are making the gesture of swearing or taking an oath in order to speak the truth. He is holding a harp, which can be taken as a sign of fair harmony and sweet melody which is found in the virtue of truth; he has at his side a crow, which signifies the first age of the world which was pure and then blackened by the sins of creatures.

Text 9

May your word be clear and true,
Apollo will remind you of it,
For he cannot abide the slightest filth
Presented under dissimulation.

Gloss 9

Apollo or Phoebus is the sun to whom the day of Sunday is assigned, as well as the metal which we call gold. Thanks to his brightness he exposes concealed things and because truth is clear and reveals secret things, it can be assigned to him—this virtue must be in the heart and mouth of every good knight. And on this topic Hermes says, "Love God and truth and give loyal advice."

Allegory 9

We can take Apollo, that is to say the sun by which we denote truth, to mean that the true knight, Jesus Christ, must have the truth on his lips and flee all falsehood. As Cassiodorus says in his sermon in praise of Saint Paul [*De laudibus Pauli homilia*], "The condition of falsehood is such that even where it has no antagonists, it collapses into itself, whereas on the contrary, the state of truth is so stable that the more adversaries it has contradicting it, the more it grows and the higher it rises." On this point Holy Scripture says, "Truth is victor over all things." [1 Esdras 3:12: *Super omnia vincit veritas.*][30]

The moon is the planet which exercises influence over melancholy and folly, and since, because of the moon, the sickness of phrenesis and melancholy befalls some according to the disposition of their bodies, it is depicted here drawing an arrow aimed downward, with the people below her melancholic and frenetic.

Text 10

Do not be like Phoebe in the least,
She is too changeable and inimical
To constancy and strong hearts,
Melancholic and lunatic.

Gloss 10

Phoebe is called the moon, after which the day Monday has been named, and the metal which we call silver is assigned to it. The moon never stops for a single moment at one fixed spot and exercises influence over fickleness and folly, and for this reason the good knight must protect himself from such vices. And on this topic Hermes says, "Make use of wisdom and be constant."

Allegory 10

The good knight, and likewise the good spirit, must not harbor Phoebe, which is the moon, which we denote as inconstancy; as Saint Ambrose says in his *Letter to Simplicianus* [*Epistola ad Simplicianum*], the fool is fickle like the moon, but the wise man is always constant in one state where fear never breaks him, power does not alter him, prosperity does not make him haughty nor sadness bring him

---

30. Christine's numbering follows that of the Vulgate, which has four books of Esdras (the Latin form of Ezra); these are divided into two books of Nehemiah and two books of Ezra in standard English versions including the King James and the RSV.

down. Where there is wisdom, there is virtue, strength, and constancy. The wise man is always of one heart, he neither shrinks nor expands when events change, he does not vacillate between different opinions but remains steadfast in Jesus Christ, grounded in charity, rooted in faith. And on the subject Holy Scripture says, "A holy man continues in wisdom as the sun: but a fool is changed as the moon." [Ecclesiaticus/Sirach 27:11: *Homo sanctus in sapiencia manet sicut sol nam stultus sicut luna mutatur.*]

Mars is the planet which exercises influence over wars and battles, and for this reason its image here below is a fully armed man.

Text 11

Mars your father, I am most certain,
You should follow well at every step,
For your noble condition
Takes its inclination from him.

Gloss 11

The day of Tuesday is named after Mars, and the metal which we call iron has been assigned to it. Mars is the planet which exercises influence over wars and battles, and for this reason every knight who loves or who follows arms and deeds of chivalry and is renowned for courage may be called a son of Mars. And Othea spoke of Hector as such for this reason even though he was the son of King Priam, and she said that he should follow his father closely, something which every good knight must do. And a wise man said that one could know the inclinations of a man from his works.

Allegory 11

Mars, the god of battle, has been well called the son of God who fought victoriously in this world, and the good spirit should follow his good father Jesus Christ by his example and fight against the vices, just as Saint Ambrose says in the first book of the *Duties of the Clergy* that whoever wishes to be God's friend must be the devil's enemy, whoever seeks to have peace in Jesus Christ must war against the vices. And just as it is useless to fight against exterior enemies in the field when the city itself is full of private spies, so too whoever does not forcefully combat the sins in his soul cannot vanquish the evils outside of it, for the most glorious victory is that of conquering oneself. And on this subject the Apostle Paul says, "For we are not contending against flesh and blood, but against the principalities, against the powers, against the world rulers of this present darkness, against the spiritual hosts of wickedness in the heavenly places." [Ephesians 6:12: *Non est vobis colluctacio adversus carnem et sanguinem sed adversus principes et potestates adversus mundi rectores tenebrarum harum contra spiritualia nequicie in celestibus.*]

Mercury is the planet having influence over fair language and was called the god of language. He holds a flower because just as the flower is pleasing to view, so too is well-wrought language a pleasure to hear. He has a full purse because one often comes to great wealth because of fair language, and so there are depicted below him wise men speaking together.[31]

Text 12

Be adorned with eloquence,
With clear and pure words,
Mercury who knows how to speak well
Will teach you this.

Gloss 12

The day Wednesday has been named after Mercury, and quicksilver has been assigned to it. Mercury is the planet which influences fair language enhanced by rhetoric and magnificent bearing. For this reason Othea tells the good knight that he should be arrayed with it as well, for magnificent bearing and fine speech well become every nobleman desiring the high prize of honor, provided he takes care not to speak too much, for Diogenes says that of all virtues, the more, the better, except speech.

Allegory 12

We can take Mercury, who is the god of language, to mean that the good knight Jesus Christ must be arrayed with forceful preaching and with eloquent teaching, and also must love and honor those who proclaim this. And Saint Gregory says in his *Homilies* that one must greatly revere the preachers of Holy Scripture, for they are the forerunners of Our Lord who follows after them. Holy preaching prepared the way so that then Our Lord comes to reside in our heart; the words

---

31. This commentary works both as a conative and as an iconographic aside, reinforcing the didactic intent of the work, before Christine segues into her crucial remarks on Minerva and Pallas. Chapters 13 and 14 are the most explicit articulation of the topos of *sapientia et fortitudo* in the *Othea*, and reveal most clearly the organizing principle of the work.

of exhortation open the path and thus truth is received by our mind. And on the point Our Lord told His apostles, "He who hears you hears me, and he who rejects you rejects me, and he who rejects me rejects him who sent me." [Luke 10:16: *Qui vos audit me audit et qui vos spernit me spernit.*]

Here ends the section on the seven planets.[32]

Text 13

Your mother Minerva,[33]
Not averse toward you,
Will deliver to you in plenty
Armor of all kinds, excellent and strong.

Gloss 13

Minerva was a lady of exceptional knowledge and she invented the craft of forging armor, for before her time, warriors armed themselves only with boiled leather; and because of her enormous erudition they called this lady a goddess. And because Hector knew how to use arms very skillfully—and this was his true calling—Othea called him the son of Minerva, although he was the son of queen Hecuba of Troy, and all lovers of arms may be called by a similar name. And on the point one ancient authority said, "Knights given to arms are subject to her, Minerva."

Allegory 13

We can interpret what was has been said, namely that the mother will deliver excellent and strong arms to the good knight, to mean the virtue of faith that is a theological virtue[34] and the mother to the good spirit. And as for the fact that she will deliver arms in plenty, Chrysostom says in his sermon *On the Creed* that faith is the light of the soul, the gate of paradise and the window of life and foundation of eternal salvation, for without faith no one can please God. And on the subject

32. This sentence appears erroneously after chapter 11 in the Harley manuscript. We moved it to the end of chapter 12, which is the last one about the planets.

33. In traditional mythology, Hector was the oldest son of King Priam and Queen Hecuba of Troy (as Christine states in the Gloss), but here she deliberately makes Minerva Hector's mother in order to underscore the importance of female maternal wisdom in the formation of the ideal knight.

34. The allegories of the next three chapters focus on the three theological virtues of faith, hope, and charity. The allegorical associations of Minerva with faith, Pallas with hope, and Penthesilea with charity are original to Christine.

the Apostle Paul said "Without faith it is impossible to please God." [Hebrews 11:6: *Sine fide impossibile est placere Deo.*]

Text 14

Unite with Pallas the goddess
Placing her together with your courage
All will go well for you if you have her,
Pallas goes well with Minerva.

Gloss 14

Afterwards Othea said that Hector should unite Pallas with Minerva who goes well with her, then one must know that Pallas and Minerva are the same thing, but these names are taken with two different meanings, for the lady whose name was Minerva was surnamed Pallas from an island named Pallene where she was born. And because she was generally wise in many things and had newly invented many crafts both fine and subtle, they called her the goddess of knowledge, and so she was called Minerva for that which related to knighthood, and Pallas for all matters belonging to wisdom. And for this reason Othea meant that Hector should add wisdom to chivalry which is quite fitting to it. And this point, that arms should be protected by faith, can be interpreted to mean what Hermes said: "Add the love of faith to wisdom."

Allegory 14

And just as Pallas who denotes wisdom should be added to knighthood, so too must the virtue of hope be added to the virtues of the spirit of knighthood without which he cannot profit. And Origen says in his sermons on the Book of Exodus that hope for things to come is the consolation of those who toil in this mortal life, just as for workers the hope of payment softens the burden of their labor, or as for champions in battle the hope of the crown of victory tempers the pain of their wounds. And on this point the Apostle Paul said, we shall "have the strongest comfort, who have fled for refuge to hold fast the hope set before us, which we have as an anchor of the soul, sure and firm." [Hebrews 6:18–19: *Fortissimum solacium habemus qui confugimus ad tenendam propositam spem quam sicut anchoram habemus anime tutam.*]

Text 15

Hold Penthesilea dear,[35]
She will be aggrieved by your death,
Such a woman must be loved well
From whom such a noble voice sprung.

Gloss 15

Penthesilea was a maiden, queen of Amazonia, and she was very pretty and exhibited extraordinary courage in arms and boldness. And because of Hector's great goodness attested by fame throughout the whole world, she loved him with great devotion, and during the great siege went to Troy from the ends of the Orient to see Hector. Yet when she found him dead, she was extraordinarily sad, and with a very large army of maidens forcefully avenged his death in the most gallant way, accomplishing great deeds of bravery and inflicting enormous damage on the Greeks. And because she was virtuous, Othea tells the good knight that he must love her, and this is to be understood to mean that every good knight must love and esteem every virtuous person, and especially a woman strong in the virtues of intellect and constancy, for such a woman grieves at the death of Hector, that is, when bravery and valor die with a knight. And a wise man said, "Goodness must be praised where it is perceived."

Allegory 15

In the case of Penthesilea, who was always prepared to help, we understand the virtue of charity, that is, the third theological virtue, which the good spirit must wholly harbor in itself. Cassiodorus said that charity is like the rain which falls in spring, for it distills drops of virtues, allowing good will to sprout, and good works to come to fruition. It is long-suffering in adversity, modest in prosperity, strong in humiliation, joyful in affliction, well-meaning to its enemies and friends alike, and ready to share its goods with its enemies. On this point the Apostle Paul observed, "Love is patient and kind; love is not jealous or boastful; it is not arrogant or rude. Love does not insist on its own way." [1 Corinthians 13:4–5: *Caritas paciens est, benigna est, caritas non emulatur, non agit perperam, non inflatur, non est ambiciosa, non querit quae sua sunt.*]

35. It is certainly no coincidence that the chapter immediately following those of Minerva and Pallas is dedicated to Penthesilea, who, as Amazon queen, represented knightly valor to the highest degree, a female exemplum for Hector of *fortitudo* (and by extension, Louis of Orléans), to contemplate.

Text 16

Do not try to be like Narcissus[36]
Decked out in too much pride
For a presumptuous knight
Has been emptied of much grace.

Gloss 16

Narcissus was a young man who, because of his beauty, had become so haughty in such overweening pride that he held all others in scorn. And because he esteemed only himself, it is said that he was so enamored and infatuated by himself that he died from it after seeing himself mirrored in a fountain, that is, his own arrogance in which he beheld himself. For this reason it is forbidden that the good knight ever mirror himself in his good deeds, by which he might turn overweening. And on the point Socrates said, "My son, take care not to be deceived by the beauty of your youth, for it is not at all a permanent thing."

Allegory 16

Now let us try to find the allegory of our argument as it applies to the seven deadly sins.[37] We understand Narcissus to mean the sin of pride, which the good spirit must protect itself from. And Origen said in his sermons, "What can ashes and dust take such pride in, or how dare a man puff himself up when he considers where he has come from and what he will become, and in what a fragile vessel his life is contained, into what filth he is plunged and what waste he incessantly throws off from his flesh and all the openings of his body?" And on this topic Holy Scripture says, "Though his height mount up to the heavens, and his head reach to the clouds, he will perish forever like his own dung." [Job 20:6–7: *Si ascenderit ad celum superbia eius et caput eius nubes tetigerit, quasi sterquilinium in fine perdetur.*]

Text 17

The goddess of madness
Made Athamas, filled with great rage,

---

36. Could the remarks on Narcissus and male vanity here be a somewhat indirect allusion to Louis's role in the *Bal des Ardents*? On this event see the Introduction, 17–18.

37. The next sections discuss the seven deadly sins: pride, wrath, envy, sloth, avarice, gluttony, and lust.

Strangle his two children.

For this reason, defend yourself against great anger.

Gloss 17

Athamas was a king, married to queen Ino, who had had roasted wheat sown in order to disinherit her stepchildren, for she had bribed the priests of the law who reported the answers of the gods so that they told the king and those in the land that the wheat which had been sown did not sprout at all because it displeased the gods that two fair and sweet children of the king had been chased away and exiled. And because the king agreed to the exile of his two children, although he had done it reluctantly and with great sorrow, the fable says that the goddess Juno wanted to take vengeance for this, and went to hell to tell the goddess of madness to go to the house of king Athamas. The horrible and fearful goddess arrived with snakes as hair, stood on the threshold of the palace, and extended her arms to the two sides of the gate. And then such strife arose between king and queen that they nearly killed each other; and when they thought they could rush out of the palace, the goddess of madness pulled two horrible snakes from her filthy hair and threw them at the laps of the king and queen. And when they saw how frightening the goddess was, both of them went mad. Athamas killed the queen out of rage, and then his two children, and he himself threw himself from a high cliff into the sea. The exposition given to this fable can be that the queen was so different from her stepchildren that, out of malice, she had them disinherited, so that then there was no peace between father and stepmother, and it can also be that he finally killed her. And because wrath is a deadly sin and so horrible that someone strongly afflicted by it has no knowledge of reason, Othea tells the good knight to protect himself carefully from rage, for it can be a great mistake indeed for a good knight to be enraged.

Allegory 17

We take Athamas, who was so filled with rage, to mean precisely the sin of wrath from which the good spirit must be purified. And Saint Augustine says in an epistle that just as vinegar or soured wine contaminates the vessel holding it if it stays there long, so too does wrath corrupt the heart in which it sours if it stays there from one day to the next. For this reason the Apostle Paul says, "Do not let the sun go down on your anger." [Ephesians 4:26: *Sol non occidat super iracundiam vestram.*]

Text 18

All your life above all else
Flee the false goddess Envy
Who made Aglauros turn greener than ivy
And changed into stone.

Gloss 18

Aglauros, the fable says, was the sister of Herse, who was herself so beautiful that she married Mercury, the god of language, and both were the daughters of Cecrops, king of Athens. But Aglauros was so jealous of her sister Herse, who had risen so high because of her beauty that she was married to a god, that so devoured by envy she became so violently agitated by the jealousy she bore her sister that she turned dried, discolored and green like an ivy leaf. One day Aglauros was sitting on the threshold of the gate and refused entry to Mercury, who wanted to enter the building, and despite his bidding to enter, she would not let him inside. Then the god became angry and said that she could forever remain as hard as her heart, whereupon Aglauros turned hard as stone. The fable may be proven when something similar happens to other people: Mercury can be taken to be a powerful and eloquent man who has his sister-in-law imprisoned or killed because of some disservice which she has done to him, and for this reason it says that she was changed to stone. And because being envious is such a horrible stain, and the opposite of kindness, Othea says to the good knight that he must protect himself from it above all else. And Socrates said, "Whoever carries the branch of envy will have eternal suffering."

Allegory 18

Just as the ancient authority forbids the good knight to feel envy, so too does Holy Scripture prohibit this same vice to the good spirit. And Saint Augustine says, "Envy is hatred for the happiness of others, ranging from where the envious man feels envy toward those greater than he because he is not as great as they, to envy toward those equal to him because he is not greater than they, and to envy toward those who are below him out of fear that they might become as great as he." Scripture says on this point: "The eye of the envious is wicked: and he turneth away his face." [Ecclesiasticus/Sirach 14:8: *Nequam est oculus invidi et avertens faciem suam.*]

Text 19

Be neither slow nor wordy
In protecting yourself from the malice
Of Ulysses, who stole the eye from the giant,
Although he was clear-sighted.

Gloss 19

A fable recounts that when Ulysses returned from Greece after the destruction
of Troy, a terrible storm took his ship to an island where there was a giant who
had a single eye of horrible size in the middle of his forehead. Ulysses, through
his craftiness, stole and robbed him of his eye, that is, he punctured it. This is to
say that the good knight should take care that sloth does not catch him with the
wiles and ambushes of the malicious so that his eye can be stolen, namely the
eye of his understanding or of his honor or of his property or of what he holds
most dear, as many unpleasant things often happen out of sloth and cowardice.
And on this point Hermes says, "Blessed is he who passes his days in appropriate
attentiveness."

Allegory 19

When it is said that the good knight should be neither slow nor long-winded, we
can take this to mean the sin of sloth which the good spirit must not have; for as
Bede says about the Proverbs of Solomon, "The slothful who does not want to la-
bor for the love of God is not worthy of reigning with God, nor is the slothful who
is a coward to enter the fields of battle worthy of receiving the crown promised
to knights." For this reason Scripture says, "The plans of the diligent lead surely
to abundance, but everyone who is hasty comes only to want." [Proverbs 21:5:
Cogitaciones robusti in abundancia, omnis autem piger in egestate erit.]

Text 20

Do not take up quarrels with frogs,
Nor dirty yourself in their swamp;
They assembled against Latona
And muddied the clear water for her.

Gloss 20

The fable says that the goddess Latona was the mother of Phoebus and Phoebe, the sun and the moon, and carried them in a single womb. Juno pursued her in every land because she was pregnant by Jupiter, her husband. One day the goddess Latona was very tired and came to a ford where she stooped down to the water to quench her great thirst. There was a large crowd of peasants bathing in the water there because of the intense heat of the sun, and they began to insult her and to muddy the waters where she wanted to drink, and despite her asking them, they would not allow it and had no pity for her plight. Therefore, she cursed them and said that they could stay in a swamp forever; as they were ugly and repulsive, and never stopped croaking and insulting, they then became wretched frogs who then never ceased croaking, as happens in summertime on this river bank. It may also have been that some peasants had displeased some great mistress who had them thrown into the river to drown, and thus became frogs. This should be taken to mean that the good knight should in no way dirty himself in the swamp of ugliness, but flee all ugly tasks which are contrary to beauty, for just as ugliness cannot abide beauty, so too can beauty not accept ugliness in itself, nor even contend or debate with someone whose behavior is ugly and manner of speaking insulting. And Plato says, "Whoever adds to his nobility the nobility of good conduct is praiseworthy, but the person for whom the nobility inherited from his parents suffices without good deeds should not be considered noble."

Allegory 20

We might take the peasants who became frogs to signify the sin of avarice, which is contrary to the good spirit; for Saint Augustine says that the avaricious man is comparable to hell, for hell cannot swallow enough souls before it says "that's enough"; and if all the treasures of the world were collected into the possession of the avaricious man, he would not be sated. And on this subject Scripture says, "The eye of the covetous man is insatiable in his portion of iniquity." [Ecclesiasticus/Sirach 14:9: *Insatiabilis oculus cupidi in partem iniquitatis non satiabitur.*]

Text 21

Never set your tune to Bacchus,
For his conditions are filthy,
His pleasures are worthless,
He turns men into swine.

Gloss 21

Bacchus was a man who was the first to plant vines in Greece, and when the inhabitants of the land felt the strength of the wine which made them drunk, they said that Bacchus was a god who had given such power to his plant, so that by Bacchus drunkenness should be understood. For this reason Othea tells the good knight that he must never abandon himself to drunkenness, as it would be an inappropriate thing and a great vice for every noble man and every man who sought to employ reason. And on this point Hippocrates said, "Excessive wines and meats destroy the body, the soul, and the virtues."

Allegory 21

With the god Bacchus we can denote the sin of gluttony from which the good spirit must protect itself. Saint Gregory, in the *Morals*, said that when the vice of gluttony begins to rule a person, he loses all the good which he had done, and when the stomach is not controlled by abstinence, all the virtues are drowned out. For this reason Saint Paul speaks of those for whom "their end is destruction, their god is the belly, and they glory in their shame, with minds set on earthly things." [Philippians 3:19: *Quorum finis est interitus, quorum Deus venter est: et gloria in confusione eorum qui terrena sapiunt.*]

Text 22

Do not become infatuated with the statue
Of Pygmalion, if you are wise,
For the beauty of the decorated figure
Is bought at too dear a price.

Gloss 22

Pygmalion was a very skillful artist at creating statues,[38] and a fable says that because of the depravity he found in the women of the city of Sidon, he despised them and said that he would create a statue where nothing could be criticized. He sculpted a statue of a woman of consummate beauty. When he had finished

---

38. Christine pointedly refers here to the *ymage* (translated here as "statue") of Pygmalion (whose gender in Middle French is both masculine and feminine). Christine switches between genders: she uses *ymage* in the feminine when making agreement with the past participle (*quant l'eut parfaite, l'ymage avoit faite*), but otherwise she refers to the lifeless image in the masculine (*un ymage de femme, il feroit un ymage, entre ses bras le prent*), and only after the statue comes to life does Christine switch to the feminine gender.

it, Amor, who knows how to steal hearts cunningly, made Pygmalion fall in love with his statue, and he was afflicted by lovesickness for it. He complained to it, with shouts mixed with pitiful sighs, but the statue, made of stone, did not hear him. Pygmalion went to the temple of Venus and he implored her with such devotion that the goddess took pity on him and, as a demonstration of this, the torch that she held by her side caught fire and blazed forth. Then the lover was joyous because of this sign, and went back to his statue and took it in his arms and warmed it on his naked flesh so long that the statue came to life and began to speak, and so Pygmalion again found joy. Several explanations can be given to this fable, and to many others in a similar manner, and for this reason the poets devised them so that men's minds would be sharpened and made more astute to detect different explanations in them. So it can be understood that Pygmalion scorned the depravity of prostitutes, and fell in love with a young woman of very great beauty who would not or could not hear his pitiful complaints any more than if she were made of stone. He made the statue, which means that he had fallen in love by thinking of her fair beauties. In the end he begged her so much and stayed around her so much that the young woman loved him back of her own free will and took him in marriage. And thus a statue, hard as stone, came to life thanks to the goddess Venus, which means that the good knight should not be smitten by such a graven image to the extent that he hates to follow the office of arms, to which he is obliged by the order of chivalry. And on this topic Apthalin[39] has said, "It is an inappropriate thing for a prince to be infatuated with something which makes him open to criticism."

Allegory 22

We take the statue of Pygmalion, with which the good knight must not fall in love, to mean the sin of lust against which the spirit of knighthood must protect its body. In a letter Saint Jerome says of lust, "O fire of hell whose mouth is gluttony, whose flame is pride, whose flares are corrupted words, whose smoke is bad reputation, whose ashes are poverty and whose end is the torment of hell." On this subject the Apostle Peter says, "They count it pleasure to revel in the daytime. They are blots and blemishes, reveling in their dissipation, carousing with you." [2 Peter 2:13: *Voluptatem existimantes delicias coiquinacionis et maculae deliciis affluentes conviviis suis luxuriantes.*]

---

39. It has been hitherto impossible to identify four authors cited by Christine in four "glosses": Apthalin here, as well as Sedechias (Gloss 65), Madarge (Gloss 85), and Zaqualquin (Gloss 86).

Text 23

Keep Diana in mind
For the purity of your body
For she abhorred a sullied life,
Deceitful and tainted.

Gloss 23

Diana is the moon, and since there is nothing so bad that it does not possess some good quality, the moon provides for chastity, and they designated the moon by a lady so named who was very chaste and remained a virgin all her life. In this way Othea proposes that purity of body well suits a good knight. On this point Hermes says, "Whoever lacks chastity cannot be perfectly wise."

Allegory 23

And to uncover here in our argument the allegorical meaning of the articles of Faith,[40] without which the good spirit cannot prosper, we take Diana to mean the God of paradise who is without any blemish, a lover of absolute purity for whom anything sullied with sin cannot be pleasing, the creator of heaven and earth, a purity which the spirit of chivalry needs. And thus the first article of Faith states, as my lord Saint Peter says, "I believe in God, the Father Almighty, Maker of Heaven and Earth." [*Credo in Deum patrem omnipotentem creatorem caeli et terre.*]

Text 24

Imitate the goddess Ceres
Who gives wheat and steals from no one
So must a good knight, well prepared,
Always be open to all.

---

40. The next twelve chapters are devoted to the Articles of Faith, that is, the twelve individual statements of belief in the Apostles' Creed which were associated with the twelve individual Apostles. Here the allegorical associations between pagan mythological figures and the Apostles are all original on Christine's part. For more on these associations see Curt F. Bühler, "The Apostles and the Creed," *Speculum* 28 (1953): 335–39.

Gloss 24

Ceres was a lady who invented the art of tilling fields, since earlier they had sown the fields without ploughing. And because the land bore more abundantly after it had been cultivated, they said that she was the goddess of wheat and designated the land from her name. Othea means that just as the land was opened up and was a generous donor of all goods, so too must the good knight be open to every person to give aid and comfort to the best of his ability. And Aristotle says, "Be a generous giver and you will have friends."

Allegory 24

We take Ceres, whom the good knight must imitate, to be the blessed Son of God whom the good spirit must follow, who has so generously endowed us with his lofty gifts; and one must firmly believe in him, just as the second article of faith puts it, citing Saint John when he said, "And I believe in one Lord, Jesus Christ, the only Son of God." [Et in Iesum Christum, Filium eius unicum, Dominum nostrum.]

Text 25

Graft and plant all virtues
In yourself; and you must build
In the same way as Isis did
To make plants and all seeds bear fruit.

Gloss 25

Similarly, the poets said that Isis was the goddess of plants and cultivation, and gave them strength and growth to multiply. For this reason Othea says to the good knight that he must prosper in all virtues and avoid every evil vice. And Hermes says in this regard, "O man, if only you knew the harm of vice, how much you would refrain from it, and if only you knew the reward of courage, how much you would love it!"

Allegory 25

We can take the place where it says that the good knight should imitate Isis, who is so fertile, to refer to the blessed conception of Jesus Christ by the Holy Spirit in the Blessed Virgin Mary, mother of grace whose great bounties could never be imagined or spoken in full, whose worthy conception the good spirit should graft into itself, embracing firmly this laudable article of faith, just as Saint James the

Greater said, "Who was conceived of the Holy Spirit and born from the Virgin Mary." [*Qui conceptus est de Spiritu Sancto, natus ex Maria Virgine.*]

Text 26

Do not hold yourself to the judgment
Of Midas, who never judged wisely,
Nor take counsel from this judgment,
Since for this reason he had donkey ears.

Gloss 26

Midas was a king of small intellect. And a fable says that Phoebus and Pan, the god of shepherds, were quarreling with each other, and that Phoebus said the sound of the lyre was more praiseworthy than the sound of the flute or the pipes. Pan maintained the opposite and said that the flute was more praiseworthy, and in this disagreement they settled upon Midas and chose him as judge. And after both had played in front of Midas, following long consideration, he judged that the sound of the pipes was worth more and was more pleasing than that of the lyre. The fable says that Phoebus, who was infuriated, scorned Midas's uncouth intellect and gave him donkey ears to show that he, having judged so foolishly, had the brain of a donkey. It could happen in this way that someone made a foolish judgment against a prince or powerful man, who punished him by making him show some sign of a fool, which can be seen in the donkey ears. This fable should be interpreted to mean that the good knight should not embrace a foolish judgment not based on reason, nor should he be judged by a verdict handed down in this way. On this topic, a philosopher has said, "The fool is like the mole which hears and understands nothing." And Diogenes compared fools to stone.

Allegory 26

With the judgment of Midas, which the good knight must not embrace, we understand Pontius Pilate, who condemned the Son of God to be taken, bound, and hung on the gibbet of the Cross like a thief, he who was pure and without blemish. Therefore it should be interpreted that the good spirit should refrain from judging the innocent and should believe the article of faith expressed by Saint Andrew, "And he suffered under Pontius Pilate, was crucified, dead, and buried." [*Passus sub Pontio Pilato, crucifixus, mortuus, et sepultus.*]

Text 27

If you have loyal companions in arms,
You must go to help them, if need be,
Even going to hell, where souls descend,
Just as Hercules did.

Gloss 27

The fable says that Pirithous and Theseus went to hell to rescue Proserpine, whom
Pluto had ravished. And they would have been badly treated if Hercules, their
companion, had not helped them: his exploits there terrified the inhabitants of
hell, and he cut the chains of Cerberus the gatekeeper. In this way Othea means
that the good knight must not fail his loyal companion out of fear of whatever
danger there may be, for loyal companionship must be like one and the same
thing. And Pythagoras said, "You must guard diligently the love of your friend."

Allegory 27

We can interpret what the authority says about the necessity of helping one's loyal
companions in arms, even all the way to hell, as did the blessed soul of Jesus
Christ, who harrowed the good souls of the holy patriarchs and prophets which
were in Limbo.[41] And, for example, the good soul should draw to itself all the
virtues and believe in the article of faith expressed by Saint Philip, "And he de-
scended into hell." [*Descendit ad infernos.*]

Text 28

May Cadmus be much beloved and esteemed
By you, and his disciples empowered,
For he conquered the serpent's fountain
With great difficulty.

Gloss 28

Cadmus was a very noble man and founded Thebes, a city of great renown. He
created a school there and he himself was a man of letters and great learning, and

---

41. This is a reference to the Harrowing of Hell, alluded to in 1 Peter 3: 19–20, and elaborated in
the later apocryphal Gospel of Nicodemus (probably mid-fourth century CE). It was believed that
between the Crucifixion and the Resurrection, Christ descended into hell to liberate the virtuous
pagans who had died before Christ's coming.

for this reason the fable said that he conquered the serpent at the fountain, which should be taken to mean knowledge and wisdom which always surge forth. The serpent denotes the difficulty and toil which a student must overcome before he has acquired knowledge. And the fable also says that he himself became a serpent, which should be taken to mean that he was the teacher and regulator of others. In this way Othea means that the good knight must love and honor cultivated scholars with a deep knowledge in all forms of learning. On this topic Aristotle said to Alexander, "Honor knowledge and strengthen it with good teachers."

Allegory 28

We can take Cadmus, who conquered the serpent at the fountain and whom the good knight must love, to represent the blessed humanity of Jesus Christ, who overcame the serpent and won the fountain, that is, the life in this world which he spent with great difficulty and with great toil, over which he triumphed completely when he was resurrected on the third day, just as Saint Thomas says, "On the third day he rose from the dead." [*Tertia die resurrexit a mortuis.*]

Text 29

Take great delight in the knowledge
Of Io more than in any other knowledge
For you will be able to learn much from this,
And take back great profit here.

Gloss 29

Io was a young noble woman, the daughter of king Inachus, who possessed great knowledge and invented many different kinds of letters in the alphabet which had not been envisaged before. As much as several fables claim that Io was Jupiter's lover and that she was turned into a cow, and then that she was a prostitute, but also as much as poets have hidden truth under the dissimulation of fiction, it can be understood that Jupiter loved her, which should be taken to mean the virtues of Jupiter found in her. She was turned into a cow, and just as cows give milk which is sweet and nourishing, she gave with the letters that she invented sweet sustenance to the mind. The fact that she was a woman who made her body accessible to all can be interpreted that her intelligence was made accessible to all, as letters are shared by all people.[42] For this reason the good knight should love

---

42. That a woman whose body was "accessible to all" (i.e., a prostitute) has a positive value may have been suggested to Christine by the interpretation of the story of Byblis in the *Ovide moralisé* (9.2533–49). Byblis's desire to commit incest with her brother was thwarted and she was turned into a fountain,

Io, who can be taken to mean the letters and writings and the histories of good writers which the good knight must gladly listen to and read and whose examples can be useful to him. And on this topic Hermes says, "Whoever endeavors to acquire science and good behavior, he will find that which pleases him in this world and in the next."

Allegory 29

We can interpret Io, who denotes letters and writings, as meaning that the good spirit must delight in reading and hearing the Holy Scriptures and have recorded them in his thoughts. And in this way he can learn to ascend to the heavens with Jesus Christ through good works and holy contemplation, and must believe the worthy article of faith expressed by Saint Bartholomew: "He ascended into heaven and sits at the right hand of God the Father Almighty." [*Ascendit ad caelos, sedet ad dexteram Dei Patris omnipotentis.*]

Text 30

Take care wherever you are
That you are not lulled to sleep by flutes:
Mercury, who sings softly,
Enchants people with his flute.

Gloss 30

A fable recounts that when Jupiter loved the fair Io, Juno became very suspicious and came down from heaven as a cloud to catch her husband in the act. But when Jupiter saw her coming, he changed his lover into a cow, which however did not change Juno's mind, so that she asked Jupiter for the cow as a gift, and Jupiter, reluctantly, granted her request as someone who did not dare refuse out of fear of suspicion. Then Juno gave the cow to Argus, her cowherd with a hundred eyes, to guard, and he watched over her day and night. Nonetheless, the god Mercury, at Jupiter's command, took his flute which plays softly, and played so long in Argus's ear that all of the eyes, one after the other, fell asleep, and then after stealing the cow, he cut off Argus's head. The exposition of the fable can be that some powerful man loved a young woman whom his wife takes to her side to watch so that her

accessible to all. The *Ovide moralisé* poet interprets this metamorphosis on the literal level as Byblis becoming a prostitute, but on the allegorical level she stands for Jesus, whose charity flows out to all humans; see Renate Blumenfeld-Kosinski, "The Scandal of Pasiphaë: Narration and Interpretation in the 'Ovide moralisé,'" *Modern Philology* 93, no. 3 (1996), 319n27. Christine here emphasizes the intellectual benefits, as she does for Io in the *City of Ladies*.

husband cannot approach her, and places strong and clear-eyed guards which are denoted by the eyes of Argus. Still, the lover, with the help of some malicious and well-spoken person, succeeded in convincing the guards to give him back his lover, and thus they were lulled to sleep by Mercury's pipes and had their heads cut off. And for this reason, Othea tells the good knight that he must not be lulled to sleep by such a flute so that he may not be robbed of what he must guard well. And on this point Hermes said, "Guard yourself from those who constantly conduct themselves by deception."

Allegory 30

We can interpret Mercury's pipes to mean that the good spirit should not be deceived by the ancient enemy, by any disbelief or otherwise, and must believe firmly the article of faith spoken by the Evangelist Matthew, who said that God will come to judge the quick and the dead when he said, "Inde venturus iudicare vivos et mortuos" [1 Peter 4:5].

Text 31

Rest assured that Pyrrhus will resemble
His father, and that he also will harass
His enemies: he will avenge
The death of Achilles by oppressing them.

Gloss 31

Pyrrhus was the son of Achilles and closely resembled his father in strength and courage, and after the death of the father, he went to Troy and relentlessly avenged his father and inflicted much damage on the Trojans. For this reason Othea tells the good knight that if someone does wrong to the father, he must beware of the son when he comes of age, and that if the father has been courageous, by the same token, his son will of course also be courageous. On this point a wise man said, "The father's death will bring on the son's vengeance."

Allegory 31

There where it is said that Pyrrhus will resemble his father we can interpret it as the Holy Spirit who proceeds from the Father, in whom the good spirit must believe firmly just as Saint James the Lesser said, "I believe in the Holy Spirit." [Credo in Spiritum Sanctum.]

Text 32

Frequent the temple and honor
The gods of heaven at all times,
And maintain the customs of Cassandra
If you wish to be considered wise.

Gloss 32

Cassandra was the daughter of King Priam, and she was a very good lady and devout in their religion: she would serve the gods and honor the temple, and rarely spoke except when necessary; and when it was useful for her to speak, she would never say something which was not true, nor was she ever caught in a lie. Cassandra was greatly learned, and for this reason Othea tells the good knight that he should resemble her, for foolish customs and lies are deeply reproachable in a knight. Therefore he must serve God and honor the temple, which means the Church and its ministers. And Pythagoras said, "It is highly praiseworthy to serve God and to sanctify his saints."

Allegory 32

The authority says that the good knight must frequent the temple; and the good spirit must do likewise: he must have singular devotion to the holy Catholic Church and to the Communion of Saints, just as the Article of Faith stated by Saint Simon expressed that speaks of "the Holy Catholic Church and the Communion of Saints." [*Sanctam ecclesiam catholicam, sanctorum communionem.*]

Text 33

If you frequently haunt the sea,
You must call upon Neptune
And celebrate his feast well
So that he will protect you from the storm.

Gloss 33

Neptune in the pagans' religion was called the sea-god, and for this reason Othea told the good knight that he must serve him. This should be taken to mean that knights who often take to sea voyages or to other different perils need to be even more devout and to serve God and the saints more than others, so that, if need be, they may be prepared to help and come to them with aid, and they must show special piety and devote prayers to one saint whom they call upon in their need. And since prayer only in the heart is not sufficient, a wise man said, "I never estimate God to have been well served only by words, but also by good works."

Allegory 33

We take Neptune, whom the good knight must call up if he often travels by sea, to mean that the good spirit which constantly sails the world's ocean, must devoutly call upon its Creator, and pray that he grants it to live so that it may have remission of its sins, and must believe in the Article of Faith spoken by Saint Jude: "the remission of sins" [*remissionem peccatorum*].

Text 34

Always be on the lookout
For Atropos and her spear
Which strikes and spares not a soul—
This will make you think of your soul.

Gloss 34

The poets called death Atropos, and for this reason Othea is saying to the good knight that he must think every day that he will not live forever in this world, but will soon leave it. For this reason, he must pay more attention to his soul's virtues than taking pleasure in his body's delights. And every Christian must think of this so that he keeps in mind taking care of his eternal soul. And on this subject Pythagoras said that just as our beginning comes from God, so too must our end be in Him.

Allegory 34

Where Othea tells the good knight to keep in mind Atropos, who denotes death, by the same token the good spirit must also keep Atropos in mind, the same good spirit which, thanks to the merits of the passion of Our Lord Jesus Christ, must have firm hope, cultivated with effort and diligence, of achieving paradise in the end. And the good spirit must believe firmly that it will be resurrected on the Day of Judgment and will have life eternal if it deserves it, as Saint Matthew says in the last Article of Faith, "the resurrection of the flesh and life everlasting. Amen." [*Carnis resurreccionem vitam eternam. Amen.*]

Text 35

May Bellerophon be exemplary
For all feats you wish to undertake—
Bellerophon who preferred dying
To risking disloyalty.

Gloss 35

Bellerophon was a knight of great beauty and truth. His stepmother was so taken with love for him that she desired him; but because he did not wish to consent to her will, she managed to have him condemned to be devoured by wild beasts. And he preferred to choose death rather than do something disloyal. For this reason, Othea tells the good knight that he must not risk committing any disloyalty out of fear of death. On this point Hermes says, "Prefer dying without cause rather than committing something unfitting."

Allegory 35

Now we have come to the Ten Commandments, and we will propose allegories of them which fit our arguments.

Bellerophon, who was so truthful, may denote God in paradise; and as His worthy grace has always abounded and may it always abound in truth for us, in this instance we can cite the First Commandment which says, "Thou shalt not worship foreign gods." In other words, as Saint Augustine said, "You shall not show that form of worship called *latria* or 'devotion' to any idol, image, depiction, or any other creature, for this honor is due only to God." And in this commandment any kind of idolatry is forbidden. Our Lord speaks of this in the Gospel, "You shall worship the Lord your God and him only shall you serve." [Matthew 4:10: *Dominum Deum tuum adorabis et illi soli servies.*]

Text 36

You must love Memnon,
Your loyal cousin, close to you in your need,
And who loves you so much that
You must arm yourself for him in his need.

Gloss 36

King Memnon was Hector's cousin, of Trojan lineage; and when Hector fought fierce battles where many times he was hard-pressed by his enemies, Memnon, who was a very brave knight, followed him close behind. And so he would often come to Hector's aid, and in skirmishes would split the enemy in two, and this was evident, for when Achilles treacherously killed Hector, Memnon severely wounded Achilles and would have killed him if sudden help for him had not arrived. For this reason Othea told the good knight that he must love Memnon and aid him if need be: and this should be interpreted as meaning that every prince and good knight with some good and loyal relative, however small or poor as he may be, must love him and must make him part of his affairs, and especially then when he feels how loyal he shows himself to be. And it happens sometimes that a great prince is better and more loyally loved by his poor relative than by a very powerful man. And on this topic the philosopher Zeno said, "Multiply your friends, for they will be prepared to help you."

Allegory 36

We can interpret Memnon the loyal relative to mean God in paradise, who truly became a loyal relative to us by taking on our humanity, a favor that we could never pay back. Therefore in this instance we can cite the Second Commandment, which says, "Thou shalt not take the name of the Lord thy God in vain," that is, as Saint Augustine said, "You should not swear falsely, neither without cause nor in order to embellish falsehood, for there can be no greater deception than to present the highest and unshakeable truth as evidence for falsehood." In this commandment all lies, all perjuries, and all blasphemies are forbidden. On this point, the law says in Exodus 20:7, "the Lord will not hold him guiltless who takes his name in vain." [*Non habebit dominus insontem eum qui assumpserit nomen domini dei sui frustra.*]

Text 37

Think long before a word
Fraught with threats, silly and foolish,
Leaves your mouth and you say too much,
And reflect on the example of Laomedon.

Gloss 37

Laomedon was the king of Troy and the father of Priam, and when Jason, Hercules, and his companions were on the way to Colchis to seek the Golden Fleece, they arrived and left ship in the port of Troy to refresh themselves, without harming the land, whereupon Laomedon, poorly advised, sent messengers ordering them with insults to depart and threatening them if they did not immediately leave his country. Thereupon the Greek commanders considered themselves so offended by this dismissal that the destruction of the first Troy was the result afterwards.[43] For this reason Othea advises the good knight that, just as threats are ugly and mean, they should be carefully weighed before being uttered, for oftentimes many great evils are the result. On this point the poet Homer said, "Whoever knows how to curb his tongue is a wise man."

Allegory 37

As menacing threats may arise from arrogance, and in like manner breaking a commandment may be presumptuousness, we can understand that no one should disregard feast-days, for this goes against the commandment which says, "Remember to sanctify the Sabbath," by which we are commanded, writes Saint Augustine, that we observe Sunday in place of the Jews' Sabbath, and celebrate it solemnly by resting the body by ceasing all menial labor and by resting the soul by ceasing all sins. And the prophet Isaiah speaks of this rest, "cease to do evil, learn to do good." [Isaiah 1:16–17: *Quiescite agere perverse, discite bene facere.*]

Text 38

Hold nothing for certain
Before attaining the truth—
Pyramus teaches you
What presuming a little brings.

Gloss 38

Pyramus was a young man in the city of Babylon, and before he had reached the age of seven, Cupid wounded him with his arrow and he was smitten with love for Thisbe, a beautiful and well-mannered young woman of the same age

---

43. In the version of Dares, supposedly an eyewitness account of the Trojan story but probably dating from the sixth century CE, Troy was destroyed the first time when, as in this Gloss, King Laomedon refused to give hospitality to the Argonauts heading to Colchis to capture the Golden Fleece. See Dictys and Dares, *The Trojan War*.

and background. And because of the frequent meetings of the two lovers, their great love was noticed and denounced by a servant to the young woman's mother, who took her daughter and shut her up in her room and told her that she would carefully protect her from Pyramus's frequent company. For this reason the two children's grief was overwhelming and their sighs and tears heartbreaking. This imprisonment lasted for a long time, but gradually as they grew older, the spark of love, which long absence never extinguished, burst into flame in them. However, as there was only a single wall between the palaces of the two lovers' parents, Thisbe once spotted a crack in the wall where the light from the other side showed through. She then stuck the bite from her belt buckle into the crack so that her lover could see her, which happened in short time, and the two lovers often met there with pitiful laments. In the end, forced by loving too much, they agreed that they would steal away at night from their sleeping parents, and would meet under a white mulberry tree, outside the city, near a fountain where they used to play together as children. When Thisbe arrived at the fountain, alone and fearful, she heard a lion rapidly approaching and, taking fright, fled and hid in a nearby bush, but as she was fleeing, her white wimple fell off her head. Pyramus arrived, and in the moonlight saw the white wimple, which the lion had completely soiled and covered with blood when he vomited on it the entrails of an animal he had devoured. Pyramus's grief was boundless, for he thought his beloved had been devoured by wild beasts, whereupon after many pitiful wails he killed himself with his sword. Thisbe leapt out from the bush, but when she heard the sobs of her dying lover, when she saw the sword and the blood, out of grief she fell on her lover who could not speak to her, and after lamenting, wailing, and fainting many times, she killed herself with the same sword. And the fable says that because of this misfortune the mulberry tree, which used to be white, turned black. And because such a terrible misadventure could arise from such a small occasion, Othea tells the good knight not to lend credence to trifles. On this topic a wise man said, "Do not endorse as certain matters which are doubtful before you have made the necessary inquiry about them."

Allegory 38

We can interpret what the wise man says about uncertainty as meaning the ignorance in which we find ourselves under the correction of father and mother, and in the good deeds which we receive from them we can understand the Fourth Commandment which says, "Honor thy father and thy mother." Saint Augustine comments on this commandment by saying that we must honor our parents in two ways: by showing them the proper respect and by helping them in their need. On this topic the wise man said, "With all your heart honor your father, and do not forget the birth pangs of your mother." [Ecclesiasticus/Sirach 7:27: *Honora patrem tuum et gemitus matris tue non obliviscaris in finem.*]

Text 39

For the health of your body
Believe the reports of Asclepius,
And not those of the sorceress
Circe, ever the deceiver.

Gloss 39

Asclepius was a very wise scholar who invented the art of medicine and wrote books about it. And for this reason Othea advises the good knight to believe Asclepius's accounts about health. This should be taken to mean that if he finds himself in need, he should turn to doctors and physicians, and never to the spells of Circe who was a sorceress. And the same can be said for those who in their illness use spells and charms and enchantments, and think that they can be healed this way—practices which are forbidden and which violate the commandment of Holy Church and which no good Christian must employ. Plato repudiated and burnt the books of enchantments and spells devised for medicine which had been long been employed, and he endorsed and adhered to those based methodically on reason and experience.

Allegory 39

We can take Asclepius, who was a physician and doctor, to mean the Fifth Commandment that says "Thou shalt not kill," that is, according to Saint Augustine, with heart, tongue, or hand. And thus all violent persecution and bodily harm are forbidden, but by the same token it is not forbidden for princes, judges, and officers of the law to put criminals to death, but only forbidden for those who have no authority in this matter except in cases of need where a man cannot escape otherwise, or in those cases, in self-defense, where the laws permit killing, but not otherwise. On this topic the Gospel says, "If anyone slays with the sword, with the sword must he be slain." [Revelation 13.10: *Qui gladio occiderit oportet eum in gladio occidi.*]

Text 40

Do not trust someone
To whom you have done too much harm

And who themselves cannot in fact take revenge for it,
For they will resent it, as Achilles's death teaches you.

Gloss 40

Achilles inflicted great harm on the Trojans and killed several children—Hector, Troilus, and others—of King Priam, who must have hated him for this. Nevertheless, Achilles trusted Queen Hecuba, the wife of Priam, whose children he had treacherously murdered, and went by night to speak to her to negotiate his marriage to her daughter Polyxena, and there Achilles was killed by Paris and his companions by the order of his mother the queen at the temple of Apollo. For this reason Othea tells the good knight that, without having first made peace or reparation, he should not trust his enemy against whom he has sinned too much. In this regard a wise man said, "Beware the ambushes of your enemy who cannot avenge himself."

Allegory 40

Since one should not trust someone against whom one has sinned too much, we take it, just as we ought to fear God's vengeance, that it is necessary to uphold the commandment which states that "Thou shalt not commit adultery," that is, sex between married people or between unmarried ones. And by this, according to Isidore, any illicit carnal intercourse outside of marriage and any disordered use of the genitals are forbidden. On this point the law says, "Both the adulterer and the adulteress shall be put to death." [Leviticus 20:10: *Morte moriantur mechus et adultera.*]

Text 41

Do not resemble in any way Busiris
Who was much worse than a thief;
His cruelty was reproachable,
Do not engage in such deeds.

Gloss 41

Busiris was a king of amazing cruelty and he took great pleasure in killing men, and in fact he himself slaughtered them with knives in his temples and made sacrifices out of them to his gods. For this reason Othea says to the good knight that he must not delight in killing human nature, for such cruelty is against God, against nature, and against all goodness. On this topic Socrates said to the good counselor, "If your prince is cruel, you must temper him with good examples."

Allegory 41

We can take Busiris, who was homicidal and contrary to human nature, to mean the prohibition which the commandment imposes on us which says, "Thou shalt not steal." By this token, according to Saint Augustine, are also forbidden the illicit usurpation of others' possessions, the confiscation of the Church's property, and the plundering and the unjustified seizing by force or by the lord's power of people's goods. And on this subject the Apostle Paul says, "Let the thief no longer steal." [Ephesians 4:28: *Qui furabatur iam non furetur.*]

Text 42

Do not hold your pleasure so dear
That you place your life,
Which you must love, in too great uncertainty—
Leander perished at sea for doing so.

Gloss 42

Leander was a young man who was smitten with too much love for the beautiful Hero. And as there was an arm of the sea separating the two lovers' estates, Leander frequently crossed it by swimming at night in order to see his beloved, whose castle lay near the shore, so that their love would not be observed. And it happened that a terrible storm arose over the sea which lasted for several days, and which interrupted the two lovers' pleasure—but it also happened that one night, Leander, aroused by excessive desire, dove into the sea while the storm raged, and the treacherous waves dragged him so far out that he could only die a miserable death. When Hero, who was waiting in great distress for her lover on the other side, saw the body floating by the shore, overcome with overwhelming grief, she threw herself into the sea, and, embracing the body, perished and was drowned. For this reason, Othea advises the good knight that he must not love his pleasure so much that he risk his life for it. A wise man has therefore said, "I am amazed to see how many risks are taken for the body's pleasure with such little regard for the well-being of the eternal soul."

Allegory 42

When the ancient authority forbids holding one's pleasure so dear, it can be taken to mean the commandment which says, "Thou shalt bear no false witness against thy neighbor." By the same token, according to Saint Augustine, are also forbidden false accusations, calumny, slander, false report, and defamation. And it should be understood, as Isidore said, that the false witness commits a base act against three parties: that is, against God, whom he scorns by invoking Him in a false oath, to the judge whom he deceives by lying, and to his neighbor by giving a false deposition against him. For this reason Scripture says, "A false witness will not go unpunished, and he who utters lies will not escape." [Proverbs 19:5: *Testis falsus non erit inpunitus et qui mendacia loquitur non effugiet.*]

Text 43

Surrender Helen if she is demanded,
For reparation lies in a great sin,
And it is better to consent to peace sooner
Than to be forced to repent later.

Gloss 43

Helen was the wife of King Menelaos, and was kidnapped in Greece by Paris. And when the Greeks descended upon Troy with a large army to avenge this deed, and before they began with any wrongdoings on land, they demanded that Helen be returned to them and that reparations for this offense be made, otherwise they would destroy the land. And because the Trojans wanted to do none of this, the terrible disaster resulted which then befell them. With this example Othea tells the good knight that if he has committed some foolish deed, it is better that he abandon it and make peace rather than pursue it so that nothing bad happens to him because of it. For this reason the philosopher Plato says, "If you have done wrong to anyone, you must not be at ease until you have come to terms and made peace with him."

Allegory 43

With the figure of Helen, who should be surrendered, can be taken the commandment which says: "Thou shalt not covet thy neighbor's wife," which forbids, according to Saint Augustine, the thought and intention of committing fornication, an act forbidden by the Sixth Commandment, for our Savior says in the Gospel, "Everyone who looks at a woman lustfully has already committed adultery with her in his heart." [Matthew 5:28: *Qui viderit mulierem ad concupiscendum eam iam mechatus est in corde suo.*]

Text 44

Do not resemble the goddess
Aurora, who gives great joy
To others when her time comes,
But for herself only holds sadness and weeps.

Gloss 44

Aurora is the dawn, and the fables tell us that she was a goddess and that she had a son killed at the siege of Troy who was called Cygnus, and that she, having the power of a goddess, changed her son's body into a swan and that the first swans are descended from this. This lady was of such great beauty that she delighted all who saw her, but for the rest of her life, she mourned her son Cygnus who had died at Troy, and she weeps for him still, the fable tells, and others say this as well, for the dew which falls from heaven at dawn are the tears of Aurora weeping for her son Cygnus. For this reason Othea advises the good knight who cheers others with his noble virtues that he must not be sad, but glad and graciously joyful. For this reason Aristotle told Alexander the Great, "No matter what sadness you have in your heart, you must always display a cheerful face to your people."

Allegory 44

With the weeping Aurora we take it that no longing should weep in us from coveting any worldly thing. And by this we can note for ourselves the Tenth Commandment which says, "Thou shalt not covet thy neighbor's house, … nor his ox, nor his ass, nor any thing that is thy neighbor's." According to this, says Saint Augustine, wanting to steal or to rob is forbidden, just as the deed itself is forbidden by the Seventh Commandment. On this topic David says in his Psalter, "Put no confidence in extortion, set no vain hopes on robbery." [Psalm 61:11 (62:10): *Nolite sperare in iniquitate rapinas nolite concupisce.*]

Text 45

Even if Pasiphaë was dissolute,
Do not follow her school lesson
That all women are like this,
For there are many ladies of great worth.

Gloss 45

Pasiphaë was a queen, and several fables say that she was of woman of great decadence, and even that she had made love to a bull, which should be taken to mean that she had been intimate with a man of lowly condition, from whom she conceived a son of extreme cruelty and astonishing strength. And because he had the appearance of a man and the nature of a bull in that he was strong, extremely harsh, and so evil that he devastated the entire land, the poets explained with a fiction that he was half-man, half-bull. And for this reason, even if this lady was so inclined, Othea counsels the good knight not to claim or maintain that all women are like her, as the contrary is manifestly true. Galen learned the science of medicine from a woman of great worth and wisdom named Cleopatra, who taught him to recognize beneficial plants and their properties.

Allegory 45

We can interpret Pasiphaë, who was dissolute, as meaning the soul having returned to God. And Saint Gregory says in his Sermons that greater joy is felt in heaven from a soul having returned to God than from a just soul who had always been so, and the captain in battle prefers the knight who had fled, then come back, and after his return inflicted heavy losses on the enemy to one who has done nothing courageous, just as someone who works the land prefers a field cleared of brambles which bears abundant fruit to one free of brambles which has never borne fruit. On this topic, God has said through His prophet, let everyone "turn from his evil way, so that I may forgive their iniquity and their sin." [Jeremiah 36:3: *Revertatur unusquisque a via sua pessima et propicius ero iniquitati et peccato ipsorum.*]

Text 46

If you have daughters to be married,[44]
You must give them in marriage
To men from whom no evil will come to you—
Then remember King Adrastus.

---

44. This chapter seems to anticipate *in nuce* the later factional strife between the Armagnacs and Burgundians. The Theban story was read throughout the Middle Ages as a paradigm of fratricidal or civil war.

Gloss 46

Adrastus was the king of Argos and was very powerful and noble. One dark night, two knights, the one named Polynices and the other Tydeus, fought under his palace's gateway, each claiming shelter there because of the bad weather and heavy rains which had tormented them all night, and by chance at that hour they were fighting there. The king, hearing the din of swords clashing on shields, got up from his bed. He went and separated the two knights and established an accord between them. Polynices was the son of the King of Thebes and Tydeus of another king in Greece, but both had been exiled from their lands. Adrastus showed great honor to the two princes and then he gave them his two beautiful daughters in marriage. Afterwards, to restore to Polynices the claims which he had on the land held by his brother Eteocles, King Adrastus assembled a large army and descended with it upon Thebes, but things turned out so badly that the great army was completely defeated, and everyone was captured and killed. And with the King's two sons-in-law dead, the two brothers at the origin of the dispute killed each other during the battle. And so no one survived except Adrastus and two of his knights. And because restoring the rights of exiled people entails great effort, Othea advises the good knight that in such a case he must take counsel and must reflect on what happened here. And because Adrastus had dreamed one night that he was giving his two daughters in marriage to a lion and a dragon who fought against each other, the interpreter of dreams says that a dream comes from the head's imagination, which can be a demonstration of good or bad events that must happen to creatures.

Allegory 46

We can interpret the passage where it says that if someone has daughters to marry, he must beware to whom he gives them, to mean that the good knight of God must consider well whom he escorts if it happens that he wants to go forth in company, as did the good Tobias [with the angel Raphael], and must fix all his thoughts in God and holy meditations. And Saint Augustine says in a letter that those who have learned from Our Lord to be benevolent and humble profit more by meditating and praying than when they read and listen. For this reason David says in the Psalms, "I meditated also on thy commandments, which I loved." [Psalm 118 (119):47: *Meditabor in mandatis tuis quae dilexi.*]

Text 47

It would please me well enough, if,
Though you are young and handsome, you acquainted yourself
With Cupid prudently, for no matter what he does,
He very much pleases the god of battle.

Gloss 47

Cupid is the god of love, and because it is never unseemly for a young knight to
be in love with a respected and wise lady—on the contrary, his status can greatly
improve from this, provided he knows how to keep the golden mean, which is
quite conducive to feats of arms—Othea tells the good knight that she well and
truly assents to his acquainting himself with Cupid. And a philosopher said that
loving honestly comes from a noble heart.

Allegory 47

The fact that becoming acquainted with Cupid very much pleases the god of bat-
tles can be interpreted as penitence. If the good spirit, repenting its sins, battling
against the vices, is young and a recent entry on the straight and narrow path, it
pleases the god of battles, that is, Jesus Christ, that he becomes acquainted with
penitence. And that Jesus Christ became our Redeemer because of his worthy
battle, Saint Bernard says: "What word," he says, "of greater mercy can one speak
to a sinner who was damned because when he had been sold by sin to the enemy
of hell and had nothing to redeem himself with, God the Father said to him: 'Take
my Son, and I give him for your sake,' and the Son says to him, 'Take me and
redeem yourself through me.'" And the Apostle Peter recalled in his First Epistle:
"You were ransomed from the futile ways inherited from your fathers, not with
perishable things such as silver or gold, but with the precious blood of Christ,
like that of a lamb without blemish or spot." [1 Peter 1:18–19: *Non corruptibilibus
auro vel argento redempti estis sed precioso sanguine quasi agni incontaminati et
inmaculati Jhesu Cristi.*]

Text 48

Do not kill the beautiful Coronis
Because of the crow's report
And news, for if you kill her,
You will regret it afterwards.

Gloss 48

Coronis was a young woman, as the fable says, whom Phoebus truly loved. The crow who then served him reported to him that it had seen his lover Coronis in bed with another young man. This news afflicted Phoebus so much that he killed his lover as soon as she returned to him, but afterwards, surprisingly, he regretted having done this. Then the crow, who expected to receive a reward from his lord for this good deed, was cursed and chased away because of this, and Phoebus changed his plumage, which used to be white, to black as a sign of grief, and ordered that from then on he be the bearer and messenger of bad news. And this tale can be taken to be that of a servant of some powerful man who reported similar news, for which he was dismissed and sent away. For this reason Othea advises that the good knight should not rush to tell his prince news which would move him by flattery to ire or anger against the well-being of others, since in the end the rewards for such reports turn out to be slight, and that he himself should not believe a report relayed to him out of flattery. On this point the philosopher Hermes says, "Someone who reports or invents news, is either lying to the person to whom he reports the news, or he is untruthful to the person from whom he got them."

Allegory 48

We take Coronis, who should not have been killed, to represent our soul, which we must not kill through sin, but rather guard well. And Saint Augustine says that the soul should be guarded like a chest full of treasure, like the castle which has been besieged by enemies, like the king resting in his retreat, and that this chamber should be shut with five doors which are nature's five senses, for shutting these doors is nothing other than withdrawing from the delights of the five senses. And should it happen that the soul must exit through these doors to go to fulfill its duties outside, it must depart with reflection, with calm, and with discretion. And just like princes, when they wish to leave their chambers, have doorkeepers go ahead of them, holding up maces to make way through the crush,[45] so too, when the soul wishes to go out to see, hear, speak, and feel, must it have fear as the doorkeeper who holds up as the mace a view of hell's sufferings and of God's judgment. And the wise man admonishes guarding one's soul this way: "Keep your heart with all vigilance; for from it flow the springs of life." [Proverbs 4:23: *Cum custodia serva cor tuum quoniam ex ipso vita procedit.*]

---

45. A mace is a weapon, but also a ceremonial symbol, denoting authority.

Text 49

Do not concern yourself with Juno too much,
If you wish to have the kernel
Of honor, rather than its shell,
For courage is worth more than possessions.

Gloss 49

Juno is the goddess of possessions according to the poets' fables, and because great effort and exertion are needed to hold and acquire possessions and riches, and because such effort can distract from acquiring honor, and since honor and valor are more praiseworthy than riches, just as the kernel is worth more than the shell, Othea advises the good knight that he should not place his thoughts and happiness so that the pursuit of valor is abandoned. On this subject Hermes says that poverty is worth more in accomplishing good than sinfully acquired riches, for worth is eternal, riches vain and frail.

Allegory 49

We can likewise take Juno, with whom it was said that one should not concern oneself too much, and who represents riches, to mean that the good spirit should scorn wealth. And Saint Bernard said, "O Adam's son, envy's prodigy, to what end do you love these earthly riches so much which are neither real nor yours, and like it or not, you must forsake at your death!" And the Gospel says that the camel would pass through the eye of a needle sooner than the rich man would enter the kingdom of heaven, for the camel only has a hump on its back, whereas the sinful rich man has two: one, his earthly possessions, and the other, his sins. One must leave behind the first hump at the moment of death, but the other one, like it or not, he will carry with him if he does not give it up before dying. On this point Our Lord said in the Gospel, "It is easier for a camel to go through the eye of a needle than for a rich man to enter into the kingdom of God." [Matthew 19:24: *Facilius est camelum per foramen acus transire quam divitem intrare in regnum celorum.*]

Text 50

Against the advice of Amphiaraus
Do not go to destroy either the city of Thebes
Or of Argos, for you will die—
Do not assemble either an army, or shields or bucklers.

Gloss 50

Amphiaraus was a very wise scholar of the city of Argos, and deeply learned. When King Adrastus wanted to descend on Thebes to destroy the city, Amphiaraus—who, thanks to his learning, knew that evil would befall him for this—told the King that he should not go there and that if he would go there, everyone would be killed and destroyed. Yet he was not believed, and things happened as he had said. For this reason, Othea advises the good knight that he should undertake nothing against the advice of wise men, but, as Solon says, "The advice of a wise man is rarely beneficial to someone unwilling to take it."

Allegory 50

We interpret the advice of Amphiaraus, against which one should not go into battle, to mean that the good spirit should follow holy preaching. And Saint Gregory says in his Sermons that just as the life of the body cannot be sustained without frequently taking bodily nourishment, so too the life of the soul cannot be sustained without frequently hearing the word of God. Therefore receive in your heart God's words which you hear with bodily ears, for when the word which is heard is not kept in the seat of memory, it is the same as when the sick stomach vomits food. And just as one despairs for the life of someone who cannot hold down food but vomits everything, so too is someone in peril of eternal death who hears preaching without retaining or implementing it. For this reason Holy Scripture says, "Man shall not live by bread alone, but by every word that proceeds from of the mouth of God." [Matthew 4:4: *Non in solo pane vivit homo sed in omni verbo quod procedit de ore Dei.*]

Text 51

Let your speech be deliberate[46]
And stay away from all evil.
To speak too much is a bad habit
And whoever has it is crazy.

Gloss 51

Saturn, as I said earlier, is a slow and sluggish planet. For this reason Othea tells the knight that his speech should resemble Saturn's, for one's speech should be

---

46. The Middle French is "saturnine," referring to the pagan god Saturn, who is associated with melancholia. Here "saturnine" could mean "slow," that is, deliberate. The French "langue" can mean both tongue and speech, and it is translated both ways in this Text.

deliberate in that one's tongue should be hesitant about speaking too much and careful not to slander anyone or say something that can be interpreted as crazy. "One knows the wise man by his speech, and the fool by his look."

Allegory 51

That the tongue that should be saturnine means that one should speak slowly. Hugh of Saint Victor[47] says in this context that a mouth without the protection of discretion is like a city without a wall, like a vessel without a cover, like a horse without a bridle, like a ship without steering. A poorly guarded tongue slithers like an eel, pierces like an arrow, takes away friends and multiplies enemies, creates uproar and sows discord, and strikes a blow killing several people. Whoever guards his tongue guards his soul, for both death and life are within the power of speech. On this topic David says in his Psalter: "What man is there who desires life, and covets many days, that he may enjoy good? Keep your tongue from evil, and your lips from speaking deceit." [Psalm 33:13–14 (34:12–13): *Quis est homo qui vult vitam, dies diliget videre bonos? Prohibe linguam a malo et labia ne loquantur dolum.*]

Text 52

Believe the crow and her advice,
Never be eager
to bring bad news,
It is best to stay away from them.

Gloss 52

The crow, so tells the fable, met the raven when he was carrying the news to Apollo about his lover Coronis who had done him wrong, and the crow so entreated him to tell her the reason of his errand that he did so. But she persuaded him not to go to Apollo by citing the example of herself, who for a similar reason had been chased away from Pallas Athena's dwelling, where she had once occupied a privileged position. But the raven did not want to believe her and had to bear the bad consequences. For this reason Othea tells the good knight that he

---

47. Hugh of Saint Victor (1096–1141), a German-born theologian and mystic, made the School of Saint-Victor in Paris a celebrated center of learning. He authored an encyclopedia, the *Didascalion*, as well as commentaries on the Scriptures and on earlier theologians' writings. See Ivan Illich, *In the Vineyard of the Text: A Commentary to Hugh's Didascalion* (Chicago: University of Chicago Press, 1993).

must believe the crow. And Plato says: "Don't be a gossip and do not see yourself as a great messenger bringing news to the king."

Allegory 52

That one should believe the crow means that the good spirit should use good counsel, just as Saint Gregory says in the *Morals* that force is worth nothing without good counsel, for force is quickly beaten down when unsupported by the gift of good counsel, and the soul that has lost within itself good counsel scatters itself on the outside through various desires. For this reason the wise man says: "For wisdom will come into your heart ...; discretion will watch over you; understanding will guard you." [Proverbs 2:10–11: *Si intraverit sapiencia cor tuum ... consilium custodiet te et prudencia servabit te.*]

Text 53

If you try beyond your strength
To engage in several games of mock combat,
Withdraw so that nothing bad happens to you,
And remember Ganymede.

Gloss 53

Ganymede was a young man of Trojan lineage, and a fable tells that Apollo and he were competing together one day to throw the discus, and as Ganymede had but little strength against that of Apollo, he was killed when the discus rebounded that Apollo had thrown so high that he had lost sight of it.[48] And for that reason Othea says that a contest between yourself and someone much stronger and more powerful than you is not a good idea, because only harm can come of it. And the wise man says: "To risk oneself in unmannerly games of mock combat with other men is a sign of arrogance and usually ends in fury."

Allegory 53

And when it is said that no one should fight against anyone stronger than himself this means that the good spirit should not undertake too severe a penance without counsel. And on that subject Saint Gregory says in the *Morals* that penance

48. This is the story of Hyacinthus rather than that of Ganymede. See *Ovide moralisé* 10:738–52 for Ganymede, and 10:852–78 for Hyacinthus. We translate Christine's "bar de fer" as discus rather than as iron bar because only a discus can lethally rebound from the ground as described in Ovid (*Metamorphoses* 10:176-85) and Gloss 53. Ovid uses the word *discus*.

without discretion profits nothing, and that the virtue of abstinence is worth
nothing unless it is so disposed that it is not harsher than the body can bear. And
for this reason he concludes that no one should undertake anything without the
counsel of someone who is more discerning than himself. For this reason the wise
man says in Proverbs: "In an abundance of counselors there is safety" [Proverbs
11:14: *Ubi multa consilia, ibi est salus*], and the common proverb: "Do everything
with good counsel and then will you not regret it later" [*Omnia fac cum consilio
et postea non penitebis*].

Text 54

Do not resemble Jason
Who conquered the Golden Fleece
With Medea's help, for which she later
Paid him back with an evil reward.

Gloss 54

Jason was a Greek knight who traveled abroad, that is, to the island of Colchis,
on the orders of his uncle Pelias, who because of envy desired his death. On this
island there was a ram with a golden fleece that was guarded by magic. And its
conquest was so difficult that not a single man who had gone there did not end
up by losing his life. Medea, who was the daughter of the king of this country,
fell so in love with Jason that she gave him spells based on the magic of which
she was a consummate mistress, and taught him magic which allowed him to
conquer the Golden Fleece. He thus gained honor over all living knights and was
saved from death by Medea, to whom he promised to be always a loyal lover. But
later he broke his word and loved another woman and left her, although she was
of outstanding beauty. For this reason we say to the good knight that he should
not resemble Jason, who was too ungrateful and disloyal to the woman who had
done him so much good. And it is a villainous act for a knight or any other noble
person to be ungrateful and show no appreciation for a good thing he has re-
ceived, be it from a lady, a young woman, or any other person; rather, he should
remember it every day, and pay them back as much as it is in his power. On this
subject says Hermes: "You should not wait to pay someone back who has done
you good, for you should remember it every day."

Allegory 54

The good spirit, who should not be ungrateful for the benefits received from his
creator, should not resemble Jason, who was ungrateful. And Saint Bernard says

in his commentary on the Canticles that ingratitude is the enemy of the soul, the diminishment of the virtues, the dispersion of merits, and the loss of graces. Ingratitude is also like a dry wind that dries out the fountain of pity, the dew of grace, and the stream of compassion. On this subject the wise man says: "For the hope of the ungrateful shall melt away like the winter's ice, and shall run off as unprofitable water." [Wisdom 16:29: *Ingrati enim spes tanquam hibernalis glacies tabescet et dispariet tamquam aqua supervacua.*]

Text 55

Beware of the serpent Gorgon,
Take care not to look at her;
Remember Perseus,
He can tell you the whole story.

Gloss 55

Gorgon, so tells a fable, was a young lady of great beauty; but because Apollo lay with her in Diana's temple the goddess was so furious that she transformed her into a serpent of horrible appearance. And this serpent had the power that any man who looked at her was immediately changed into a stone. And because she was the source of so much evil, Perseus the valiant knight went to do battle with the fierce beast; and in order not to look at the evil serpent he reflected his gaze through his splendid shield—made entirely of gold—and he succeeded so well that he cut off her head. Several different interpretations can be attached to this fable: the Gorgon can stand for a city or town that once possessed great goodness, but through the vices of its inhabitants turned into a venomous serpent, which means that they committed great evils against their neighboring regions, such as robbing and pillaging them; and merchants and travelers were captured and detained and put into a confining prison, which means they were turned into stone. Perseus reflected himself in his shield, that is, in the force of chivalry, and went to fight against this city and conquered it and took away its power to do evil. And [the Gorgon] can also be a very beautiful but evil lady who through her greed ruined many people; and even more meanings can be found. For this reason Othea wants to say to the good knight that he should guard against bad things that could lead him to evil. And Aristotle says: "Flee people who are filled with iniquity, but rather follow wise men and study their books and reflect on their deeds."

Allegory 55

That one should not look at the Gorgon means that the good spirit should not look at or think about any pleasures but should mirror itself in the shield of perfection. And one should flee from vices, says Saint Chrysostom, because just as it is impossible for fire to burn in water, so is it impossible that the heart's compunction can exist in the midst of the pleasures of this world. These are two contrary things that destroy each other, for compunction is the mother of tears and pleasures bring forth laughter; compunction restrains the heart and pleasures enlarge it. On this subject the Scriptures say: "May those who sow in tears reap with shouts of joy." [Psalm 125:5 (126:5): *Qui seminant in lacrimis, in exultacione metent.*]

Text 56

If Love shortens your night
Beware that Phoebus does not harm you.
Through him you could be taken
By surprise in Vulcan's bonds.

Gloss 56

A fable recounts that Mars and Venus were lovers. It happened one night that Phoebus, who could see clearly, surprised and saw them and denounced them to Vulcan, Venus's husband. Then he, who was the blacksmith of the heavens and could work with great subtlety, saw them in this situation, forged a bronze lock and chain, and bound the two together so that they could not move. And thus he took them by surprise and went to get the other gods and showed them his shame. And the fable says that he who would fall into a similar predicament laughs about it. This fable can be interpreted in various ways; first, it could make a reference to alchemy for those who know how to understand it in a subtle manner. But for our purposes it means that the good knight must watch out so that he is not surprised through forgetfulness. And a wise man says: "There is hardly anything that is so secret that it does not become known."

Allegory 56

When the authority says, "If love shortens your night," we say that the good spirit must protect itself against the snares of the enemy. On this subject pope Saint Leo the Great says that the ancient enemy who transfigures himself into an angel of light never stops laying out the snares of his temptations and lying in wait trying to corrupt the faith of the believers. He waits for the person whom he will set on fire with desire, whom he will inflame with ardent voluptuousness, to whom he will propose the attractions of gluttony; he examines all the habits and hearts, makes suppositions regarding people's affections, and he seeks an occasion to do harm in that moment when he finds the creature most inclined to be flighty and busy. For this reason Saint Peter says: "Be sober, be watchful. Your adversary the devil prowls around like a roaring lion, seeking someone to devour." [1 Peter 5:8: *Sobrii estote et vigilate, quia adversarius vester dyabolus tanquam leo rugiens circuit querens quem devoret.*]

Text 57

Do not scorn Thamaris
Although she is a woman,
Remember the narrows where Cyrus was trapped,
For he dearly paid for his contempt.

Gloss 57

Thamaris was the queen of Amazonia, a very valiant lady full of prowess and daring, and well versed in the arts of war and government.[49] Cyrus, the great king of Persia, who had conquered many regions, assembled a large army to attack this realm of Feminia,[50] whose strength he greatly underestimated. But the queen, who was a skillful expert in the military profession, let him enter her realm without doing anything until he was trapped in narrow passages between the mountains where the landscape was very rough. Then Thamaris devised an ambush and Cyrus was attacked from all sides by the women's army until he was finally cornered and taken prisoner with all his men either dead or captured. The queen had him led before her, had him beheaded, and threw his head into a bucket filled with the blood of his men, whom she had beheaded in his presence. Then Thamaris spoke as follows: "Cyrus, you who in the past could not get enough of human blood, now you can drink your fill." And this was the end of Cyrus, the great king of Persia, who had never before been vanquished in any battle. For this reason it is said to the good knight that he should not be presumptuous, for there is no doubt that by some chance a misfortune could befall him and diminish him. And on this subject Plato says: "Do not underestimate someone for his small strength for his virtues may be great."

---

49. Christine mentions Thamaris (also spelled Tomyris) in the *Mutacion de fortune* and the *Cité des dames.*

50. Another name for the reign of the Amazons.

Allegory 57

Thamaris, who should not be scorned just for being a woman, means that the good spirit should not disdain or hate the state of humility, whether in religion or elsewhere. And to prove that humility should be praised, John Cassian says that the edifice of virtues can be neither built nor erected in our soul if we do not first savor in our heart the foundations of true humility,[51] which, once they are firmly set, can support the lofty construction of perfection and charity. And for this reason the wise man says, "The greater you become, the more humble you should become; then the Lord will be pleased with you." [Ecclesiasticus/Sirach 3:18: *Quanto maior es, humilia te ipsum in omnibus et coram Deo inveniens gratiam.*]

Text 58

Do not let your good sense be destroyed
By foolish delight, nor let anyone
Take away your belongings even if they ask.
Think of Medea.

Gloss 58

Medea was one of the most learned women in telling fortunes and she was the most knowledgeable woman of all, according to accounts about her. And nevertheless she let her good sense be destroyed by her willingness to fulfill her desire when she let herself be dominated by foolish love so much that she gave her heart to Jason, ceding to him her honor, body, and belongings. He later paid her back very badly for this. For this reason we say that the good knight should not let his reason be conquered by foolish delight for whatever cause if he wants to employ the virtue of strength. And Plato says, "A flighty man is soon bored by what he loves."

Allegory 58

That the good spirit should not let his good sense be destroyed by foolish delight can signify that he should never stop to exert control over his will, for if the dominion of self-will were to cease, there would be no hell, nor would the fires of hell have any dominion except over the person who lets his self-will dominate. For self-will struggles against God and turns proud; it is what despoils paradise,

---

51. St. John Cassian (ca. 360–435), also known as John the Ascetic and John Cassian the Roman, was a monk and theologian who spent many years in the Middle East before returning to France to establish a monastery near present-day Marseille.

fills up hell, voids the value of the blood of Jesus Christ, and subjects the world to the servitude of the enemy. On this topic the wise man says, "The rod and reproof give wisdom, but a child left to himself brings shame to his mother." [Proverbs 29:15: *Virga atque correccio tribuent sapienciam; puer autem qui dimititur proprie voluntati confundet matrem suam.*]

Text 59

If you are subject to the god Cupid
Beware of the enraged giant
So that the rock will not be thrown
On Acis and Galatea.

Gloss 59

Galatea was a nymph or goddess who loved a young man named Acis. An ugly giant was enamored of Galatea, who did not deign to love him. And he spied on them until he perceived both of them in the hollow of a rock. And overcome by a sudden rage he brought down the rock so that it crushed Acis completely. But Galatea, who was a nymph, threw herself into the sea and thus escaped. And this means that the good knight should beware of being surprised by someone powerful who wants to harm him.

Allegory 59

That the good spirit should beware of the giant in Cupid's thrall means that he should guard against paying too much attention to the world and worldly things and should always remember that all worldly things are of short duration. And Saint Jerome comments on Jeremiah, saying that there is nothing among things that come to an end that should be considered long-lasting, nor should our time by comparison with everlasting eternity. On this subject the wise man says, "All those things are passed away like a shadow, and like a post that runneth on." [Wisdom 5:9: *Transierunt omnia velut umbra et tanquam nuncius percurrens.*]

Text 60

Flee the goddess of discord,
Evil are her chains and her ropes.
She disturbed the wedding of Peleus,
Where later many people assembled.

Gloss 60

Discord is a goddess with evil preoccupations; a fable tells that when Peleus married the goddess Thetis, from whom later Achilles was born, Jupiter and all the gods and goddesses were at the wedding, but for the goddess of discord, who had not been invited. And for this reason she was envious and arrived unbidden; but she did not come in vain, for she did her job there. The three powerful goddesses Pallas, Juno, and Venus were seated at the dinner table; the goddess of discord arrived and threw on the table a golden apple on which was written, "May it be given to the most beautiful." Then the feast was disrupted, for each one of them maintained that she should have it, and they went before Jupiter so that he would resolve this conflict, but he did not want to please one to displease another. For this reason they put the question to Paris, who was a shepherd. Because his mother had dreamt when she was pregnant with him that he would be the cause of the destruction of Troy, he was sent into the woods to a shepherd whose son he believed himself to be. And now Mercury, who led the ladies to him, told him whose son he was. Then he left the sheep herding and went to Troy to claim his great lineage. Thus the fable testifies where the true story is hidden under a poetic cover.[52] And because often great troubles arose and still arise because of discord and conflicts, it is said to the good knight that he should beware of discord, for it is a very unpleasant habit to be contentious and cause riots.[53]

Allegory 60

Just as it is said that one should flee discord, the good spirit should flee all obstacles to his conscience and avoid fights and riots. Cassiodorus comments on the Psalter: "Most of all, he says, flee conflicts and riots, for to fight against peace is madness; to fight against one's sovereign is madness; to fight against one's subject is great villainy." On this subject Saint Paul says: "… not in quarreling and jealousy" [Romans 13:13: *non in contencione et emulacione*].

Text 61

Never forget a misdeed
That you committed against anyone,
For it will come back to haunt you;

---

52. See the Introduction for the vocabulary of *integumentum* or *involucrum*, that is, the veil or covering of allegory.

53. See Margaret J. Ehrhart, *The Judgment of the Trojan Prince Paris in Medieval Literature* (Philadelphia: University of Pennsylvania Press, 1987), for the great popularity of this story in medieval literature.

Laomedon was destroyed by it.[54]

Gloss 61

Laomedon, as I have said above, was king of Troy; and he acted disgracefully toward the Greek barons when he dismissed them from his country, a fact they never forgot. But Laomedon had forgotten it when the Greeks attacked him and surprised him unprepared; thus they destroyed and killed him. For this reason we say to the good knight that if he has committed any misdeed, he must be on his guard, for he can be certain that it will not be forgotten but avenged at an opportune time and place. On this subject Hermes says, "Make sure that your enemies do not surprise you unprepared."

Allegory 61

That someone should not forget a misdeed that he has done to someone else can be understood as meaning that when the good spirit feels it is sinning by lacking the strength to resist, it can be sure that it will be punished, just as it happens to the damned if they do not repent. And on this subject Saint Gregory says that at present God's justice moves slowly, but in the future it will mete out just deserts more harshly. God's mercy is therefore still a long way off.[55] The prophet Joel says in this context: "Turn to the Lord your God: for he is gracious and merciful, patient and rich in mercy, and ready to repent of the evil."[56] [Joel 2:13: *Convertimini ad Dominum Deum vestrum qui et benignus et misericors est, paciens et multe misericordie prestabilis super maliciam.*]

Text 62

Should it happen that you go crazy because of love,
At least watch out to whom you speak.
Remember Semele,
So that your deeds do not get you into trouble.

Gloss 62

The fable tells that Semele was a young woman whom Jupiter truly loved. Juno, who was jealous of this love, took on the shape of an old woman, came to Semele,

54. His story also appears in Chapters 37 and 66. See note 43 for the destruction of the first Troy.

55. According to Parussa, *Epistre d'Othea*, 429, this phrase is obscure and cannot be attributed to any of Saint Gregory's writings.

56. Cited from the Douay-Rheims version, which is more accurate here than the RSV.

and began to talk to her with sweet words. And she went on for so long that Semele revealed her love and that of her lover for her, and boasted how well she was loved and satisfied by him. Then Juno said to the young woman, who was not aware of the deception, that she did not yet know true love, but that when she was again with her lover she should ask him for a gift. Then, when he had promised her the gift, she should ask him that he should embrace her in the same manner in which he embraced Juno, his wife, when he wanted to make love with her, and in this manner she would be able to discern her lover's true love. Semele did not forget, and when she had made the request of Jupiter and he had promised her the gift which, as a god, he could not take back, he was most upset and knew that she had been deceived. So Jupiter took on the shape of fire and embraced his beloved, who quickly was all burnt and charred, and this event deeply weighed upon Jupiter. This fable can be interpreted in different ways, and can even have a significance for astronomy, as the masters say. But it can also mean that a young woman was somehow deceived by her lover's wife, and that because of this deception he then inadvertently caused her death. And for this reason we say to the good knight that he should be careful when he speaks of things that he wants to conceal, and watch out to whom he speaks and what he says, for circumstances may well permit for these things to be heard. For this reason Hermes says, "Do not reveal the secrets of your thoughts to anyone whom you have not well tested."

Allegory 62

That he should watch out to whom he speaks can mean that the good spirit, whatever his thoughts may be, should be careful in all cases where he could arouse someone's suspicion. As says Saint Augustine in the *Book of Sheep*, that we must not only take care to have a clear conscience, but also, as much as our infirmity, as much as the diligence of human weakness permits, that we do nothing which might arouse the evil suspicion of our frail brothers. In this context Saint Paul says, "Show yourself in all respects a model of good works." [Titus 2:7: *In omnibus prebe te exemplum bonorum operum.*]

Text 63

Do not spend too much time with the pastime
Of Diana, for it is not suitable for those
Who aspire to chivalry
To amuse themselves with hunting.

Gloss 63

Diana is called the goddess of the woods and hunting. So Othea says that the good knight who aspires to the high honor of arms should not amuse himself too much with the pastime of hunting, for this is something people with too much leisure do. And Aristotle says that idleness leads to all kinds of trouble.

Allegory 63

The good spirit can also take note of the exhortation not to follow the pastime of Diana, which stands for idleness. And Saint Jerome says that one should avoid idleness: "Always do some good deeds so that the devil will always find you occupied with some good practices." On this topic one says of the wise woman, "She looks well to the ways of her household, and does not eat the bread of idleness." [Proverbs 31:27: *Consideravit semittas domus sue et panem occiosa non commedit.*]

Text 64

Do not boast, for something bad happened
To Arachne who so erred that she
Boasted in front of Pallas.
As a result the goddess worked magic on her.

Gloss 64

Arachne, so tells a fable, was a young woman much skilled in the art of weaving and spinning, but she was too conceited about her skill and in fact boasted about herself in front of Pallas, who became so angry with her that she turned her into a spider and said to her, "Because you so boasted about your spinning and weaving, you will now forever spin and weave fabrics of no value." And this is the origin of spiders who to this day never stop spinning and weaving. This could mean that a woman boasted in front of her mistress and that something bad happened to her because of it. For this reason Othea tells the knight that he should not boast about himself, for it is unseemly for a knight to be boastful, and he could besmirch his reputation for goodness. And in this vein Plato says, "If you do something better than someone else be careful not to boast about it, for this would diminish your reputation."

Allegory 64

That he should not boast of himself we can take to mean that the good spirit should guard against bragging, for Saint Augustine, speaking against boastfulness in Book Twelve of the *City of God*, says that bragging is not a vice of human praise, but a vice of the perverse soul which loves human praise and scorns the true witness of his own conscience. On this subject the wise man says, "What has pride profited us? Or what advantage has the boasting of riches brought us?" [Wisdom 5:8: *Quid profuit nobis superbia? Aut diviarum jactancia quid contulit nobis?*]

Text 65

If you are pursued by a great desire
To overdo your love of hunting,
At least remember Adonis
Who was killed by a wild boar.

Gloss 65

Adonis was a very brave young man of great beauty. Venus truly loved him, but because he took too much pleasure in hunting, Venus, who was afraid that harm might come to him through some misadventure, begged him many times not to hunt wild animals. But Adonis did not comply and was killed by a wild boar. For this reason Othea tells the good knight that if he insists on hunting he should at least avoid a hunt where he could get hurt. On this topic Sedechias, [57] the philosopher, says that a king should not let his son go hunting too often or indulge in idleness, but rather have him instructed in good conduct and make him avoid vanity.

Allegory 65

That he should remember Adonis can mean that if the good spirit is led astray in any way it should at least remember the great danger of obstinacy. For, as the devil has great power over sinners, Saint Peter says in his second epistle (2:19), sinners are the serfs of corruption and the devil has power over them. For a man who is vanquished by another in a battle has become that man's serf. And as a sign of this it is said in the Apocalypse: "Authority was given to the beast over every tribe and people." [Revelation 13:7: *Data est bestie potestas in omnem tribum et populum.*]

57. Christine's source for Sedechias is Guillaume de Tignonville's *Dits moraux des philosophes*; he nevertheless remains unidentified.

Text 66

If it happens that your enemies attack you,
Be careful that you and your army do not rush out
Against them and leave the city empty:
Remember the example of the first Troy.[58]

Gloss 66

When Hercules attacked the first Troy with a multitude of Greeks and King
Laomedon heard of their coming, he and all the people he could gather rushed
out of the city and attacked them on the riverbank. There they met in fierce battle
and the city was left empty of people. Then Ajax Telamonius, who was hiding
with a great army near the city walls, penetrated the city and in this way the first
Troy was captured. For this reason Othea says to the good knight that he should
beware of being deceived by his enemies with such tricks. And Hermes says, "Be-
ware of your enemies' ambushes."

Allegory 66

That he should be careful not to empty out his city when his enemies attack means
that the good spirit should always be in possession of and filled with virtues.
And Saint Augustine says on this subject that just as in times of war men at arms
should not let go of their weapons and never take them off, neither during the day
nor during the night, so the good spirit should not be stripped of its virtues in the
present life. For he whom the devil finds without virtues is like the man whom
the enemy found without weapons. And for this reason the Evangelist says: "Fully
armed, he guards his own palace." [Luke 11:21: *Fortis armatus custodit atrium
suum.*]

Text 67

Do not be too besotted by Orpheus's lyre.
If you choose to make arms
Your principal business
You have no business yearning for instruments.

58. See note 43 to Gloss 37.

Gloss 67

Orpheus was a poet, and the fable says that he played the lyre so well that even rivers reversed course, and birds, wild animals, and fierce serpents forgot their cruelty and stopped in order to listen to the sounds of his lyre. This means that he played so well that everyone, no matter what background they came from, took delight in hearing the poet play. And because such instruments often infatuate the hearts of men, we say to the good knight that he should not take too much delight, for it is not suitable for the sons of knights to amuse themselves with instruments and other idle pastimes. On this subject one authority says, "The sound of an instrument is the serpent's snare." And Plato says, "The man who gets his pleasure from carnal delights is even more servile than an actual slave."

Allegory 67

The lyre of Orpheus with which one should not be infatuated signifies that the chivalrous spirit should not stupidly amuse itself in worldly company, whether they be his relatives or other people. Saint Augustine says in his book *The Singularity of Clerics*[59] that the solitary man who avoids the company of pleasure-seekers is less excited by the pinpricks of the flesh, and that he who does not see the world's wealthy feels less the torments of greed. And on this subject David says: "I lie awake; I am like a lonely bird on a housetop." [Psalm 101:8 (102:7): *Vigilavi et factus sum sicut passer solitarius in tecto.*]

Text 68

Do not base a great enterprise,
Whether right or wrong,
On a dream vision or a foolish illusion.
Remember Paris.

Gloss 68

Because Paris had dreamed that in Greece he would abduct Helen, a great army was sent from Troy to Greece, where Paris kidnapped Helen. In order to avenge this injustice, all the Greek powers attacked Troy. Greece was then such a large country that it reached all the way to Apulia and Calabria in Italy; then it was called *Parva* Graecia, Little Greece,[60] and from there came Achilles and the

---

59. See note 16

60. "Little" because at the time of the Trojans Greece did not include Apulia and Calabria, as does "Great Greece."

Myrmidons, who were such valiant fighters. This great mass of people vanquished Troy and the surrounding country. For this reason Othea says to the good knight that he should not undertake any important action because of a dream vision, for great harm and danger can be the result. And Plato says that a great action should not be undertaken without lengthy deliberations and counsel: "Do not do anything that you have not examined in depth beforehand."

Allegory 68

That a great enterprise should not be undertaken because of a dream vision means that the good spirit should not be presumptuous and rise up in arrogance, however much grace it may have been granted by God. And Saint Gregory says in his *Morals* that there are four things in which all the conceit of the arrogant is demonstrated: the first is when they claim that what they have achieved they did all by themselves; the second when they believe that they deserve all the good things they have and that they have received them because of their merit; the third is when they boast of goods they do not actually possess; and the fourth when they despise others and want people to recognize the good things that reside in them. Against this vice the wise man of the Proverbs says: "Pride and arrogance … and perverted speech I hate." [Proverbs 8:13: *Arroganciam et superbiam … et os bilingue detestor.*]

Text 69

If you like dogs and birds,
Remember Actaeon, the polite young man,
Who became a stag. And take care
That the same does not happen to you.

Gloss 69

Actaeon was a very courtly young man and of a very gentle disposition who loved dogs and birds too much.[61] And the fable recounts that one day, as he was hunting all alone in a dense forest, his men lost track of him. Then the goddess of the forest, Diana, who had been hunting in the woods until noon, was so hot because of the sun's heat that she had the idea of taking a bath in a clear and beautiful fountain that was located there. And when she was completely naked in the fountain, surrounded by the nymphs and the goddesses that served her,

---

61. On this story see Jacqueline Cerquiglini-Toulet, "Sexualité et politique: Le mythe d'Actéon chez Christine de Pizan," in *Une femme de lettres au Moyen Age: Etudes autour de Christine de Pizan*, ed. Liliane Dulac and Bernard Ribémont (Orléans: Paradigme, 1995), 83–90.

Actaeon, completely heedless, burst in upon her and saw her totally naked; she, because of her great chastity, blushed deeply and was very upset. So she said to him, "Because I know that young men have the habit of boasting about women and young girls, and so that you will not be able to boast that you have seen me naked, I will take away your ability to speak." Then she cursed him and he turned into a wild stag, and from his human form he retained only his intelligence. Filled with great pain and sudden fear he fled into the woods. And soon he was spotted by his own dogs and cornered by his own men who were looking for him in the woods, but now that they had found him they did not recognize him. At that spot Actaeon, weeping copiously, was brought down, and he would have cried for mercy had he been able to speak. And from this moment on stags were able to weep. At that place Actaeon was killed and painfully slaughtered by his own men and dogs that within a very short span of time devoured him completely. This fable can be interpreted in a variety of ways, but for our present purposes let us say that Actaeon stands for a young man who gave himself over to idleness and spent all his fortune and property on bodily delights, on the pleasure of hunting, and devoting his household to idle pursuits. And with this we can say that he was hated by Diana, who signifies chastity, and devoured by his own household. For this reason Othea says to the good knight that he should guard against being destroyed in the same manner. A wise man says, "Idleness engenders ignorance and error."

Allegory 69

We can take Actaeon, who became a stag, as the true penitent who used to be a sinner; he has vanquished his own flesh and subjugated it to the spirit and adopted a state of penitence. And Saint Augustine interprets the Psalms by saying that penitence is quite an easy load and a light burden and it should not even be called the load of a man weighted down but rather the wings of birds in flight, for just as the birds carry on earth the burden of their wings and their wings carry them to heaven, so too we carry on earth the burden of penitence and it will carry us to heaven. On that topic the Gospel says, "Repent, for the kingdom of heaven is at hand." [Matthew 3:2: *Penetenciam agite, appropinquabit enim regnum celorum.*]

Text 70

Do not go to the iron gates
In order to seek Eurydice in hell.
Orpheus gained little there with his lyre,
As I have heard said.

Gloss 70

Orpheus, the poet who played the harp so well, so says a fable, was about to marry the beautiful Eurydice. But on their wedding day she entertained herself by walking in a meadow, barefoot because of the sun's great heat. A shepherd lusted after the beautiful woman and in order to rape her ran after her and she, who was fleeing in fear of him, was bitten by a snake hidden in the grass. A short while later she died from the bite. Orpheus was deeply grieved by this terrible accident; he took his lyre and went to the gates of iron, in the dark valley before the infernal palace, and he began to play a sorrowful song. And he sang so sweetly that all the torments in hell stood still and all the infernal occupations ceased so that the sound of his lyre could be heard, and even Proserpine, the goddess of hell, was moved by great pity. Then Pluto, Lucifer, Cerberus, and Charon, who noticed that their minions had stopped inflicting hell's pains because of the harp player, gave him back his wife on the condition that he go in front and she behind until they exited the infernal valley, and that he not turn around, for if he were to turn around he would lose her. Through this agreement Eurydice was returned to him, and so Orpheus walked in front and his beloved behind him. But he who loved her too much could not resist turning around because he had such a strong desire to see his beloved; and immediately Eurydice was separated from him and returned to hell, and he could not get her back. This fable can be understood in several ways. It could mean a man whose wife was taken from him, and then given back, and then lost again; or it could be a castle or some other possession, but for our purposes we can say that a person who seeks Eurydice in hell seeks the impossible, and one should not turn melancholic over trying to recover the impossible. And even Solomon says, "It is the height of folly to try and seek that which is impossible to have."

Allegory 70

That he should not seek Eurydice in hell can be understood to mean that the good spirit should not aspire to nor request from God something miraculous or marvelous, for that is called tempting God. And Saint Augustine comments on the Gospel of John, saying that the request a creature makes to God is not fulfilled when he asks for something that cannot or should not be done, or something that would be misused or would hurt his soul if it were given. On this topic Saint James the apostle says in his letter, "You ask and you do not receive, because you ask wrongly." [James 4:3: *Petitis et non accipitis quod male petatis.*]

Text 71

If you want to recognize true knights
Even if they are enclosed in a convent for nuns,
The test that Achilles was subjected to
Will teach you to recognize them.

Gloss 71

Achilles, so tells a fable, was the son of the goddess Thetis, and because she knew that if her son were to go to war he would die, she, who loved him deeply, hid him under women's garments and had him veiled as a nun in the abbey of the goddess Vesta. Achilles was hidden for a long time until he had grown up. And the fable says that he fathered Pyrrhus with the daughter of king Hystrus. Then the great Trojan Wars began and the Greeks learned through their oracles that they needed Achilles with them. He was sought everywhere but his whereabouts were unknown. Ulysses, who was very clever, and looked for him everywhere, came to the temple, but since he could not ferret out the truth he came up with a clever ruse and trick. Ulysses took rings, wimples, belts, and all kinds of women's jewels together with beautiful chivalric weapons and threw everything down in front of the ladies and said that each of them should take what pleased them the most. And then, as every object is drawn to its own nature, the ladies ran toward the jewels, while Achilles seized the arms. And then Ulysses went up to him and told him that he was the one he was looking for. And because knights should be drawn more toward arms than pretty baubles that are fitting for ladies, the authority says that by this one can recognize the true knight. On this topic Leginon[62] says, "The knight is recognized only by his arms." And Hermes says, "Test men before you firmly believe in them."

Allegory 71

Where it is said, "If you want to recognize a true knight," we can take this to mean that the knight Jesus Christ should be recognized in the arms of good deeds; and Saint Jerome says in a letter that this knight should have the recompense that is due good people, and that just as God's justice does not leave any bad deed unpunished it does not leave any good deed unrewarded. So to good people no labor should seem hard and no time span should seem long, when they await

---

62. This could be John of Legnano (1320–1386), a jurist and canon lawyer from Bologna, whose other important works included treatises on warfare and on the virtues and vices. Christine uses John of Legnano as one of her sources in her later *Livre des fais d'armes et de chevalerie*. Parussa thinks this could be a reference to an author of fables named Lokman.

everlasting glory as their reward. For this reason Holy Scripture says, "Take courage and let not your hands be weakened, for there shall be a reward for your work." [2 Paralipomenon (Chronicles) 15:7: *Confortamini et non dissolvantur manus vestre, erit enim merces operi vestro.*]

Text 72

Do not compete with Atalanta,
For she has a greater talent for
Running than you. It is her job.
You have no need of such races.

Gloss 72

Atalanta was a nymph of great beauty, but her destiny was strange since several people lost their lives because of her. This young woman, for her great beauty, was desired in marriage by many men, but an edict was issued that no one would have her unless he defeated her in a race, but if she won then the man would have to die. Atalanta was incredibly fast and no one could equal her in a race, and thus several men died. This race can be interpreted in many ways: it could mean that something much coveted by several people cannot be attained without great effort. The race that she ran is the defense or resistance against this thing; or the fable could mean that people make a great effort unnecessarily. The authority wants to say that a strong and courageous man should neither pay attention to nor strive for useless things that do not regard his honor or should not interest him. For great harm has often resulted from such efforts. And Basil of Caesarea says, "You should do what is most profitable for your body and most fitting for your soul and avoid the opposite."

Allegory 72

We can take "Do not compete with Atalanta" to mean that the good spirit should not be too preoccupied with things going on in the world or worry too much over the place in life in which it may find itself. And Saint Augustine says in a letter that the world is more perilous when it treats people softly than when it is harsh; but the more one sees it as disturbing, the less one should preoccupy oneself with it, especially when it draws one to love it rather than when it gives occasion to be despised. On this topic Saint John the Evangelist says in his first letter, "If any one loves the world, the love for the Father is not in him." [1 John 2:15: *Si quis diligit mundum non est caritas Patris in eo.*]

Text 73

Do not judge like Paris.[63]
For one receives quite a paltry meal
By handing out bad judgments,
And many have had a bad return for this.

Gloss 73

The fable says that three powerful goddesses, that is, Pallas, the goddess of wisdom; Juno, the goddess of riches; and Venus, the goddess of love, came before Paris holding a golden apple on which was written: "May this be given to the most beautiful and most powerful woman." A great dispute erupted from this apple, for every one of them said that she should have it. And because they came before Paris because of this dispute, Paris diligently wanted to find out for himself what each one's strength and power was. Then Pallas said, "I am the goddess of chivalry and wisdom, and through me arms are given to the knights and wisdom to the scholars, and if you deign to give the apple to me you should know that I will make you more chivalrous than anyone else and that you will surpass everyone in all sciences." Juno, the goddess of riches and dominion, spoke after her: "Through me are granted great treasures to the world, and if you give me the apple I will make you richer and more powerful than anyone else." Then Venus spoke a great deal about love and said, "I am the one who teaches about love and gaiety and who makes foolish people wise and wise people foolish, who turns the rich into beggars and the exiles into the rich; there is no power that can be compared to mine, and if you deign to give me the apple I will grant you the love of the beautiful Helen of Greece, a love which is worth more than any wealth." Then Paris delivered his judgment and renounced chivalry, wisdom, and riches for the sake of Venus, to whom he gave the apple; and for this reason Troy was later destroyed. This means that because Paris was not chivalrous and did not really care much about riches but turned all his thoughts toward love, he gave the apple to Venus. And for this reason Othea advises the good knight not to act in the same way. And Pythagoras says, "The judge who does not judge justly deserves all evil."

Allegory 73

Paris, who judged foolishly, stands for the good spirit who must guard against judging someone else. Saint Augustine speaks to this topic in his treatise against the Manicheans when he says that we should avoid especially two things: judging other people, first, since we do not know in what spirit these things were done

---

63. For another version of this story see Chapter 60.

and therefore condemning them is extremely presumptuous; we should rather interpret them in the best possible way. Second, because we do not know who at present is good or bad. On this point our Lord says in the Gospel: "Judge not, that you be not judged. For with the judgment you pronounce you will be judged." [Matthew 7:1-2: *Nolite iudicare et non iudicabimini; in quo enim iudicio iudicaveritis iudicabimini.*]

Text 74

Do not trust in Fortune, the great goddess,
nor in her promises.
For she changes in a very short time,
And often throws the most exalted in the mud.

Gloss 74

Fortune, according to the way of speaking of the poets, can rightly be called a great goddess, for we can see how she rules over the course of worldly things. And because she promises many people great prosperity and sometimes even gives it to some, and then takes it back quickly when it pleases her, we say to the good knight that he should not trust her promises or be discouraged when things go wrong. And Socrates says, "The machinations of Fortune are ruses."

Allegory 74

By saying that the good spirit should not trust Fortune, we mean that it must flee and scorn the delights of the world. Boethius says in the third book of his *Consolation* that the happiness of the Epicureans must be called unhappiness, for it is the true, full, and perfect happiness that makes man self-sufficient, powerful, revered, famous, and joyous, but these conditions, in which worldly people place their happiness, do not offer these things.[64] For this reason God speaks through the prophet and says, "My people, those that call thee blessed, the same deceive thee."[65] [Isaiah 3:12: *Popule meus, qui te beatum dicunt, ipsi te decipiunt.*]

64. Boethius, *Consolation of Philosophy,* book 3, prose 9. Among many available translations, see that of Victor Watts, rev. ed. (London: Penguin, 1999).The late antique philosopher Boethius wrote his *Consolation of Philosophy* in prison before his execution in 524. This was an extremely popular text in the Middle Ages, featuring both prose and verse passages.

65. This phrase of the Vulgate is not translated in the RSV; the translation is taken from Douay-Rheims.

Text 75

To undertake and succeed in war
Do not put Paris in charge,
For I do not doubt that he would know much better
How to take his pleasure in his lover's fair arms.

Gloss 75

Paris had absolutely no aptitude for war, but only for love. And for this reason
Othea advises the good knight not to appoint as chief of his army or his battles
a knight who has no aptitude for warfare. And this is why Aristotle said to Al-
exander, "You should appoint as commander of your troops the man whom you
consider wise and experienced in warfare."

Allegory 75

That you should not put Paris in charge of starting a war means that the good
spirit, aspiring only to celestial chivalry, should remove himself from all worldly
things and elect the contemplative life. And Saint Gregory says in his commen-
tary on Ezekiel that the contemplative life is rightly to be preferred over the active
life as the most worthy and the greatest; for the active life is preoccupied with the
troubles of the present life, but the contemplative life already begins to taste the
savor of future rest. And for this reason the Gospel says of Mary Magdalene, who
signifies contemplation: "Mary has chosen the good portion, which shall not ever
be taken away from her." [Luke 10:42: *Optimam partem elegit sibi Maria que non
aufferetur ab ea in eternum.*][66]

Text 76

Take no interest in spying on anyone
But stick to your own path.
Cephalus with his javelin
And Lot's wife teach you this lesson.

---

66. On interpretations of the Judgment of Paris as a choice between three lives see Ehrhart, *The Judg-
ment of Paris.* On Mary and Martha, see Giles Constable, "The Interpretation of Mary and Martha,"
in *Three Studies in Medieval Religious and Social Thought* (Cambridge: Cambridge University Press,
1995), 1–141.

Gloss 76

Cephalus was a knight in antiquity, and a fable says that all his life he took plea-
sure and delight in the pastime of hunting, and he had a marvelous talent for
throwing his javelin, which had the characteristic that it was never thrown in
vain, for it killed everything it hit. And because he had the habit of getting up
early to go to the forest in order to lie in wait for wild game, his wife, fearing that
he loved another woman, became very jealous. And in order to discover the truth
she spied on him. And Cephalus, who was in the woods, upon hearing the leaves
crackle from his wife's hiding place, thought that it was a wild animal. Immediate-
ly he threw his javelin, hit his wife, and killed her. Cephalus was deeply sorrowful
about this mishap but there was no remedy for it. Lot's wife, as Holy Scripture tells
us, hearing the five cities falling into ruins behind her, turned around against the
orders of the angel; and for this reason she was transformed into a pillar of salt.
And because all these things have a figural meaning, one can understand them in
many different ways. On the level of truth we offer this example: no knight should
take pleasure in spying on things that do not concern him. And because no one
wants to be spied upon, Hermes says, "Do not do to your companion what you do
not want him to do to you, and do not lay snares to catch men and do not cause
them harm through traps or tricks, for in the end this will turn against you."

Allegory 76

That spying on anyone should not interest the good spirit can mean that it should
not try to discover things about other people's deeds or inquire about other peo-
ple's news. And Saint John Chrysostom says about the gospel of Saint Matthew,
"How do you see so many small defects in the deeds of others, and in your own
you tolerate such big defects? If you love yourself more than your neighbor why
are you so preoccupied with his deeds and pay no attention to your own? Above
all, be diligent in thinking about your own deeds and only then about someone
else's." On this topic our Lord says in the Gospels, "Why do you notice the speck
that is in your brother's eye, but do not notice the log that is in your own eye?"
[Matthew 7:3: *Quid autem vides festucam in oculo fratris tui, trabem autem in
oculo tuo non vides?*]

Text 77

Do not despise the counsel of Helenus,
I advise you,
For often great harm is done
By not wanting to believe wise men.

Gloss 77

Helenus was Hector's brother and the son of Priam, King of Troy; he was a wise and learned man and advised as much as he could against Paris going to Greece to abduct Helen, but no one believed him, and great harm ensued for the Trojans. For this reason Othea tells the good knight that he should believe wise men and their counsel. And Hermes says, "Whoever honors wise men and uses their counsel will last forever."

Allegory 77

Helenus, who advised against war, means that the good spirit should avoid temptations. And Saint Jerome says that the sinner has absolutely no excuse if he lets himself be overcome by temptation, for the enemy tempter is so weak that he can only overcome those who wish to give themselves to him. And about this topic the Apostle Paul says, "God is faithful and will not let you be tested beyond your strength, but with the temptation will also provide the way of escape, that you may be able to endure it." [1 Corinthians 10:13: *Fidelis Deus qui non pacietur vos temptari supra id quod potestis, sed faciet etiam cum temptacione proventum ut possitis sustinere.*]

Text 78

Neither rejoice too much nor let yourself be troubled
By obscure dream visions
Of Morpheus, who is the messenger
Of the god who sleeps and makes us dream.

Gloss 78

Morpheus, so says a fable, is the son and the messenger of the god of sleep, and he is the god of dreams and makes people dream. And because a dream is a very dark and obscure thing and often signifies nothing or the contrary of what one has dreamt, no one is wise enough to speak of it correctly, despite whatever the dream interpreters may say. This is why Othea says to the good knight that he should neither rejoice nor be troubled too much by these dream visions, which one cannot interpret with certainty, nor can one tell what they predict. And likewise one should not be overjoyed or troubled by the things Fortune brings, which are transitory; as Socrates states, "You as a man should neither be overjoyed nor troubled by any event."

Allegory 78

When we say that one should neither be overjoyed nor troubled by dream visions we mean that the good spirit should be neither too overjoyed nor too troubled by anything that might happen; and that he should bear his tribulations patiently Augustine says with reference to the Psalms, "My good son, if you weep over the harm that you feel, you weep under your father's correction. If you weep over the tribulations that happen to you, be careful not to weep out of indignation or pride, for the adversities that God sends you are medicine and not pain, they are punishment, not damnation. Do not reject your father's rod if you do not want him to expel you from his realm, and do not think of the pain you have to suffer from his flail, but consider what place you have in his testament." On this topic the wise man says, "Let be what shall be brought upon thee, and in thy sorrow endure, and in thy humiliation keep patience." [Ecclesiasticus/Sirach 2:4: *Esse quod tibi applicatum fuerit accipe et in dolorem sustine et in humilitate pacienciam habe.*]

Text 79

If you want to embark on a
Dangerous sea voyage
Take Alcyone's advice,
She will tell you about Ceyx's misfortune.

Gloss 79

Ceyx was a very valiant king and much beloved by his wife Alcyone. He had the desire to make a very dangerous sea voyage. He set out to sea during a storm but Alcyone, his wife, who loved him passionately, went to great pains to dissuade him from this voyage and begged him with weeping and tears, but she did not succeed. He did not want to let her accompany him, which she wanted to do at all costs, so she threw herself onto the departing ship. However, king Ceyx comforted her and forced her to stay behind, which left her most anxious and distressed, for she was extremely worried when she saw Aeolus, the wind god, moving over the sea. Ceyx, the king, perished at sea within a few brief days, and when Alcyone learned of this misfortune she threw herself into the sea.[67] And the fable says that the gods took pity on them and transformed the bodies of the two lovers into two birds, so that their great love would be remembered forever. And so the birds still fly above the sea; they are called halcyons and have white

---

67. Christine reuses this myth in her own fictionalized life story in Part 1 of the *Mutacion de Fortune.* For an interpretation of this very moving passage, see Blumenfeld-Kosinski, *Reading Myth,* 184–87.

plumage. When sailors see them they are certain that there will be a storm. The correct interpretation of this fable may be that two lovers loved each other in marriage in such a way that the poet compared them to two birds, and such was their fate and their fortune. And Othea means that the good knight should not undertake a perilous voyage against the advice of his friends. And Assaron says, "The wise man makes an effort to stay away from harm, the fool strives to find it."

Allegory 79

That one should believe Alcyone means that if the good spirit is hindered through some evil temptation by some error or doubt in his thoughts it should refer to the opinion of the Church. And Saint Ambrose says in the second book of his *Offices* that the man who despises the counsel of the Church is out of his senses; for Joseph helped the Pharaoh much more profitably through his prudent counsel than if he had given him gold or silver, for money could not have taken care of the famine in Egypt as did Joseph's advice, which provided a remedy for the famine in Egypt for seven years. And he concluded, "Believe the advice and you will not regret it." On this topic the wise man says in the Proverbs, speaking in the person of the Church, "Keep my law and counsel and they will be life for your soul." [Proverbs 3:21–22: *Custodi legem meam atque consilium et erit vita anime tue.*]

Text 80

Do not trust in the counsel of a child
And remember Troilus.
Believe older and wise men
And only put in charge of arms skilled men.

Gloss 80

When King Priam had Troy rebuilt, which because of the expulsion of those who had gone to Colchis had been destroyed,[68] he wanted to take revenge. So he assembled his council, which consisted of many great barons and wise men, and inquired whether it was a good idea that his son, Paris, should go to Greece and abduct Helen in retaliation for Hesione, his sister who had been taken by Ajax Telamonius and enslaved. However, all the sages agreed that he should not do it because of all the prophecies and writings that said that Troy would be destroyed through this abduction. Then Troilus, who was a child and the youngest of Priam's sons, said that, when it came to advice about war, one should not believe these old men and the priests who advised doing nothing because of their love of leisure.

68. See note to Gloss 61.

So it was decided that they should go ahead. The advice of Troilus was heeded, and great harm resulted from it. For this reason Othea says to the good knight that he should not heed or believe a child's advice that is by nature superficial and of slight intelligence. On this topic an authority says, "The land is cursed whose ruler is a child."[69]

Allegory 80

That he should not agree to the advice of a child means that the good spirit should not be ignorant, but rather wise and knowledgeable about what can be profitable for its salvation. And against the ignorant, Saint Augustine says, "Ignorance is a very evil mother with very evil daughters, that is, falsity and doubt: the first is evil, the second causes misery; the first is vicious but the second is more harmful. And both of them are extinguished by wisdom." On this topic says the wise man, "For regarding not wisdom, they did not only slip in this, that they were ignorant of good things, but left also unto men a memorial of their folly." [Wisdom 10:8: *Sapienciam pretereuntes non tamen in hoc lapsi sunt ut ignorent bona, sed insipiencie sue relinquerunt hominibus memoriam.*]

Text 81

Hate Calchas and his accomplices
Whose infinite malice
Betrays kingdoms and empires;
There are no worse people in the world.

Gloss 81

Calchas was a subtle learned man in the city of Troy, and when King Priam realized that the Greeks were approaching him a with a great army he sent Calchas to Delphi in order to learn from the god Apollo how he would fare in the war. But after the god's answer, that said that after ten years the Greeks would be victorious, Calchas went over to the Greeks and met Achilles, who had come to Delphi for the same reason. Together with him, Calchas went to the Greeks, whom he helped with his counsel against his own city, and many a time did he prevent peace being made between the Greeks and the Trojans. And because he was a traitor Othea says to the good knight that he should hate such subtle and evil people, for their treacheries, strategically designed, can wreak havoc on kingdoms, empires, and all people. For this reason Plato says, "The subtle enemy who is poor and powerless can be more harmful than a rich and powerful but clueless enemy."

69. Ecclesiastes 10:16.

Allegory 81

That Calchas should be hated can mean that the good spirit should hate all fraudulent malice against its fellows and should never consent to it. And Saint Jerome says that the traitor does not become more malleable through good company, nor through the intimacy of eating and drinking together, nor through being served graciously, nor through an abundance of benefits. Of this vice the Apostle Paul says, "Men will be lovers of money, arrogant, proud, … treacherous, inclined to evil, conceited" [2 Timothy 3: 2, 4: *Erunt homines cupidi, elati, superbi, … proditores, protervi, timidi*].

Text 82

Do not be cold-hearted in granting
What you can put to good use.
Reflect on Hermaphroditus
Who suffered harm for his refusal.

Gloss 82

Hermaphroditus was a young man of great beauty. A nymph was smitten with him, but he did not deign to love her even though she pursued him everywhere. And once it happened that the young man was very tired from a strenuous day-long hunt; he arrived at the fountain of Salmacis, where there was a beautiful pond, clear and pure. Then he suddenly felt inclined to bathe, took off his clothes, and dove into the water. When the nymph saw him all naked, she stripped, jumped in after him, and began to embrace the young man with great love, but he, full of malice, rudely pushed her away, and she could not soften his heart with her entreaties. Then the nymph, filled with sorrow, prayed to the gods with fervent intent that she should never be separated from this man she loved, but who had pushed her away. The gods mercifully granted her devout prayer and immediately transformed the two bodies into one body with both genders. This fable can be understood in a variety of ways, and just as the great learned philosophers hid their great secrets under the cover of fables, we can interpret this story as relating to the science of astronomy or alchemy, as the masters say. And because the subject of love is so much more pleasant to listen to than any other, they usually constructed their fictions around love, so that they would be more delightful even for the unlearned who eat nothing but a fruit's peel, and even more delicious for the learned who suck out the fruit's juice.[70] But for our present purposes we can interpret it by saying that it is an ugly and villainous thing to refuse or to grant

70. See the Introduction (11) for this interpretive metaphor.

only with great reluctance something that cannot turn out to be harmful or vicious if granted.

Allegory 82

The good spirit must not be cold-hearted in granting something where it sees need, but comfort the needy as much as possible. Saint Gregory says in his *Morals* that if we want to comfort someone afflicted in his sadness, we must mourn with him, for no one can truly comfort a sufferer without trying to feel his pain. Just as one cannot join two pieces of iron if both are not heated and softened in the fire, we cannot raise someone up if our heart is not softened by compassion. On this topic Holy Scripture says, "Strengthen the weak hands and make firm the feeble knees." [Isaiah 35:3: *Confortate manus dissolutas et genua debilia roborate.*]

Text 83

You may well amuse yourself
With Ulysses's games every now and then
For they are subtle and honorable
In times of truce and celebrations.

Gloss 83

Ulysses was a Greek baron of great cleverness. And during the time of the long siege before Troy which lasted ten years, when there was a truce, Ulysses invented subtle and beautiful games to entertain the knights while they were resting. And some say that he invented the game of chess and other similar games. For this reason Othea tells the good knight that in appropriate moments he can well entertain himself with such games. And Solinus says, "Anything subtle and honest is an honorable thing to do."

Allegory 83

Ulysses's games can be understood to mean that when the good spirit is weary of praying and devoting himself to contemplation, he can entertain himself by reading the Holy Scriptures. For as Saint Jerome says in his *Morals,* "Holy Scripture is proposed to the eyes of our heart as a mirror so that we can see in it the entire face of our soul. There we can see our good face and our bad face; there we can see how much we have advanced and how far we still are from advancing further. On this topic our Lord says in the gospels, "You search the scriptures, because you think that in them you have eternal life." [John 5:39: *Scrutamini scripturas in quibus putatis vitam eternam habere.*]

Text 84

If you want to give your heart to Cupid
And abandon everything
Be careful not to be too close to Briseis,
For her heart is too flighty.

Gloss 84

Briseis was a young woman of great beauty; she was very pretty, inconstant, and attractive. Troilus, the youngest of Priam's sons, who was filled with prowess, beauty, and gentleness, loved her passionately, and she had given him her love forever and promised never to be false to him. Calchas, the young woman's father, who had the foreknowledge that Troy would be destroyed, succeeded in getting his daughter back, taking her out of the city and back to the besieging Greeks where he was. The sorrow of the two lovers was great at this separation, and their complaints were very pitiful. Nonetheless, within a very short time, Diomedes, who was a great baron of the Greeks, became acquainted with Briseis, and pursued her so much that she fell in love with him and forgot her loyal beloved Troilus. And because Briseis has such a flighty heart we say to the good knight that if he wants to abandon his heart to love he should be careful not to become acquainted with a lady who resembles Briseis. And Hermes says, "Avoid the company of evil people so that you will not become one of them."

Allegory 84

Briseis, with whom the good spirit should not become acquainted, is vainglory, which it should not approach but flee from as best it can, because it is a facile thing and it appears too quickly. And Saint Augustine says in *On the Psalms* that the person who has learned through experience how to overcome the different degrees of the vices has come to the realization that vainglory is the vice that above all has to be avoided by perfect human beings, for among all vices this is the one that is most difficult to vanquish. And on this topic says Saint Paul, the apostle, "Let him who boasts, boast of the Lord." [2 Corinthians 10:17: *Qui gloriatur in Domine glorietur.*]

Text 85

When you will have killed Patroclus
Beware of Achilles.
Believe me, they are like one person,
They hold their goods in common.

Gloss 85

Patroclus and Achilles were companions and such close friends that never two
brothers loved each other more, and what belonged to one belonged to the other.
And because Hector killed Patroclus in battle, Achilles began to greatly hate Hec-
tor and swore his death. But because he feared his great strength, he kept on
watching him in order to ambush him when he was not on his guard. Thus Othea
says to Hector, as a kind of prophecy of what is to come, that when he will have
killed Patroclus he should beware of Achilles. And this means that any man who
has killed or harmed the loyal companion of another man should know that that
man will take revenge on him. On this topic says Madarge,[71] "Wherever you may
be with your enemy, always be suspicious of him, even if you are stronger than
he."

Allegory 85

When it is said "when you will have killed Patroclus beware of Achilles," this
means that if the good spirit slides toward sin because of the devil, it must fear ev-
erlasting death. And as Job says, "The present life is nothing but military service,
and to signify this the present life is called warlike, by contrast to the next one
which is called triumphant, for it has already vanquished its enemies."[72] On this
topic Saint Paul the apostle says, "Put on the whole armor of God, that you may be
able to stand against the wiles of the devil." [Ephesians 6:11: *Induite vos armature
Dei ut possitis stare adversus insidias diaboli.*]

Text 86

Be careful not to reject Echo
And not to despise her pitiful complaints.
If you cannot resist her desire
You do not know what might happen to you.

---

71. In Guillaume de Tignonville's *Dits moraux des philosophes*, ed. Robert Eder, *Romanische Forschun-
gen* 33 (1915): 851–1022, this mysterious name is given as Macdarge.

72. See Job 7:1.

Gloss 86

Echo, so says a fable, was a nymph, and because she was in the habit of being a great gossip and one day betrayed Juno who was jealously spying on her husband, the goddess was furious and said, "From now on you will not speak first, only after someone else." Echo was in love with the beautiful Narcissus, but whatever entreaty or sign of friendship she offered him, he did not deign to have pity on her, until she finally died of love for him. But while dying she prayed to the gods that she might be avenged on him in whom she had found so much cruelty and that they should make him feel the sting of love, so that he would experience the great pain that courtly lovers feel when they are rejected, and from which she must now die. Thus Echo came to her end but her voice remains to this day; and the gods made her voice everlasting in order to commemorate this story, and it calls back to people in valleys and across rivers after someone else's voice, but it cannot speak first. Echo can signify a person who urgently entreats another. The voice that remained means that needy people have been left behind, and that they cannot speak without the help of someone else. For this reason we say to the good knight that he should have pity on the needy people who entreat him. And Zaqualquin[73] says, "Whoever wants to protect the law must help his friends with his goods and lend money to the needy; he should be gracious and not deny justice to his enemy and guard against all vices and dishonor."

Allegory 86

Echo, who should not be rejected, can stand for mercy that the good spirit should have within himself. And Saint Augustine says in his book on the Sermon of Our Lord on the Mount that blessed are those who gladly help the poor who are in misery, for they deserve that God's mercy deliver them from their misery. And it is just that whoever wants to be helped by a more powerful sovereign should aid the man inferior to him, for he is more powerful than that man. For this reason the wise man says in the Proverbs, "He that is inclined to mercy shall be blessed."[74] [Proverbs 22:9: *Qui pronus est ad misericordiam benedicetur.*]

Text 87

If you want to earn the laurel crown
Which is worth more than any other possession,

73. Zaqualquin (alternatively spelled Aqualquin) is named, but not further identified, as a philosopher by Guillaume de Tignonville. See *Les dits moraux*, 921.

74. This is again the Douay-Rheims version, more accurate here than the RSV.

You must pursue Daphne,
Whom you will catch if you follow her well.

Gloss 87

The fable says that Daphne was a young woman with whom Phoebus Apollo was in love and whom he pursued, but she would not yield. One day it happened that he saw the beauty walking on a path, and when she saw him coming she began to flee and the god ran after her. And when he was so close that she saw well that she could not escape, she prayed to the goddess Diana to protect her virginity. Then the girl's body was transformed into a green laurel tree, and when Phoebus was close to it he took the branches of this tree and made himself a wreath as a sign of his victory; and since then the laurel wreath signifies victory. And still in the time of Rome's great prosperity they crowned the victors with laurel. The fable can have several meanings: it can happen that a powerful man with great effort pursued a lady and that he attained his desire under a laurel tree, and that for this reason he loves the laurel tree and features it in his heraldry as a sign of the victory he achieved in his love life under the laurel tree. And the laurel tree can also stand for gold, which signifies nobility. And because the laurel tree signifies honor we say to the good knight that he should pursue Daphne if he wants to have the laurel crown. On this topic Homer says, "With great diligence one arrives at honor and perfection."

Allegory 87

That he should pursue Daphne in order to gain the laurel crown can mean that if the good spirit wants to have a glorious victory, it needs perseverance that will lead it to the victory of paradise, of which the joys are infinite. As says Saint Gregory, "What kind of tongue could suffice to tell about and what kind of understanding could comprehend how manifold are the joys of this sovereign city of paradise. To be always present among the orders of the angels with the blessed spirits, to witness the glory of the Creator, to behold the face of God, to see the indescribable light, to be assured not to have to fear death anymore, to enjoy the gift of eternal incorruptibility." On this topic David says in the Psalms, "Glorious things are spoken of you, city of God." [Psalm 86:3 (87:3): *Gloriosa dicta sunt de te, civitas Dei.*]

Text 88

I also mention Andromache to you:
You should not disregard the dream vision

Of your wife, nor those
Of other learned women.

Gloss 88

Andromache was Hector's wife, and the night before he was killed the lady saw
in a dream vision that if Hector went into battle on that day, he would be killed
without fail. So Andromache with great sighs and weeping did all she could to
stop him from going into battle, but Hector did not want to believe her and was
killed. And for this reason we say to the good knight that he should not disregard
the dream visions of his wife, that is, the counsel and advice of his wife, if she is
wise and of good conduct, and likewise that of other wise women. And Plato says,
"You should not disregard the advice of an unimportant wise person for, even if
you are old, you should not be ashamed to learn things, even if it is a child that
shows you things, for sometimes those without knowledge can advise the wise
man."

Allegory 88

That one should not disregard Andromache's dream vision means that the knight
of Jesus Christ should not throw away the good words sent by the Holy Spirit, but
use them as best he can. On this topic says Saint Gregory in his *Morals* that the
good spirit admonishes us, moves us, and teaches us to do good. It admonishes
our memory, it moves our willpower, and teaches our understanding. The sweet
and mild spirit does not tolerate that even a tiny piece of straw remains in the
dwelling of the heart where he finds inspiration, but rather burns it with his subtle
circumspection. For this reason the Apostle Paul says, "Do not quench the spirit."
[1 Thessalonians 5:19: *Spiritus nolite extinguere.*]

Text 89

If you confront a difficulty or danger
Do not trust in Babylon's strength,
For it was taken by Ninus: no one
Should have confidence in its strength.

Gloss 89

Great Babylon was founded by the giant Nimrod, and it was the strongest city
ever built, but nonetheless it was taken by king Ninus. For this reason we say to
the good knight that he should never trust in the strength of his city or his castle

in times of war unless he has at his disposal people and everything else that he needs for an effective defense. And Plato says, "The man who relies only on his force is often vanquished."

Allegory 89

That one should not trust Babylon's strength means that the good spirit should not trust in or expect anything that the world promises. And on this topic Saint Augustine states in his book *On the Singularity of Clerics* that it is too foolish a conviction to consider one's life safe in face of the perils of this life. And it is a foolish hope to believe to be safe among the bites of sin, for victory is still uncertain as long as one finds oneself in the midst of the enemies' darts, and whoever is surrounded by flames cannot easily escape without being burnt. "Believe the one who has experience, if the world is joyful toward you do not trust it, put all your hopes into God." On this topic David says, "It is better to take refuge in the Lord than to take confidence in man." [Psalm 117:8 (118:8): *Bonum est confidere in domino quam confidere in homine.*]

Text 90

Hector, I have to predict your death;
Because of it great pain gnaws at my heart.
This will happen when you will not believe
King Priam, who will come and entreat you.

Gloss 90

On the day that Hector was killed in battle, his wife Andromache came to king Priam to beg him with great plaints and weeping that he should not let Hector go into battle, for without fail he would be killed if he went; this had been announced to her by Mars, the god of battles, and Minerva, the goddess of arms, who had appeared to her in her sleep. Priam tried as hard as he could to keep Hector from fighting that day, but Hector stole away from his father, left the city by an underground passage, and went into the battle where he was killed. And because he had never disobeyed his father before, except on that day, one can say that the moment he disobeyed his father he died. And this can mean that in truth no one should disobey his sovereign or his good friends if they are wise. And for this reason Aristotle said to Alexander, "As long as you believe the advice of those who employ wisdom and who love you loyally you will reign gloriously."

Allegory 90

Where she said to Hector that she had to predict his death means that the good spirit should always hold in its memory the hour of its death. On this topic Saint Bernard says that among human things nothing is more certain than death or less certain than the hour of our death, for death shows no mercy to poverty, nor does it honor riches; it does not spare anyone because of wisdom, good morals, or age. Of death one has no other certainty except that it stands at the door of the old and lies in wait for the young. On this topic the wise man says, "Remember that death will not be slow." [Ecclesiasticus/Sirach 14:12: *Memor esto quoniam mors non tardabit*.]

Text 91

Again I want to make you wise
So that you do not adopt the habit
Of taking off your armor in battle,
For that will expose you to death.

Gloss 91

During the battle Hector was found without his armor and was then killed. And for this reason we say that one should not take off one's arms in battle. And Hermes says, "Death is like the shot of an arrow, and life also is like an arrow that takes its time to arrive."

Allegory 91

Where it is said that one should always be covered by one's armor, we mean that the good spirit should always keep its senses close to itself and not let them wander about. On this topic Saint Gregory says that the person who takes leave of his senses is like the juggler who finds no worse abode than his own, because he is always away from home. Similarly, the man who does not keep his senses close to him is always wandering about outside of the house of his conscience. And he is also like the open hall into which one can enter from all sides. Therefore our Lord says in the Gospels, "Shut the door and pray to your Father who is in secret." [Matthew 6:6: *Clausio hostio ora Patrem tuum in abscondito*.]

Text 92

Do not covet Polybetes's arms.
They are cursed.
For by stripping them off as spoil, your death will follow
At the hands of the one who pursues you.

Gloss 92

Polybetes was a very powerful king whom Hector killed in battle, after he had
done many great deeds that day. And because he was armed with beautiful weap-
ons, Hector coveted them and bent down over the neck of his horse in order to
strip them off as spoil. And immediately Achilles, who had followed him with
the intention of attacking him when he was uncovered, struck him from below in
the gap in his armor and with one stroke struck him dead. This was a great loss,
for never, out of all those whom historical works mention, did a more valiant
knight gird himself with a sword. And that such covetousness can be harmful in
such a place is obvious in this story. Therefore the philosopher says, "Disordered
covetousness leads a man to death."

Allegory 92

That you should not covet Polybetes's arms means that the good spirit should not
covet any worldly things, and because covetousness leads man to death, Pope In-
nocent says in his book on the *Misery of the Human Condition* that covetousness
is like a fire that one cannot extinguish, for the covetous man is never content
with having that which he desires; when he has the thing he desires he always
wants more.[75] And his goal is always to have what he still expects to have and not
what he already has. Avarice and covetousness are two bloodsuckers that will not
stop saying, "Bring me things, bring me things." And as the value of one's money
increases, so too does the love of money increase. Covetousness is the path to
spiritual death and often to physical death. Therefore the Apostle Paul says, "The
love of money is the root of all evils." [1 Timothy 6:10: *Radix omnium malorum
cupiditas est.*]

Text 93

Do not become infatuated with foreign love;
Think about the deeds of Achilles

---

75. As Parussa notes, this is a reference to the entry "Cupiditas" in the *Manipulus florum*.

Who foolishly intended to take his
Enemy as his beloved.

Gloss 93

Achilles was foolishly in love with Polyxena, the beautiful young woman who
was Hector's sister. Achilles saw her at the first anniversary of Hector's funeral
ceremonies, at the time where there was a truce during which several Greeks went
to Troy in order to see Troy's nobles and the rich funeral ceremonies which were
celebrated with the greatest solemnity ever accorded the body of a knight. There
Achilles saw Polyxena and was overwhelmed by a love that could not last. He
approached Queen Hecuba about negotiating a marriage, saying that he would
stop the war and lift the siege, and would always be their friend. For a long time
Achilles did not take up arms against the Trojans because of this love, and he tried
everything to get the army to leave but could not do it. And after this Achilles
killed Troilus, who was well the equal of his brother Hector, even though he was
younger. And Queen Hecuba was so pained by this that she asked Achilles to
come to Troy to negotiate the marriage, and he went and was killed there. There-
fore Othea says to the good knight that he should not become infatuated with
foreign loves, for because of love in faraway lands much harm has been done. And
on this topic a wise man says, "If your enemies do not have a chance to avenge
themselves, then you must be on your guard."

Allegory 93

That he should not become infatuated with foreign loves means that the good
spirit should not love anything that does not come from God or have its end in
Him, and that it should flee from foreign things, that is, from the world. And that
one should hate the world says Saint Augustine in his interpretation of the letter
of Saint John, "The world and its concupiscence pass. Oh reasonable man, what
do you prefer: to love the temporal world that passes with time or to love Jesus
Christ and to live with Him in eternity?" On this topic Saint John says in his first
epistle, "Do not love the world or the things in the world." [1 John 2:15: *Nolite
diligere mundum neque ea que in mundo sunt.*]

Text 94

Do not use arms foolishly;
It is dangerous for body and soul,
If you fight with a naked arm and without a shield.
You can learn this from Ajax.

Gloss 94

Ajax was a Greek knight, very proud and overweening, but he was good at handling arms, and because of pride and gallantry he took up his arms, with one arm naked and unprotected by his shield, and thus he was pierced through and through and killed. And therefore we say to the good knight that to handle arms that way is not honorable; rather, it is a sign of folly and pride and is very dangerous. And therefore Aristotle says, "Many err through ignorance and lack of knowledge and do not know what to do and what not to do, and others fail through arrogance and pride."

Allegory 94

That he should not handle arms foolishly means that the good spirit should not trust in its own fragility. Saint Augustine says in a sermon that no one should take himself for granted when he says something, nor should he trust in his strength when he faces temptation, for when we wisely utter good words they come from God and not from our wisdom, and when we endure adversities with steadfastness, it comes from God and not from our patience. On this topic the Apostle Paul says, "Such is the confidence that we have through Christ toward God. Not that we are sufficient of ourselves to claim anything as coming from us." [2 Corinthians 3:4–5: *Fiduciam talem habemus per Cristum ad Deum, non quod sumus sufficientes aliquid cogitare ex nobis, tanquam ex nobis.*]

Text 95

Exile and chase away Antenor
Who perpetrated false and disloyal
Treason against his country.
He received a bad recompense for it.[76]

Gloss 95

Antenor was a Trojan baron, and when the end of the great battle for Troy was near, the Greeks, who had besieged the city for a long time, did not know how to succeed in finally taking the city, for it was too strong. Then Antenor, who was angry at king Priam, incited them to pretend to make peace with Priam, because this way he himself would let them into the city and give them safe passage. This

---

76. Antenor was seen as the proverbial traitor in the tradition of the Troy story. In Dante's *Divine Comedy* he ended up in Hell's Circle of Treachery, reserved for those who have betrayed cities, countries, and political parties: *Inferno,* Circle 9, cantos 32–33.

is what he did and Troy was betrayed. And because his treachery and evilness were so great we say to the good knight that whenever he may meet men like this he should exile and chase them away, for such people are to be hated. Plato says, "Deception is the captain and governor of evil people."

Allegory 95

That Antenor should be chased away means that the good spirit should chase away from itself anything that could harm him. On this topic Saint Augustine says that the person who does not take care to avoid harm resembles a moth that turns around the lamplight until its wings are burnt and then drowns in the oil; and the bird that flies around the branch covered with glue so long that it loses its feathers. The example is Saint Peter, who remained so long in the judge's court that he came to such harm as to renounce his master. Therefore the wise man says, "Do not enter the path of the wicked, do not go on it." [Proverbs 4:14–15: *Fuge a via malorum, ne transeas per eam.*]

Text 96

Do not let your enemies offer gifts
At Minerva's temple.
Reflect on the wooden horse;
Troy would still exist if it had not [existed].

Gloss 96

When, through the treachery of Antenor, the Greeks had pretended to make peace with the Trojans, they said that they had vowed a gift to the goddess Minerva that they wanted to offer, and they had made a wooden horse of marvelous size that was filled with armed knights; and it was so large that it was necessary to break down the gates of the city so that it could enter. The horse was set on wheels and they dragged it all the way to the temple. And when night had fallen the knights jumped out of the horse and let in those who were still outside the city, and they killed everyone, and burned and destroyed the city. Therefore Othea says to the good knight that he should not trust in such deceit or in this kind of offering. On this topic the wise man says, "One should fear the subtleties and the traps of one's enemy if he is clever, and if he is foolish, his evilness."

Allegory 96

We can understand Minerva's temple as Holy Church, where nothing should be offered except prayer. Saint Augustine says in his book *On Faith* that without the presence of Holy Church and baptism no one can thrive, and the works of mercy are worthless, and there will be no eternal life: there can be no salvation outside of the bosom of Holy Church. Therefore David says in the Psalms, "With you is my praise in a great church." [Psalm 21:26 (22:25): *Apud te laus mea in ecclesia magna.*]

Text 97

Do not take your possessions for granted,
For Ilion, the strong fortress,
Was taken and burned, as was Tunis also.
Everything is in Fortune's hands.

Gloss 97

Ilion was the principal fortress of Troy and the strongest and most beautiful castle ever built among those that are written about in histories, and nonetheless it was taken, burned, and reduced to nothing, and so was the city of Tunis, which used to be so great. And because such ruin is caused by the mutability of Fortune, the good knight should not be proud nor believe himself to be safe because of his strength. Therefore Ptolemy says, "The higher a realm is elevated, the more perilous is its ruin."

Allegory 97

That the good spirit should not take its possessions for granted can mean that it should not value or regret any kind of delight, for delights are transitory, not certain, and lead to damnation, and Saint Jerome says that it is impossible that a person could pass from delight to delight and then leap from the delights of this world to the delights of paradise, that here he can fill his belly and there his soul, for the divine condition is released [from delights], nor has it been given at all to those who think that they can possess the eternal world in delights. On this topic it is written in the Apocalypse, "As she glorified herself and played the wanton, so give her a like measure of torment and mourning."[77] [Revelation 18:7: *Quantum glorificavit se et in deliciis fuit, tantum date ei tormentum et lutum.*]

---

77. The feminine is the city of Babylon here.

Text 98

You should avoid the port of Circe
Where Ulysses's knights
Were all changed into pigs.
Remember her ways.

Gloss 98

Circe was a queen who had her kingdom on the Italian sea, and she was a great enchantress and knew much about oracles and magic.[78] And when Ulysses, who traveled by sea after the destruction of Troy since he planned to return to his country after the great and dangerous torments he had suffered, arrived at the port of this land, he asked the queen through his knights whether he could safely land in her harbor. Circe received the knights, and in a show of courtesy she had them served with a drink that was delicious; but the potion had such power that suddenly the knights were transformed into pigs. Circe can be understood in several ways. She can stand for a land or a country where the knights were put into a dirty and vile prison. And she can represent a lady full of idleness by whom several knights errant, that is, knights who took up arms, and who were among Ulysses's followers, that is, who were malicious and crafty, were kept like pigs. And for this reason we say to the good knight that he should not linger at such sojourn. And Aristotle says, "He who is wholly inclined toward fornication cannot be praised in the end."

Allegory 98

We can interpret the port of Circe as hypocrisy, which the good spirit should avoid above all other things. And against the hypocrites Saint Gregory says in his *Morals* that the life of hypocrites is nothing but a fantastic vision and an imaginary fantasy that show through an outward image what is not inside in true reality. On this topic Our Lord says in the Gospels, "Woe unto you, scribes and Pharisees, hypocrites! For you are like whitewashed tombs, which outwardly appear beautiful but within they are full of dead men's bones." (Matthew 23:27: *Ve vobis ypocrite, qui similes estis sepulchris dealbatis que a foris apparent hominibus speciosa, intus vera plena sunt ossibus mortuorum.*]

---

78. Christine speaks of Circe in *Autres ballades* (Other Ballads) 17, and will also mention her in the *Mutacion de Fortune* and the *City of Ladies*, each time with a different meaning, ranging from the personal to the moral/sexual and the political. See Blumenfeld-Kosinski, *Reading Myth*, 176–80 and 186.

Text 99

You should not offer beautiful arguments
To someone unable to understand them.
Take good notice, I believe,
Of Ino who sowed baked wheat kernels.

Gloss 99

Ino was a queen who sowed baked wheat kernels that did not sprout, and this means for the good knight that beautiful, well ordered arguments and words from wise authorities should not be offered to people of primitive understanding and to those who cannot understand them, for they would be squandered. Therefore Aristotle says, "Just like rain is useless for wheat sown on stone, so are arguments offered to the ignorant."

Allegory 99

Beautiful words should not be offered to primitive and ignorant people who could not understand them because they would thus be squandered, and that one should rather blame ignorance says Saint Bernard in a book on the *Fifteen Degrees of Humility;* he states that those who use frailty and ignorance as excuses sin more freely, for they are willfully frail and ignorant. And many things that one should know are sometimes ignored, sometimes by negligence in learning them, or by laziness in asking about them, or by shame in inquiring about them. And all these kinds of ignorance have no excuse. Therefore Saint Paul the apostle says, "If one does not recognize this, he is not recognized." [1 Corinthians 14:38: *Si quis ignorat ignorabitur.*]

Text 100

I have written down one hundred authorities for you;
May you not despise them,
For Augustus learned from a woman
Who reprimanded him for being worshipped.

Gloss 100

Caesar Augustus was the emperor of the Romans and of the entire world; and because at the time he reigned there was peace throughout the world and he governed peacefully,[79] foolish and impious people maintained that peace existed because of his goodness. But this was not so, for this peace existed because of Jesus Christ who was born of the Virgin Mary and already lived on earth; and as long as he lived there was peace in the entire world. All the same, they wanted to worship Caesar as God, but then the Sibyl of Cumae told him not to let himself be worshipped, for there was only one God who had created everything.[80] And then she led him to a high mountain outside of the city, and in the sun, by the will of Our Lord, there appeared a Virgin holding a child. The Sibyl showed this to him, and told him that this was the true God who should be worshipped; and Caesar worshipped Him. And because Caesar who was the ruler of the entire world learned to recognize God and the true faith through a woman, one can cite on this topic the authority of Hermes: "It should not be shameful to you to hear the truth and good teaching from whoever may pronounce them; for the truth ennobles the person who tells it."

Allegory 100

Where Othea says that she wrote down one hundred authorities to him and that Augustus learned from a woman means that good words and good teaching are praiseworthy for whoever may have pronounced them. Regarding this, Hugh of Saint Victor says in his book called *Didascalion*[81] that the wise man listens gladly to everyone and learns gladly from each, and reads gladly all kinds of teachings; he does not despise Scripture; he does not despise the person; he does not despise doctrine; he searches equally everywhere and everything he sees for that which he lacks; he does not consider who speaks but rather that which is said; he does not pay attention to how much he knows, but to what he does not know. On this topic the wise man says, "A good ear should hear wisdom with all its desire." [Ecclesiasticus/Sirach 3:31: *Auris bona audiet cum omni concupiscencia sapienciam.*]

Here ends Othea's letter.

79. The Emperor Augustus lived from 63 BCE to 14 CE. The *pax Augusta*, or Augustan Peace, was declared in 17 BCE.

80. The story of the Sibyl and the Emperor August us comes from the *Golden Legend* by Jacobus de Voragine, *The Golden Legend,* trans. William Granger Ryan (Princeton, NJ: Princeton University Press, 1995), 1:40. Written in Latin in the thirteenth century, it was soon translated into many vernacular languages, including French (by Jean de Vignay). Christine identifies the unnamed Sibyl from the *Golden Legend* as the Sibyl of Cumae, who, as Parussa points out (455), was named by Saint Augustine in his *City of God.* In the *City of Ladies* Christine opens Book 2 with an account of all the Sibyls. On their important role in the Middle Ages see Bernard McGinn, "*Teste David cum Sibylla:* The Significance of the Sibylline Tradition in the Middle Ages," in *Women of the Medieval World*, edited by Julius Kirshner and Suzanne F. Wemple (Oxford: Basil Blackwell, 1985), 7–35.

81. For Hugh of Saint Victor, see the note to Allegory 51.

Appendix

Copy editor Cheryl Lemmens originally constructed the table in this appendix in an attempt to track down the various sources used by Christine in the allegory sections of the *Othea*. I believe it demonstrates clearly that Christine's competence in Latin—a subject of debate for most of the twentieth century—can no longer be called into question.

In his 1924 study of the sources of the *Othea*, P.G.C. Campbell concluded more or less in passing that Christine could not read Latin fluently.[1] Some fifteen years later Suzanne Solente contested this conclusion in the very careful notes to her edition of the biography of Charles V, *Le livre des fais et bonnes meurs* (vol. 1, pp. xxxv–vi), pointing out, among other Latin sources, Christine's knowledge of the works of Thomas Aquinas. Despite Solente's detailed documentation, Charity Cannon Willard concluded in her examination of the Latin epigraphs beginning each chapter of her edition of the *Livre de la paix* that Campbell's assessment of Christine's Latin was correct.[2] This conclusion remained unchallenged in Christine studies until 1995, when Christine Reno and Liliane Dulac, returning to Solente's source studies, demonstrated an even more profound knowledge of Aquinas' works on Christine's part than Solente had assumed,[3] and, when, again in 1995, independently, I re-examined the Patristic sources of the *Othea* and concluded that Christine's use of these authors went beyond mere mechanical citations from the homiletic handbook called the *Manipulus florum* ("Handful of Flowers").[4] The definitive refutation of both Campbell's and Willard's argument was made by Constant J. Mews, an experienced medieval Latinist, who re-examined the original manuscripts of the *Livre de paix* and discovered that Willard had made mistakes in transcribing the Latin epigraphs there. Willard's Latin, not Christine's, was at fault.[5] Thelma Fenster has gone on to show in detail how

1. Campbell, *L'Épitre d'Othéa: Étude sur les sources de Christine de Pisan* (Paris: Champion, 1924), 132n.

2. Willard, *The "Livre de la Paix,"* based on Willard's 1940 Harvard Ph.D. dissertation.

3. Liliane Dulac and Christine Reno, "L'humanisme vers 1400, essai d'exploration à partir d'un cas marginal: Christine de Pizan, traductrice de Thomas d'Aquin," *Pratiques de la culture écrite en France au XVe siècle : Actes du Colloque international du CNRS, Paris, 16–18 mai 1992, organisé en l'honneur de Gilbert Ouy par l'unité de recherche "Culture écrite du Moyen Âge tardif,"* ed. Monique Ornato and Nicole Pons (Louvain-la-Neuve: Fédération internationale des instituts d'études médiévales, 1995), 161–78.

4. Earl Jeffrey Richards, "In Search of a Feminist Patrology: Christine de Pizan and *les glorieux dotteurs*," in Dulac and Ribémont, *Une femme de lettres au Moyen Âge*, 281–95.

5. Constant J. Mews, "Latin Learning in Christine de Pizan's *Livre de paix*," in *Healing the Body Politic: The Political Thought of Christine de Pizan,*, ed. Karen Green and Constant J. Mews (Turnhout: Brepols, 2005), 61–80.

Christine was sensitive to stylistic registers in a range of genres in both Middle French and Latin.[6] Now, as this appendix shows, questions about Christine's fluency in Latin can be put to rest.

Moreover, unknown to both Campbell and Willard, is an aside found in the still unpublished *Livre de la Prod'ommie de l'homme* (1405–1407, "The Book of Man's Probity"). Christine comments there in passing on the Latin competence of Louis d'Orléans, the younger brother of Charles VI to whom she dedicated the *Othea*, shortly before his assassination in 1407: *"Et je vous ouïe descrire tant bien et tant notablement, allegant a propos auctoritez sainctes, tant en latin comme en françois, par preuves vraies, come legiste de la prodommie du noble et vertueux homme..."* (Vatican, Reg. lat. 1238, f. 2 r°–v°, "And I used to hear you describe [probity] so well and so remarkably, citing holy authorities, both in Latin and in French, in cogent proofs on this subject, as the legal advocate of the gallantry of the noble and virtuous man"). What Christine casually describes here is the bilingual nature of the French royal court, where Latin actually remained the official language until 1539. Thanks to the efforts of Louis's father, the king Charles V, the royal court had experienced something of a Latin renaissance. In her biography of Charles V, Christine notes that while Charles himself had a fairly good competence in Latin, he commissioned the translation of many Latin works so that he could understand them better. At the same time, he surrounded himself with intellectuals who were as fluent in Latin as in French. This pattern continued during the reign of Charles VI. This flourishing of a bilingual royal court culture in the reigns of Charles V and Charles VI is associated with the names of Nicole Oresme, Raoul de Presles, Philippe de Mézières, Évrart de Conty, Laurent de Premierfait, and Jean Gerson, to name only a few. Christine in effect tells us in her description of Louis d'Orléans that she was perfectly integrated in this bilingual environment, and, in the future, scholars must be sensitive to the bilingual or even multilingual practice underlying Christine's work, a multilingual "situated literacy."[7]

Earl Jeffrey Richards

6. Thelma Fenster, "'Perdre son latin': Christine de Pizan and Vernacular Humanism," in *Christine de Pizan and the Categories of Difference*, ed. Marilynn Desmond (Minneapolis: University of Minnesota Press, 1998), 91–107.

7. See the essays assembled by editors David Barton, Mary Hamilton, and Roz Ivanič in *Situated Literacies: Theorising Reading and Writing in Context* (London: Routledge, 2000).

Authors and Works Cited in the Allegories

Prepared by Cheryl Lemmens[1]

**Allegory
Number**

1   Christine's source for Augustine on the utility of prudence is taken from *Manipulus florum,* "Prudencia siue prouidencia," a: "Vbicumque fuerit prouidencia, frustrantur uniuersa contraria."[2] However, *De singularitate clericorum* (CSEL 3.3, ed. Wilhelm Hartel) is now attributed to the Pseudo-Cyprianus Carthaginensis, and the text cited is found there in chapter 42, p. 217, ll. 15–16. This work was a treatise in favor of clerical celibacy; the title may be translated literally as "on the singleness of priests." The same work is cited in Allegories 67 and 89.

2   Here Christine cites Augustine on temperance from *Manipulus florum,* "Temperancia," a: "Munus temperantiae est in coercendis sedandisque cupiditatibus." This text is Thomas Aquinas' paraphrase (in *Summa* II, ii, 141.4.1) of Augustine, *De moribus ecclesiae catholicae et de moribus Man-ichaeorum,* 1.19 (CSEL 90, ed. J.B. Bauer, pp. 39–40, ll. 2–8).

3   Ambrose on fortitude is taken from *Manipulus florum,* "Fortitudo," d (also the source of the quotation in Allegory 10 below), and the text is not from Ambrose's *De officiis,* but from Ambrose's letter to Simplician, written in 387. See Ambrosius Mediolanensis, *Epistulae,* 7, 5 (CSEL 82.1, ed. Otto Faller, p. 45, ll. 34–41): "Sapiens enim non metu frangitur, non potestate mutatur, non attollitur prosperis, non tristibus mergitur." (*Please note:* This letter is numbered as 37 in other editions; see, e.g., PL 16, col. 1131.) The previous quotation in *Manipulus florum* ("Fortitudo," c) is the one taken from *De officiis.* The citation error is due to a *lapsus oculi* either on Christine's part or on the part of the scribe who copied the manuscript.

4   Saint Bernard on justice is based on *Manipulus florum,* "Iusticia et iustus," s, which is taken from Bernard de Clairvaux, *Sermons,* 3, 4–6 (SBO 4, ed. Jean Leclercq, C.H. Talbot, and H.M. Rochais, at p. 178, ll. 4–8, 16–18, and

1. I would like to thank Renate Blumenfeld-Kosinski and Earl Jeffrey Richards for their generosity in including this table as an appendix to their edition of *Othea.* I am also grateful to Prof. Richards for his assistance in tracking down sources, making revisions and corrections where necessary, and adding valuable information about Christine and the milieu in which she lived and wrote.

2. The earliest printed editions of the *Manipulus florum* (Piacenza, 1483; Venice, 1550; Lyon, 1567) follow the alphabetically arranged format of topics originally found in the manuscripts, and reference citations for each topic by using a small letter. Chris L. Nighman's online edition follows this format, so that "Prudencia siue prouidencia, a" refers to the first citation under this topic.

p. 179, ll. 10–12). The precept of justice as "rendering to each his own" is, as stated in the footnote, originally taken from the *Institutes* of Justinian, Book I, Title I, "Of Justice and Law," section 3: "The precepts of the law are these: to live honestly, to injure no one, and to give every man his due." See *The Institutes of Justinian*, ed. John Baron Moyle, 5th ed. (Oxford: Clarendon Press, 1913), p. 3.

5   Parussa (p. 495) notes that Christine is alluding to Augustine's *Livre de correccion* ("Book of Correction"), a reference to Sermon 355, preached some time after the Christmas of 425: Augustinus Hipponensis, *Sermones* (CPL 0284), sermo 355, p. 124: "duae res sunt conscientia et fama, conscientia tibi, fama proximo tuo." See Siegfried Wenzel, trans., *Preaching in the Age of Chaucer: Selected Sermons in Translation* (Washington, DC: Catholic University of America Press, 2008), 149: "Augustine further says in his common sermon for the clergy: 'You need to have two things, [a good] conscience and reputation—conscience for yourself, and reputation for your neighbor. A person who relies on his conscience but neglects his reputation is cruel.'" See also Augustine, "Sermon 355: First Sermon on the Way of Life of his Clergy," in *Sermons (341–400) on Liturgical Seasons*, ed. John E. Rotelle, with translation and notes by Edmund Hill (Hyde Park, NY: New City Press, 1995), 165–72, where the relevant text is found on page 165. The date of 425 is also given on this page, with the following endnote: "The sermon was preached after Christmas, either at the end of December or the beginning of January; at any rate, shortly before Epiphany, 426" (171). Chaucer uses both this text and another text attributed to Augustine (see the note on Allegory 20) in *The Tale of Melibee*.

6   Saint Jerome, "Letter to Nepotian": The text quoted here ("I do not remember to have read or heard that anyone has died a bad death who freely did works of mercy, for mercy has many intercessors and it is impossible that the prayers of many not be granted") is taken from *Manipulus florum*, "Misericordia," m. However, the attribution to Jerome there is false, and the text given there abridges a much longer passage first attributed to Augustine, although the direct source is Pseudo-Augustinus Belgicus, *Sermones ad fratres in eremo commorantes*, 44 (PL 40, col. 1319): "Nunquam recordor me legisse mala morte perisse qui libenter in hac uita opera charitatis uel pietatis uoluerit exercere."

7   Christine has cited Cassiodorus on the Psalms from *Manipulus florum*, "Superbia," az: "Superbia de angelo dyabolum fecit." This concise text is somewhat more rhetorically pointed than the original quotation from Cassiodorus, which is taken from *Expositio Psalmorum*, 18, 14 (CCSL 97, ed. Marcus Adriaen, p. 176, ll. 285–290): "Quantum enim in malo magnum sit,

hinc datur intellegi, quae ex angelo diabolum fecit, quae homini mortem intulit et concessa beatitudine uacuauit."

8 This allusion to Gregory's *Morals on the Book of Job* is taken from *Manipulus florum*, "Iudex sive iudicium," u: "Diuina iudicia dum nesciuntur non audaci sermoni discutienda sunt, sed formidoloso silentio ueneranda." See Gregorius Magnus, *Moralia in Iob*, 32, 1 (CCSL 143B, ed. Marcus Adriaen, p. 1626, ll. 51–55). The *Moralia* can also be read online in English from a British edition of 1844; here, the translated text reads: "when the Divine judgments are not known, they are not to be discussed with bold words, but to be venerated with awful silence." See <http://www.lectionarycentral.com/GregoryMoralia/Book32.html>.

9 The sermon of Cassiodorus [*recte*: Chrysostom] in praise of Saint Paul [*De laudibus Pauli homilia*] cited here is excerpted in *Manipulus florum*, "Veritas," x: "Talis est condition falsitatis uel erroris, ecitam nullo sibi obsistente consenescit ac defluit" ("The condition of falsehood is such that even where it has no antagonists, it collapses into itself"). The text is based on Iohannes Chrysostomus, *De laudibus sancti Pauli apostoli homiliae*, 4 (PG 50, col. 496).

10 *Manipulus florum*, "Fortitudo," d, "Stultus sicut luna mutatur," is taken from Saint Ambrose, "Sed multo hoc prius Solomon dixit qui ait: Stultus sicut luna mutatur." See Ambrosius Mediolanensis, *Epistulae*, 7, 5 (CSEL 82.1, ed. Otto Faller, p. 45, ll. 34–41). See also the note to Chapter 3 above.

11 The reference to Saint Ambrose, *On the Duties of the Clergy* [*De officiis*], Book 1, is taken from *Manipulus florum* ("Bellum," m, with variants at "Gula," n), but the attribution to Ambrose is incorrect in "Bellum"; the correct source is Saint Gregory, *Moralia in Iob*, 30, 18 (CCSL 143B, ed. Marcus Adriaen, p. 1530, ll. 27–29). See also <http://www.lectionarycentral.com/GregoryMoralia/Book30.html> for the 1844 translation.

12 Saint Gregory's remark in *Homilies*—that "one must greatly revere the preachers of Holy Scripture, for they are the forerunners of Our Lord who follows after them"—seems to be a somewhat attenuated allusion to Gregorius Magnus, *Homiliae in euangelia* (CPL 1711, lib. 1, homilia 17, p. 117): "Praedicatores enim suos Dominus sequitur, quia praedicatio praeuenit" ("for the Lord follows his preachers, since their preaching is a forerunner").

13 Saint John Chrysostom's sermon *On the Creed*—"faith is the light of the soul, the gate of paradise and the window of life and foundation of eternal salvation"—is taken from *Manipulus florum*, "Fides siue fidelitas," al: "Fides religioinis catholice lumen est anime, hostium uite, fundamentum salutis

eterne." While Christine follows the *Manipulus florum* in giving Chrysostom as her source, the actual source is Eusebius "Gallicanus," *Collectio homiliarum* (CPL 0966, SL 101, hom. 10, l.1): "Fides religionis catholicae, lumen est animae, ostium uitae, fundamentum salutis aeternae." Aquinas repeats a similar formula in *Super Ad Hebraeos reportatio* ("lumen animae est fides"), so one can assume that this formula was frequently used by preachers.

14   The quotation from Origen's sermons on the Book of Exodus, "hope for things to come is the consolation of those who toil in this mortal life, just as for workers the hope of payment softens the burden of their labor," is taken from *Manipulus florum*, "Spes," r: "Futurorum spes laborantibus requiem parit, sicut in agone positis dolorem uulnerum mitigate spes corone." This closely follows Origenes, *In Exodum homeliae*, 6, 7 (SC 321, ed. Marcel Borret, p. 186, ll. 5–7).

15   Cassiodorus on charity as "the rain which falls in spring," distilling drops of virtues, is cited in *Manipulus florum*, "Caritas," z: "Caritas Dei quedam uernalis est pluuia vuirtutum." This is a close quotation from Cassiodorus, *Expositio Psalmorum*, 12, 1 (CCSL 97, ed. Marcus Adriaen, p. 122, ll. 7–11).

16   Origen's remark on pride—"What can ashes and dust take such pride in, or how dare a man puff himself up when he considers where he has come from and what he will become"—has been taken from *Manipulus florum*, "Superbia," ar. This text accurately cites Origenes, *In Ezechielem homeliae*, 9, 2 (SC 352, ed. Marcel Borret, p. 304, ll. 21–25): "quid *superbit terra et cinis* (Eccles. 8:9), ut homo arrogantia sublevetur oblitus quid erit et quam fragili vasculo contineatur et quibus stercoribus immersus sit et qualia semper purgamenta de sua carne proiciat?"

17   Augustine on wrath compared to vinegar is taken from *Manipulus florum*, "Ira" b, where the quotation there accurately cites Augustinus Hipponensis, *Epistulae*, 210, 2 (CSEL 57, ed. Alois Goldbacher, p. 355, ll. 22–25): "sicut acetum corrumpit uas, si diutius ibi fuerit, sic ira corrumpit cor, si in alium diem durauerit." See also Stefano Mazza and Yoshikatsu Murooka, "Vinegars Through the Ages," in *Vinegars of the World*, ed. Laura Solieri and Paolo Giuduci (Milan: Springer, 2009), p. 24, in which the authors quote Augustine in both Latin and English, noting that "the famous Christian philosopher refers to a chemical property of vinegar, of which people were already well aware at the dawn of medieval Europe."

18   Augustine, "Envy is hatred for the happiness of others," cites *Manipulus florum*, "Inuidia," d, "Inuidia est odium aliene felicitatis," and is taken from Augustine's *Enarrationes in Psalmos* (CPL 0283, SL 40, ed. Eligius Dekkers and Jean Fraipont), psalmus 104, par. 17, l. 18. For an English translation,

see Augustine, *The Literal Meaning of Genesis*, translated and annotated by John Hammond Taylor, Vol. 2: *Books 7–12* (New York and Mahwah, NJ: Newman Press, 1982), p. 146. The connection between *invidia* and *odium* was already proverbial among Latin pagan authors, beginning with Cicero.

19   Bede's remarks on sloth, commenting on the Proverbs of Solomon, is based on *Manipulus florum*, "Accidia," f: "Vult et non uult piger; recte pigri uocabulo denotatur qui uult regnare cum Deo, et non laborare pro Deo." This text closely follows Bede's Latin; see Beda Venerabilis, *In Prouerbia Salomonis libri III*, 2, 13 (CCSL 119B, ed. David Hurst and J.E. Hudson, pp. 78–79, ll. 5–8).

20   Augustine's comparison of the avaricious man to hell, "for hell cannot swallow enough souls before it says 'that's enough,'" is cited in *Manipulus florum*, "Auaricia," c: "Auarus uir inferno est similis. Infernus enim quantoscumque deuorauerit, numquam dicit: satis est." The precise author is uncertain, with a possible attribution to Augustine mentioned in the *Liber exhortationis, uulgo de salutaribus documentis ad quemdam comitem*, 30 (PL 40, col. 1058). This saying also appears in Chaucer's *Tale of Melibee*: "And therfore seith Seint Augustyn that the avaricious man is likned unto Helle, that the moore it swelweth, the moore desir it hath to swelwe and devoure." A recent edition of *The Canterbury Tales* notes: "The reference to St. Augustine has not been identified. Skeat cites a familiarity with Proverbs 27:20. Hell was frequently depicted visually in the Middle Ages as a great, monstrous mouth swallowing its victims." See Geoffrey Chaucer, *The Canterbury Tales*, edited by Robert Boenig and Andrew Taylor, 2nd ed. (Peterborough, ON: Broadview Press, 2008), p. 321n1.

21   The quotation from Gregory cited by Christine comes from *Manipulus florum*, "Gula," k: "Dominante gule uicio omne quod homines fortiter egerunt perdunt, et dum uenter non restringitur, simul cuncte uirtutes obruuntur"). This text cites a paraphrase by Thomas Aquinas in the *Summa*, II, ii, 148.2.4, of a passage drawn from Gregorius Magnus, *Moralia in Iob*, 30.18 (CCSL 143B, ed. Marcus Adriaen, p. 1530, ll. 35–39). See also the English translation at <http://www.lectionarycentral.com/GregoryMoralia/Book30.html>.

22   Jerome's description of gluttony as the mouth of the fire of hell is taken from *Manipulus florum*, "Luxuria," k, "O ignis infernalis luxuria, cuius material gula, cuius flamma superbia," and in fact appears to come from the variant text in Alanus ab Insulis (Alain de Lille), *Summa de arte praedicatoria*, 5 (PL 210, cols. 121–122): "O miserabilis ignis luxuriate! Ubi gula material, flamma concupiscentia …" The early church reformer Jan Hus, however,

in three sermons, and apparently working with a copy of the *Manipulus florum*, also attributes this same quotation to Jerome.

23-34 In the next twelve chapters, based on the sections of the Apostles' Creed, Christine does not cite any Patristic sources. See Curt F. Bühler, "The Apostles and The Creed," *Speculum* 28 (1953): 355–59, which analyzes the traditional division of the Creed into sections corresponding to each of the twelve Apostles.

35 Although Augustine is cited here and in the following chapters devoted to the Ten Commandments, the specific combination of images, creatures, devotion, and *latria* ("idolatry") given in Allegory 35 is found only in Thomas Aquinas, *Summa*, III, 25.3, responsio 2: "Secundo, propter res quarum erant *imagines*, statuebant enim *imagines* aliquibus *creaturis*, quas in eis *veneratione latriae* venerabantur." The major source for Christine here would appear to be Augustine's discussion of the Ten Commandments in his Sermon 250, preached during Easter Week in 416. See PL 38, cols. 1166–1167, or SC 116, ed. Suzanne Poque, 308–324; another version of the text can be found in *Sermons 230–272B on Liturgical Seasons*, ed. John E. Rotelle, translation and notes by Edmund Hill (Hyde Park, NY: New City Press, 1993), 122. Augustine also speaks about the Commandments in *Quaestiones in Exodum* [*Questions on Exodus*], particularly Question 71 (on this point, see the *Catholic Encyclopedia* entry at <http://www.newad vent.org/cathen/04153a.htm>). Specific verbal echoes between the texts of Christine and Augustine, however, are difficult to ascertain. Jonathan Hall's essay "St. Augustine and the Decalogue," accessible at <https://sites. google.com/site/miscelleneatheologica/home/augustinedec>, provides an excellent summary and analysis.

36 Saint Augustine on the Second Commandment ("You should not swear falsely, neither without cause nor in order to embellish falsehood, for there can be no greater deception than to present the highest and unshakeable truth as evidence for falsehood"): From Sermon 250. See also Augustine's letter to Publicola (Letter 47), in which he says, "Nevertheless it is, beyond all doubt, worse to swear falsely by the true God than to swear truly by the false gods; for the greater the holiness of that by which we swear, the greater is the sin of perjury." This letter can be read online at <http://www. newadvent.org/fathers/1102047.htm>.

37 Saint Augustine on the Third Commandment (observance of Sunday as the Sabbath): From Sermon 250; see also *De civitate Dei* [*The City of God*], Book 22, chapter 30.

38   Saint Augustine on the Fourth Commandment ("Honor thy father and thy mother"): From Sermon 250.

39   Saint Augustine on the Fifth Commandment ("Thou shalt not kill"): From Sermon 250. As Jonathan Hall notes in the essay cited above (Allegory 35), "[t]he fifth and sixth commandments are sometimes switched," and Augustine does this in Sermon 250: "*Non mœchaberis:* habes quintum. *Non homicidium facies:* habes sextum."

40   Isidore on the Sixth Commandment ("Thou shalt not commit adultery"). From Sermon 250; sometimes transposed by Augustine with the Fifth Commandment, as noted above. Isidore discusses adultery in his *Etymologies* as one of several "Crimes written in the law (*De criminibus in lege conscriptis*)": see Book 5, chapter 26, section 13 (*Etymologies*, ed. Barney et al., 123).

41   Augustine on the Seventh Commandment ("Thou shalt not steal"): From Sermon 250.

42   Augustine and Isidore on the Eighth Commandment ("Thou shalt bear no false witness against thy neighbor"). For Augustine: see Sermon 250, as noted above. The citation from Isidore is taken from *Manipulus florum*, "Testimonium," d: "Testibus falsidicus tribus est personis obnoxious: primum Deo quem periurando contempnit, et sequent iudici quem menciendo fallit, postremo innocenti quem falso testimonio ledit." This text cites Isidore exactly: see *Sententiae*, Book 3, 55, 2 (CCSL 111, ed. Pierre Cazier, p. 310, ll. 5–8).

43   Augustine on the Ninth Commandment ("Thou shalt not covet thy neighbor's wife"). As Jonathan Hall observes, Augustine sometimes transposes not just the Fifth and Sixth Commandments, but the Ninth and Tenth as well. He does this in Sermon 250: "*Non concupisces rem proximi tui:* habes nonum. *Non concupisces uxorem proximi tui:* habes decinum."

44   Augustine on the Tenth Commandment ("Thou shalt not covet thy neighbor's goods"): Transposed with the Ninth Commandment in Sermon 250, as noted above.

45   The allusion to Gregory's homily on the Parable of the Lost Sheep, written and preached in the years 591 and 592, has been taken from *Manipulus florum*, "Conversio," q, which rather accurately cites Gregorius Magnus, *Homiliae in euangelia*, 2, 34, 4 (CCSL 141, ed. Raymond Étaix, p. 303, ll. 87–94): "Maius de peccatore conuerso quam de iusto stante gaudium fit in celo quia et dux in prelio plus eum militem diligit qui post fugam reuersus

hostem fortiter premit quam illum qui nunquam terga prebuit et nunquam aliquid fortiter fecit."

46   Saint Augustine on meditation and prayer is cited from his Letter 147, "De videndo Deo" ["On seeing God"], which is the basis for the entry from *Manipulus florum*, "Contemplacio," b: "Qui didicerunt a Domino Ihesu Christo mites esse et humiles corde plus cogitando et orando proficient quam legend et audiendo." This quotation exactly reproduces the text from Augustinus Hipponensis, *Epistulae*, 147 (CSEL 44, ed. Alois Goldbacher, p. 275, ll.13–15).

47   Although Christine credits her discussion of Christ as redeemer to Bernard de Clairvaux (an attribution that makes total sense given the ongoing influence of Bernard's Christology in her work, particularly her subsequent use of Bernard in her later Passion narrative, the *Heures de contemplation de la passion Nostre Seigneur*), this section is taken from Anselm of Canterbury's highly influential *Cur deus homo*, II, 20. This text encapsulates his satisfaction theory of atonement (that Christ's suffering served as a substitute for the sins of humanity, linking his incarnation with his crucifixion). The citation here is found in *Opera omnia*, ed. F.S. Schmitt, vol. 2 (Edinburgh: Thomas Nelson, 1946), p. 131:

    Capitulum XX. Quam magna et quam iusta sit misericordia Dei.

        Misericordiam vero Dei quae tibi perire videbatur, cum iustitiam Dei et peccatum hominis considerabamus, tam magnam tam que concordem iustitiae invenimus, ut nec maior nec iustior cogitari possit. Nempe quid misericordius intelligi valet, quam cum peccatori tormentis aeternis damnato et unde se redimat non habenti Deus pater dicit: accipe unigenitum meum et da pro te; et ipse filius: tolle me et redime te?

    (Chapter 20: How great and how just is God's mercy.

        We have indeed found God's mercy—which seemed lost to you when we were considering God's justice and man's sin—to be so great and so in accord with justice that nothing greater nor more just can be conceived. Without doubt, what can be understood as more merciful than when God the Father says to the sinner damned to eternal torments, not having the means to redeem himself: 'accept my only-begotten Son and offer him for yourself' and when the Son himself says 'take me and redeem yourself'?)

48   Although Augustine is given as the source, it would seem that this allusion reveals the influence of contemporary oral sermon culture in Christine's Paris, for the key element of this passage is the concept of the soul as girded with five gates, gates that are associated with the five senses. This thematic

combination is not found, to the best of our knowledge, in Augustine, but rather in a sermon by Guillaume d'Auvergne, the Bishop of Paris from 1228 to 1249 and builder of the present structure of Notre-Dame de Paris. See Guillelmus Alvernus, *Sermones de tempore*, sermo 152 (Dominica in ramis palmarum), CM 230A, p. 71, l. 61: "Item aliter quelibet *anima* bona ciuitas Dei est, scilicet Ierusalem, habens *quinque portas*, scilicet *quinque sensus*."

49   Bernard de Clairvaux's remarks on the need to forsake earthly riches is taken from *Manipulus florum*, "Diuicie," y: "Filii Adam, genus auarum: quid uobis cum terrenis diuiciis que nec uere nec uestre sunt? Aurum et argentum uere terra est rubea et alba quam solus hominum error facit aut magis reputat preciosa; denique si uestra sunt, tollite ea uobiscum," which abridges somewhat Bernardus Claraeuallensis, *Sermones in adventu Domini*, 4, 1 (SBO 4, ed. Jean Leclerq, C.H. Talbot, and H.M. Rochais, p. 182, ll. 13–17).

50   While the general analogy made by Gregory between nourishment of the body and sustenance of the soul is found in many of his sermons, the passage here seems to allude most closely to Gregorius Magnus, *Homiliae in Hiezechihelem prophetam* (CPL 1710), lib. 2, hom. 1, l. 243: "uerbum uitae auditoribus praedicat, animabus simul et corporibus necessaria ministrat" ("he preaches the word of life to his listeners, and administers what is necessary at the same time to souls and bodies"). Parussa sees a link to the section of the *Manipulus florum* dedicated to preaching ("Predicacio") which we cannot verify, but which may be a detail helpful in identifying the manuscript that Christine actually used.

51   While Christine claims to be citing Hugh of Saint Victor's *Didascalicon*, in fact her connections between verbal indiscretion and a slippery eel, a piercing arrow, etc., combine a verse from Proverbs 25:28, "sicut urbs patens et absque murorum ambitu ita vir qui non potest in loquendo cohibere spiritum suum," with a passage from *Manipulus florum*, "Loquacitas," u:

> Lingua dicitur, quia lingit. Lingit adulando, mordet detrahendo, occidit mentiendo. Ligat, et ligari non potest: labilis est, et teneri non potest; sed labitur et fallitur. Labitur ut anguilla, penetrat ut sagitta; tollit amicos, multiplicat inimicos; movet rixas, seminat discordias. Uno ictu multos percutit et interfici. Blanda est et subdola, lata et parata ad exhaurienda bona, et miscenda mala. Qui custodit linguam suam, custodit animam suam (Prov. XXI, 23); quoniam mors et vita in potestate linguae est (Prov. XVIII, 21).

This text is attributed to Pseudo-Bernardus Claraeuallensis, *Tractatus de interiori domo*, 28 (PL 184, col. 537B–C).

52 Gregory's observation that force is worth nothing without good counsel is taken from *Manipulus florum*, "Fortitudo," l, which is an accurate citation: "fortitudo destruitur nisi per consilium fulciatur, quia quo plus se posse conspicit eo uirtus sine rationis moderamine deterius in praeceps ruit." See Gregorius Magnus, *Moralia in Iob*, 1, 32 (CCSL 143, ed. Marcus Adriaen, p. 49, ll. 30–35), as well as the English translation of the *Moralia* online at <http://www.lectionarycentral.com/GregoryMoralia/Book01.html>.

53 Christine's allusion to Gregory is found in *Moralia in Iob*, 20, 41 (CCSL 143A, ed. Marcus Adriaen, p. 1061, ll. 14–16, and is accurately cited in *Manipulus florum*, "Abstinencia," m: "uirtus abstinentiae aut omnino nulla est, si tantum quisque corpus non edomat quantum ualet; aut ualde inordinata est, si corpus atterit plus quam ualet" ("the virtue of abstinence is worth nothing unless it is so disposed that it is not harsher than the body can bear"). See also the English translation at <http://www.lectionarycentral. com/GregoryMoralia/Book20.html>.

54 Christine cites Bernard on ingratitude from *Manipulus florum*, "Ingratitudo," b: "Ingratitudo inimica est animae, exinanitio meritorum, virtutum dispersio, beneficiorum perditio" ("Ingratitude is the enemy of the soul, the diminishment of the virtues, the dispersion of merits, and the loss of graces"). See *Sermones super Cantica canticorum*, 51, 6 (SBO 2, ed. Jean Leclerq, C.H. Talbot, and H.M. Rochais, p. 87, ll. 18–20).

55 The quotation from Chrysostom on compunction is from *Manipulus florum*, "Delicie," f: "sicut inpossible est, ut ignis inflammetur in aqua, ita inpossible est conpunctionem cordis vigere in deliciis. Contaria haec enim sibi invicem sunt et peremptoria. Illa enim mater fletus, haec mater est risus, illa cor constringit, ista dissolvit." ("just as it is impossible for fire to burn in water, so is it impossible that the heart's compunction can exist in the midst of the pleasures of this world. These are two contrary things that destroy each other, for compunction is the mother of tears and pleasures bring forth laughter; compunction restrains the heart and pleasures enlarge it"). See Iohannes Chrysostomus, *De cordis conpunctione*, 2, 3, ed. Wilhelm Schmitz [Monumenta Tachygraphica Cod. Paris. Lat. 2718] (Hannover: Hahn, 1883), fasc. alter, p. 25, ll. 25–31. This quotation appeared in the second of Chrysostom's two texts on compunction, addressed to his friend Stelechius (PG 47, 411–422); the first was addressed to his friend Demetrius. The two texts were translated into Latin under the title *De cordis conpunctione*.

56 Christine has taken this allusion to Leo the Great from *Manipulus florum*, "Temptatio," ah, which cites a sermon given on Christmas Day, 451: "Non

enim desinit hostis antiquus, transfigurans se in angelum lucis, deceptio-
num laqueos ubique praetendere, et ut quoquo modo fidem credentium
corrumpat." See Leo Magnus, *Tractatus septem et nonaginta*, 27, 3 (CCSL
138, ed. Antoine Chavasse, p. 134, ll. 60–69). For an English translation,
see *St. Leo the Great: Sermons*, trans. Jane Patricia Freeland and Agnes Jo-
sephine Conway (Washington, DC: Catholic University of America Press
[The Fathers of the Church 93], 1996), 112–13.

57 The quotation from John Cassian on "the edifice of virtues" is taken from
Manipulus florum, "Humilitas," ar, which accurately cites him: "Nullo enim
modo poterit in anima nostra uirtutum structura consurgere, nisi prius
iacta fuerint uerae humilitatis in nostro corde fundamina, quae firmissime
conlocata perfectionis et caritatis culmen ualeant sustinere." See Iohannes
Cassianus, *De institutis coenobiorum*, 12, 32, 1 (CSEL 17, ed. Michael
Petschenig, p. 230, ll. 2–8).

58 Although Christine does not cite an author in the allegory section of this
chapter, her source for her remarks on the consequences of will at war with
God are based on a quotation from Guibert de Nogent found in *Manipu-
lus florum*, "Voluntas," x: "Propria siquidem voluntas Deum impugnat, et
adversus eum extollitur. Ipsa est quae paradisum spoliat, et ditat infernum:
quae sanguinem Christi evacuat, et ditioni diaboli subjugat mundum."
See Guibertus de Nouigento, *Sermo in verba sapientiae*, 14 (PL 184, col.
1040A–B).

59 The allusion to Jerome here is from *Manipulus florum*, "Tempus siue tem-
porale," d: "Nil longum quod finem habet. Eternitate comparatum, omne
tempus breue est." This text combines two remarks from Jerome's com-
mentary on Ezekiel; see Hieronymus Stridonensis, *Commentariorum in
Hiezechielem libri XIV*, preface and 9, 30 (CCSL 75, ed. François Glorie, p.
91, ll. 1–4, and p. 424, ll. 1225–1236).

60 Although Christine cites Cassiodorus' commentary on the Psalms, follow-
ing the attribution given in *Manipulus florum*, "Discordia," q, the quotation
there combines the Pseudo-Guillaume de Conches ("summopere autem
fuge iurgia")," from *Moralium dogma philosophorum* (ed. John Holmberg
[Uppsala: Almqvist and Wiksells, 1929], section I.D. 2, p. 50, l. 1), with a
citation from Seneca ("cum pare contendere anceps est, cum superior fu-
riosum, cum inferior sordidum"), from *De ira* (ed. L.D. Reynolds [Oxford:
Clarendon Press, 1977], 2, 34, 1, p. 88, ll. 21–22).

61 While Christine gives Gregory as her source for the quotation on the slow-
ness of divine justice, the original source is probably a comment found
in Rufinus' translation of Origen's commentary on Paul's Epistle to the

Romans, 3:26. The Vulgate text of Paul's letter reads: "*in sustentatione Dei ad ostensionem iustitiae eius in hoc tempore*" ("in God's deferral for showing his justice at this time"). Origen's commentary, as translated by Rufinus, reads: "However he adds quite well, 'in this time,' for in the world's time, the justice of God is in deferral, in the future it lies in retribution" ("Bene autem addidit, 'in hoc tempore'; praesentis enim saeculi tempore in sustentatione est iustitia Dei, futuri uero in retribution"). See Origenes sec. translationem Rufini, *In Epistulam Pauli ad Romanos explanationum libri* (CPL 0198 M (A), ed. C. P. Hammond Bammel, v. 16, lib. 3, cap. 5, p. 246).

62   Christine follows *Manipulus florum*, "Exemplum," c, in attributing the quotation on the need for vigilant regard to human fraility to Saint Augustine's *Book of Sheep* [*De ovibus*]: "Curemus ... non tantum (…) habere bonam conscientiam, sed quantum potest nostra infirmitas, quantum uigilantia fragilitatis humanae, curemus nihil etiam facere quod ueniat in malam suspicionem infirmo fratri" ("Let us take care not so much as to have a good conscience, but, as best our fraility allows, let us take care not to do anything which would arouse evil suspicion in a frail brother"). However, this text is actually somewhat abridged from Augustine's *Sermones de uetere testamento*, 47, 14 (CCSL 41, ed. Cyrille Lambot, p. 584, ll. 377–384). Christine apparently had a copy of the *Manipulus florum* which read *diligentia* for *vigilantia*.

63   The citation given in *Manipulus florum*, "Ociositas," e, "semper aliquis operis facito ut te dyabolus inueniat occupatum," is a slight paraphrase of Jerome popularized by Petrus Lombardus, *Sententiae in IV. Libri distinctae*, libri 4, distinctio 1, cap. 5, 4 (Spicilegium Bonauenturianum 5, 3rd ed. [1981], p. 235, ll. 13–16). The original is found in Jerome's letter to Rusticus, a young monk in Toulouse, written in 411. See *Epistulae*, 125, 11 (CSEL 56, ed. Isidor Hilberg, p. 130, ll. 6–7): "facet aliquid operis, ut semper te diabolus inueniat occupatum." Dame Prudence quotes this text in Chaucer's *Tale of Melibee*, and the same theme opens the *Second Nun's Prologue*, ll. 1–14.

64   Christine's source for Augustine's condemnation of boastfulness is *Manipulus florum*, "Iactantia," b: "Iactancia non est vicium laudis humane, sed vicium anime peruerse amantis humanam laudem spreto testimonio consciencie" ("Boasting is not a vice of human praise, but a vice of the perverse soul loving human praise with the testimony of conscience having been scorned"), where the citation is identified as coming from "Book Twelve of the *City of God*" (Book 12, chapter 8). The citation in the *Manipulus florum* closely follows the original Latin, *De ciuitate Dei*, 12, 8 (CCSL 48, ed. Bernhard Dombart, pp. 362–63, ll. 11–22).

65   No author cited.

66   Augustine's remarks on the good spirit not being disarmed with virtues
      is not in the *Manipulus florum*, but instead appears to have been adopted
      from a sermon by a very influential Dominican, Étienne de Bourbon: see
      Stephanus de Borbone, *Tractatus de diuersis materiis praedicabilibus (pro-
      logus et prima pars)*, 1, 8, 8, l. 634 VII: "o, quia in tempore belli et in loco
      certaminis arma uirtutum proicit." For another text that appears to draw
      on the *Tractatus*, see the note to Allegory 91 below.

67   Christine's source is *Manipulus florum*, "Solitudo et tumultus," a, which
      follows closely the text, attributed there to Augustine, but now published
      under the authorship of the Pseudo-Cyprianus Carthaginensis: *De singu-
      laritate clericorum* (CSEL 3.3, ed. Wilhelm Hartel). The text cited is found
      in chapter 4, p. 177, ll. 2–7: "minus uoluptatibus stimulatur, qui non est, ubi
      frequentia est uoluptatum. et minus auaritiae molestias patitur qui diuitias
      non uidet" ("He who is not where there is a concentration of lust is less ex-
      cited by lust, and he who does not see riches suffers less from the torments
      of greed"). The same work is cited in Allegories 1 and 89.

68   Christine has taken these four manifestations of arrogance outlined by
      Gregory the Great from *Manipulus florum*, "Superbia," af, which closely
      follows *Moralia in Iob*, 23, 6 (CCSL 143B, ed. Marcus Adriaen, p. 1153, ll.
      7–12). See also the English translation of the *Moralia* online at <http://
      www.lectionarycentral.com/GregoryMoralia/Book23.html>.

69   Christine has taken Augustine's remarks on the lightness of penitence
      (based on Matthew 11: 28–30) from *Manipulus florum*, "Penitencia," h: "Iu-
      gum meum leue [*sic*; *recte*: lene] est et sarcina mea leuis" ("my yoke is light,
      and my load is light"), which paraphases sermon 164 (PL 38, col. 898). The
      confusion of n and u/v is frequent.

70   Christine adapts somewhat Augustine's commentary on the Gospel of John
      as found in *Manipulus florum*, "Peticio," b, which carefully cites the origi-
      nal: "Male ergo usurus eo quod uult accipere, Deo potius miserante non
      accipit. Proinde si hoc ab illo petitur unde homo laedatur exauditus, magis
      metuendum est ne quod posset non dare propitius, det iratus" ("What one,
      therefore, wishes to receive, in order to turn to an improper use, God in
      His mercy rather refuses to bestow. Nay, more, if a man asks what would,
      if answered, only tend to his injury, there is surely greater cause to fear, lest
      what God could not withhold with kindness, He should give in His anger").
      See Augustinus Hipponensis, *In Iohannis euangelium tractatus CXXIV.*, 73,
      1 (CCSL 36, ed. Radbod Willems, pp. 509–10, ll. 9–12).

71 Jerome's remark that God's justice leaves no bad deed unpunished nor any good deed unrewarded picks up the phrase *nullum malum inpunitum et nullum bonum irremuneratum*, which seems to have been repeated in innumerable sermons beginning with Aelred of Rievaulx, if not earlier. Other sources do attribute it to Augustine, from the sermon *De caritate* (which the Patrologia Latina identifies as the Pseudo-Augustine, *Sermo* 270, 5, PL 39, 2250), and to Boethius, *De consolatione philosophiae*, lib 4, prosa 3,1 (CChr 94, 70, 2).

72 Augustine's observation that "the world is more perilous when it treats people softly than when it is harsh" has been taken from *Manipulus florum*, "Mundus," a, which accurately cites his correspondence. See Augustinus Hipponensis, *Epistulae*, 145, 2 (CSEL 44, ed. Alois Goldbacher, p. 267, ll. 15–17): "mundus quippe iste periculosior est blandus quam molestus et magis cauendus, cum se inlicit diligi, quam cum admonet cogit que contemni."

73 Augustine's warning about judging others is taken from *Manipulus florum*, "Iudex siue iudicium," b, which precisely quotes Augustine's treatise on the Sermon on the Mount: "Duo sunt autem in quibus temerarium iudicium cauere debemus: cum incertum est quo animo quidque factum sit, uel cum incertum est qualis futurus sit qui nunc uel malus uel bonus apparet" ("There are two things, moreover, in which we ought to beware of rash judgment; when it is uncertain with what intention anything is done; or when it is uncertain what sort of a person he is going to be, who at present is manifestly either good or bad"). See Augustinus Hipponensis, *De sermone Domini in monte*, 2, 18, 61 (CCSL 35, ed. Almut Mutzenbecher, p. 157, ll. 1393–1396).

74 Christine herself identifies the origin of this passage: Boethius, *The Consolation of Philosophy*, III.9, on happiness. Which particular medieval French translation she used is open to dispute. The striking feature of this passage is the term for happiness that Christine uses. "Félicité," a word which Christine employs more than fifty times in her work, while not infrequent, turns up especially in the writings of Nicole Oresme and Évrart de Conty, writers attached to the court of Charles V, and Christine's use of this term reveals a lexical affinity to these writers at court. In contrast, the antonym which Christine also employs here, "infelicité," was relatively rare, but turns up in Denis Foulechat and Philippe de Mézières, also writers associated with the court of Charles V. Neither term is used in the medieval French translations of Boethius.

75 Christine has taken Gregory's remarks on the superiority of the contempla-
tive life from *Manipulus florum*, "Contemplacio," k, which cites his sermon
on Ezekiel: "Contemplatiua autem maior est merito quam actiua, quia haec
in usu praesentis operis laborat, illa uero sapore intimo uenturam iam re-
quiem degustat." See Gregorius Magnus, *Homeliae in Hiezechielem prophe-
tam*, 1, 3, 9 (CCSL 142, ed. Marcus Adriaen, p. 37, ll. 148–150).

76 Christine's remarks on the lack of tolerance for others' faults seems loosely
based on *Manipulus florum*, "Consideracio sui," u: "alter alterius culpam
cito intelligit, suam autem difficile: quia homo in causa alterius tranquillum
cor habet, in sua autem turbatum. Perturbacio autem cordis non permittit,
hominem considerare quod bonum est" ("One person quickly perceives
the fault of the other, but his own with difficulty because one has a tranquil
mind in the matters of another, but in his own a troubled one. However, a
troubled mind does permit a man to judge what is good"). See Pseudo-
Chrysostomus, *Opus imperfectum in Matthaeum*, 45 (PG 56, col. 886).

77 Although Jerome frequently speaks about temptation (a subject later cel-
ebrated in painting, notably by Giorgio Vasari and Juan de Valdés Leal), it
has not been possible to identify the source of this observation.

78 Christine translates accurately Augustine's advice on the correct reasons
for weeping from his exposition of the Psalms as cited in *Manipulus florum*,
"Paciencia," d: "Fili, si ploras, sub patre plora; noli cum indignatione, noli
cum typho superbiae. Quod pateris, unde plangis, medicina est, non poena;
castigatio est, non damnatio." See Augustinus Hipponensis, *Enarrationes in
Psalmos*, 102, 20 (CCSL 40, ed. Eligius Dekkers and Jean Fraipont, p. 1469,
ll. 6–11).

79 Christine's invocation of the wisdom of Joseph's advice to the Pharaoh
translates closely a passage from Ambrose on the duties of the clergy given
in *Manipulus florum*, "Consilium," d: "Quanto utilius regem Pharaonem
sanctus Ioseph consilio prouidentiae iuuit quam si contulisset pecuniam!
Pecunia enim unius ciuitatis non redemit ubertatem, prospicientia totius
Aegypti per quinquennium famem reppulit" ("How much more usefully
did holy Joseph help King Pharaoh with his cautious advice than if he had
amassed wealth, for wealth does not restore fertility, and so he warded off,
through his foresight, hunger in all of Egypt for five years"). See Ambro-
sius Mediolanensis, *De officiis*, 2, 15 (CCSL 15, ed. Maurice Testard, p.
123, ll. 49–58). Christine, however, makes two additions, neither found
in Ambrose: the warning that one would be mad to ignore the advice of
the Church (and this in the midst of the Great Schism), followed by a

conclusion. She has also corrected Ambrose's five years of famine to the seven years mentioned in Genesis 41.

80   Christine follows the attribution of this quotation to Augustine as found in *Manipulus florum*, "Ignorancia," b, even though it actually stems from Bernard de Clairvaux: "Pessimae matris ignorantiae, pessimae itidem filiae duae sunt: falsitas et dubietas, illa miserior, ista miserabilior; perniciosior illa, ista molestior" ("There are two daughters of ignorance, that horrible mother, as horrible as she is, and they are falsity and doubt. The former is more wretched, the latter more pitiful; the first more pernicious, the later more irksome"). See Bernardus Claraeuallensis, *Sermones super Cantica canticorum*, 17, 3 (SBO 1, ed. Jean Leclercq, C.H. Talbot, and H.M. Rochais, p. 99, ll. 25–27).

81   Christine's generalizes Jerome's description of Judas to apply to all traitors, adapting *Manipulus florum*, "Prodicio," a: "Iudas de apostolatus fastigio in proditionis tartarum labitur et nec familiaritate conuiuii nec intinctione buccellae nec osculi gratia frangitur, ne quasi hominem tradat, quem filium Dei nouerat" ("Judas slips from the peak of the apostolate into the hell of perdition, and he is stopped neither by the familiarity of a banquet nor by the dipping of the sop [John 13:26] nor the grace of a kiss [Matt 26:49] from betraying the man whom he had known as the Son of God"). See Hieronymus Stridonensis, *Epistulae*, 125, 1 (CSEL 56, ed. Isidor Hilberg, p. 119, ll. 3–6).

82   The excerpt from Gregory's *Moralia in Iob* on comforting someone afflicted in his sadness is taken from *Manipulus florum*, "Compassio," b: "Cum uero alienae infirmitati compatimur, ualentius a nostra roboramur; ut amore futurorum mens ad praesentia aduersa se praeparet et cruciatus corporis quos timebat exspectet" ("When we truly feel compassion for the weakness of a stranger, we are more powerfully strengthened by our own, so that, out of love for future things, the mind will prepare itself for present adversities and will look out for the bodily torments that it used to fear"). See Gregorius Magnus, *Moralia in Iob*, 7, 14 (CCSL 143, ed. Marcus Adriaen, p. 345, ll. 8–11), as well as the English translation online at <http://www.lectionarycentral.com/GregoryMoralia/Book07.html>.

83   Christine mistakenly attributes this passage to Jerome, even though she quotes from a passage attributed to Gregory the Great in the *Manipulus florum*, "Scriptura sacra," af: "Scriptura sacra mentis oculis quasi quoddam speculum opponitur, ut interna nostra facies in ipsa uideatur. Ibi etenim foeda ibi pulchra nostra cognoscimus. Ibi sentimus quantum proficimus, ibi a prouectu quam longe distamus" ("Holy Scripture is presented to the

eyes of the mind as a kind of mirror so that our inner face may appear in it, for truly there do we come to know our deformity, and also there our beauty. There we sense how far we have come, there how far we stand from advancement"). See Gregorius Magnus, *Moralia in Iob*, 2, 1 (CCSL 143, ed. Marcus Adriaen, p. 59, ll. 1–4); see also the English translation of the *Moralia* online at <http://www.lectionarycentral.com/GregoryMoralia/Book02.html>. Given the increasing digitization of manuscripts, this particular mistake by Christine may help in the future to identify the specific manuscript she was citing in writing the *Othea*. Christine has made an interesting error in translation here: she renders *interna nostra facies*, "our inner face," as *l'enterine face de nostre ame*, "the entire face of our soul," whereby *de nostre ame* renders somewhat indirectly "our inner face."

84 Christine first introduces her citation here from Augustine with a quotation from Paul, "Let anyone who boasts, boast in the Lord" (1 Corinthians 1: 31), which then invokes Augustine's exposition of the Psalms as cited in *Manipulus florum*, "Gloria male siue uana," b: "Qui autem bene didicit uel expertus est uitiorum superandorum gradus, intellegit hoc uitium inanis gloriae uel solum uel maxime cauendum esse perfectis. Quo primo enim uitio lapsa est anima, hoc ultimum uincit" ("Who, however, has learned well, or has learned by experience the steps in overcoming vices, recognizes this vice of vainglory as the only or the worst vice to be avoided by those who seek to perfect themselves, for the soul which lapsed into this vice first, overcomes it as the last one"). See Augustinus Hipponensis, *Enarrationes in Psalmos*, 7, 4 (CCSL 38, ed. Eligius Dekkers and Jean Fraipont, p. 39, ll. 23–26).

85 No author cited.

86 Christine has taken her text here, translated closely, from *Manipulus florum*, "Misericordia," d, which combines two separate passages from Augustine's treatise devoted to the Sermon on the Mount: "Beatos esse dicit qui subueniunt miseris, quoniam eis ita rependitur, ut de miseria liberentur (…) Est autem iustum consilium, ut qui se a potentiore adiuuari uult, adiuuet infirmiorem in quo est ipse potentior." See Augustinus Hipponensis, *De sermone Domini in monte*, 1 (CCSL 35, ed. Almut Mutzenbecher, p. 5, ll. 100–101; p. 8, ll. 167–169).

87 Christine cites here the text found in *Manipulus florum*, including its incorrect attribution to Augustine rather than to Gregory the Great, "Gloria eterna," r: "Quae autem lingua dicere, uel quis intellectus capere sufficit illa supernae ciuitatis quanta sint gaudia, angelorum choris interesse, cum beatissimis spiritibus gloriae conditoris assistere, praesentem Dei uultum

cernere, incircumscriptum lumen uidere, nullo mortis metu affici, incorruptionis perpetuae munere laetari?" ("However, what tongue or what intellect would suffice to express how great the joys of the sovereign city are, with the chorus of angels, where the most blessed spirits are present as the authors of glory, seeing directly the face of God, beholding the uncircumscribed light, untouched by the fear of death, and rejoicing in the reward of perpetual incorruption?") See Gregorius Magnus, *Homiliae in euangelia*, 37, 1 (CCSL 141, ed. Raymond Étaix, p. 348, ll. 1–12).

88   Christine's source here, including its incorrect attribution to Gregory the Great rather than Bernard de Clairvaux, is *Manipulus florum*, "Spiritus sanctus," d: "Porro ad faciendum bonum quid in nobis bonus Spiritus operator? Profecto monet, et movet, et docet. Monet memoriam, rationem docet, movet voluntatem" ("Yet does not the good spirit [the Holy Spirit] move us to do good? Indeed it admonishes us, it moves us, and it teaches us: it admonishes our memory, it teaches us reason, it moves our will"). See Bernardus Claraeuallensis, *Sermones in die Pentecostes*, 1, 5 (SBO 5, ed. Jean Leclercq, C.H. Talbot, and H.M. Rochais, p. 163, ll. 13–14).

89   Christine follows *Manipulus florum*, "Confidencia," a: "Aduersaria est confidentia quae periculis uitam suam pro certo commendat, et lubrica spes est quae inter fomenta peccati saluari se sperat. Incerta victoria est inter hostilia arma pugnare, et impossibilis liberatio est flammis circumdari nec ardere" ("Willful is the assurance which, confronted with dangers, considers its life safe, and slippery is the hope that weens itself to be safe among the enticements of sin. That victory is uncertain which is fought in the midst of hostile arms, and impossible is the escape, when surrounded by flames, from being burned"). See Pseudo-Cyprianus Carthaginensis, *De singularitate clericorum*, 2 (CSEL 3.3, ed. Wilhelm Hartel, p. 175, ll. 6–9). The same work is cited in Allegories 1 and 67.

90   Christine excerpts Bernard de Clairvaux's remarks on the certainty of death from *Manipulus florum*, "Mors," as: "Quid vero in rebus humanis certius morte, quid hora mortis incertius invenitur? Non miseratur inopiam, non divitias reveretur, non generi cuiuslibet, non moribus, non ipsi denique parcit aetati" ("What indeed is more certain than death in human affairs, what can be found more uncertain than the hour of death? It takes no mercy on poverty, it does not respect riches, and lastly it takes no mercy on any gender whatsoever, on good morals, or on any age"). See Bernardus Claraeuallensis, *Sermo de conversione ad clericos*, 16 (SBO 4, ed. Jean Leclerq, C.H. Talbot, and H.M. Rochais, p. 90, ll. 5–9).

91   When Christine attributes to Saint Gregory an observation such as "the
      person who takes leave of his senses is like the juggler who finds no worse
      abode than his own, because he is always away from home," she seems to be
      invoking the quotation in Allegory 51, attributed to Hugh of Saint Victor,
      but actually from Pseudo-Bernardus Claravellensis, *Tractatus de interiori
      domo*. Since the Medieval Latin term for juggler, *ioculator*, is rarely attested
      before the mid-twelfth-century works of Petrus Cantor and of Hildegard of
      Bingen, the mid-thirteenth-century sermons of Guillaume d'Auvergne, and
      the late-thirteenth-century *Cronica* of Salimbene de Adam, the quotation
      here attributed to Saint Gregory is certainly spurious. It plays on the fact
      that *ioculatores* were members of wandering troupes, so that they had no
      fixed abode. The closest source would seem to be Stephanus de Borbone,
      Tractatus de diuersis materiis praedicabilibus, III, 4, 11, p. 128: "Eccli. 14 f:
      Beatus uir qui in sapientia morabitur, etc.; et ne sit sicut homo ioculator
      qui nunquam uel raro moratur in domo sua, ut ibi affligatur uidens multos
      eius defectus et in quibus non est facile consilium apponere" ("Sirach 14:22:
      Blessed is the man who will dwell in wisdom, etc., lest he be like a wander-
      ing juggler who never or rarely resides in his home, so that he does not have
      to be afflicted there seeing his many defects which are not easy to remedy").

92   The source for Christine's remarks on cupidity from Innocent III's popular
      treatise *On the Misery of the Human Condition* is *Manipulus florum*, "Cu-
      piditas," y: "Ignis inextinguibilis cupiditas insaciabilis! Quis unquam cupi-
      dus primo fuit voto contentus? Cum adipiscitur quod optaverat, desiderat
      ampliora semper in habendis et nunquam in habitis finem constituit. (…)
      'Sanguisuge due sunt filie dicentes: '*Affer, affer*' [Prou. 30:15]. Nam 'crescit
      amor nummi, quantum ipsa pecunia crescit'" ("Insatiable cupidity, an inex-
      tinguishable fire! When in the first place was a covetous man ever content
      with his longings? When he obtains what he had selected, he always desires
      having more and never finds an end in what he has already acquired. (…)
      There are two daughters of the bloodsucker which say, 'Give, give' [Prov.
      30.25]. For 'as money increases, so does the love of money' [Juvenal, *Satu-
      rae* 14:139]." See Innocent III, *De miseria condicionis humane*, ed. Robert
      E. Lewis (Athens: Georgia University Press, 1978), Part 2, section 6, p. 153,
      ll. 1–11. The Juvenal citation here had achieved proverbial status among
      Medieval Latin authors.

93   Christine has taken her remarks on concupiscence from *Manipulus florum*,
      "Mundus," d, which excerpts Augustine's second sermon on the First Epis-
      tle of John (1 John 2: 12–17): "Et mundus transit et concupiscencia [*recte*:
      desideria] (…) ejus: (…) Quid vis? utrum amare temporalia, et transire
      cum tempore; an mundum non amare, et in aeternum vivere cum Deo?"

("And the world passes away and its concupiscence as well. (…) What do you want? Either to love temporal things which pass away with time, or not to love the world and live with God in eternity?"). See Augustinus Hipponensis, *In epistolam Johannis ad Parthos tractatus*, 2, 2 (PL 35, col. 1994).

94   For Augustine's remarks on presumption, Christine has cited *Manipulus florum*, "Confidencia," c: "Nemo ergo de suo corde praesumat, quando profert sermonem; nemo de suis viribus confidat, quando suffert tentationem: quia et ut bona prudenter loquamur, ab illo est nostra sapientia; et ut mala fortiter perferamus, ab illo est nostra patientia" ("Therefore, no one should presume from the heart, when he speaks, no one should trust in his strength when he undergoes temptation, for, in order for us to speak wisely about good things, our wisdom comes from Him, and in order for us to endure strongly evil things, our patience comes from Him"). See Augustinus Hipponensis, *Sermones*, 276, 1 (PL 38, col. 1256).

95   It has not been possible to identify Christine's source for Saint Augustine: "the person who does not take care to avoid harm resembles a moth that turns around the lamplight until its wings are burnt and then drowns in the oil; and the bird that flies around the branch covered with glue so long that it loses its feathers." Both of its motifs, however, were well known from classical times onward, and are discussed below.

> (i) The moth drawn to the flame, a symbol of self-annihilation, has been used to represent both the recklessness of love and the Sufi mystical experience. The element of peril is emphasized in later emblems, such as the image of a candle with one moth flying into the flame and dead moths on the table below, and the inscription "Qui amat periculum in isto perit" ("He who loves danger perishes here"). Augustine uses the moth not in this respect, but rather—following Matthew 6:19–21—as a metaphor for the transitory nature of earthly goods and riches: see *On True Religion* [*De vera religione*], 3.4.

> (ii) By contrast, the image of the bird ensnared by a lime-covered branch was used by Augustine in a number of his writings. The work of a fowler is discussed in *The Teacher* [*De magistro*]. Later, in both *On the Profit of Believing* [*De utilitate credendi*], section 2, and *Confessions*, 3.6.10, the fowler represents the persuasive but dangerous Manicheans. In the former, the Manicheans are described as "crafty fowlers … who set branches smeared with bird-lime beside water to deceive thirsty birds."

As Gunner Mikkelsen points out, the use of birdlime—made from dried mistletoe berries blended with oil—was common in the Roman empire;

Pliny the Elder briefly explains its preparation and use in his *Natural History*, written ca. 77–79 CE. Mikkelsen notes (as cited below, 423) that "[s]nare imagery is prevalent in the Old Testament, especially the *Psalms* in which are mentioned the deliverance and escape from the snares of fowlers (*Ps.* 91.3 and 124.7)." And Ecclesiastes 9:12 extends this imagery: "as fishes are taken with the hook, and as birds are caught with the snare, so men are taken in the evil time." The "harm" that one must "take care to avoid," then, is spiritual, but it is described using a metaphor of everyday life that all would understand. See Gunner Mikkelsen, "Augustine and His Sources: The 'Devil's Snares and Birdlime' in the Mouths of Manichaeans in East and West," in *In Search of Truth: Augustine, Manichaeism and Other Gnosticism: Studies for Johannes van Oort at Sixty*, edited by Jacob Albert van den Berg et al. (Leiden and Boston: Brill, 2011), 419–25.

96   On the power of the Church and of the sacrament of baptism, Christine cites in part from *Manipulus florum*, "Ecclesia," a, which attributes to Augustine two excerpts from Ambrose and Fulgentius Ruspensis. Christine's source is ultimately the latter: "Sicut enim sine Ecclesiae catholicae societate nec baptismus alicui potest prodesse, nec opera misericordiae" ("For just as without the company of the Catholic Church and without baptism, no one can prosper, nor the works of mercy"). See Fulgentius Ruspensis, *De fide ad Petrum*, 44 (CCSL 91A, ed. Jean Fraipont, p. 741, ll. 904–909).

97   Christine abridges Jerome's arguments on the incompatibility of earthly and heavenly delights, *Manipulus florum*, "Prosperitas," g: "difficile, immo inpossibile, (…) ut de deliciis transeat ad delicias, (…) ut et in terra et in caelo appareat gloriosus" ("It is difficult, indeed impossible, […] to pass from delights to delights, to appear in glory both on earth and in heaven"). See Hieronymus Stridonensis, *Epistulae*, 118, 6 (CSEL 55, ed. Isidor Hilberg, p. 444, ll. 5–8).

98   Christine's source is *Manipulus florum*, "Ipocrisis," t: "Quid est uita hypocritae, nisi quaedam uisio phantasmatis quae hoc ostendit in imagine, quod non habet ex ueritate?" ("What is the life of a hypocrite but a fantastic vision which displays as an imitation what it does not truly possess?"). See Gregorius Magnus, *Moralia in Iob*, 15, 6 (CCSL 143A, ed. Marcus Adriaen, p. 752, ll. 2-4).

99   Christine cites here *Manipulus florum*, "Ignorancia," f, a chapter which in fact combines a brief excerpt from Jerome's Epistula 61 with a short extract from Bernard of Clairvaux's book on the "twelve" steps of humility, although Christine speaks instead of fifteen steps (a detail which, again, might help to identify the manuscript she used). The passage for Christine's

text is: "Frustra sibi de infirmitate vel ignorantia blandiuntur, qui ut liberius peccent, libenter ignorant vel infirmantur" ("Those who are gladly ignorant or weak in order to sin more freely delude themselves in vain with weakness or ignorance"). See *Liber de gradibus humilitatis et superbiae*, 19 (SBO 3, ed. Jean Leclerq, C.H. Talbot, and H.M. Rochais, p. 30, ll. 12–13).

100   Christine's source for the *Didascalicon* of Hugh of Saint Victor is *Manipulus florum*, "Studium," n: "Prudens igitur lector omnes libenter audit, omnia legit, non scripturam, non personam, non doctrinam spernit. Indifferenter ab omnibus quod sibi deesse videt quaerit, nec quantum sciat, sed quantum ignoret, considerat" ("Therefore the prudent reader freely listens to all people, reads all things, and scorns neither Scripture, nor person nor doctrine. He seeks equally from all people for what he sees himself to lack, and always has in mind how much he does not know, not how much he knows"). See Hugo de Sancto Victore, *Didascalicon de studio legendi*, ed. C.H. Buttimer (Washington, DC: Catholic University Press, 1939), Book 3, Chapter 13, p. 62, ll. 20–23. On Hugh of Saint Victor, see also the footnote to Allegory 51.

Bibliography

Texts by Christine de Pizan, with Selected Translations

Le chemin de longue étude. Edited by Andrea Tarnowski, with modern French translation on facing pages. Paris : Librairie générale française, 2000.

Le débat sur le Roman de la Rose. Edited and translated by Eric Hicks. Paris: Honoré Champion, 1977.

- *Le livre des epistres de debat sus le "Rommant de la Rose."* Edited by Andrea Valentini. Paris: Garnier, 2014. A new edition of the Debate on the *Romance of the Rose*, based on MS British Library Harley 4431, that reflects Christine's own ordering of the debate documents.
- *Debate of the* Romance of the Rose. Edited and translated by David F. Hult. Chicago: University of Chicago Press, 2010.
- *Le Débat sur le Roman de la Rose.* Modern French translation by Virginie Greene. Paris: Champion, 2006.

Debating the Roman de la Rose*: A Critical Anthology.* Edited by Christine McWebb. Introduction and Latin translations by Earl Jeffrey Richards. New York: Routledge, 2007. Reprint 2011.

Le ditié de Jehanne d'Arc. Edited and translated by Angus J. Kennedy and Kenneth Varty. Oxford: Society for the Study of Mediaeval Languages and Literature, 1977.

The Epistle of the Prison of Human Life with an Epistle to the Queen of France and Lament on the Evils of Civil War. Edited and translated by Josette A. Wisman. New York: Garland, 1984.

Epistre d'Othea. Edited by Gabriella Parussa. Geneva: Droz, 1999.

- *Christine de Pizan's Letter of Othea to Hector.* Translated by Jane Chance. Newburyport, MA: Focus Information Group, 1990.
- *Lettre d'Othéa, déesse de prudence, à un jeune chevalier, Hector.* Modern French translation and adaptation by Hélène Basso, with a preface by Jacqueline Cerquiglini-Toulet. 2 vols. Paris: Presses universitaires de France, 2008.

Le Livre des fais d'armes et de chevalerie/Das Buoch von dem vechten und der ritterschaft. Edited by Danielle Buschinger, Earl Jeffrey Richards, and Phillip Jeserich. Berlin: Berlin/Brandenburg Academy of Sciences. Forthcoming.

- *The Book of Deeds of Arms and of Chivalry.* Edited by Charity Cannon Willard. Translated by Sumner Willard. University Park: Pennsylvania State University Press, 1999.

Le livre de l'advision Cristine. Edited by Christine Reno and Liliane Dulac. Paris: Honoré Champion, 2001.

- *The Vision of Christine de Pizan.* Translated by Glenda McLeod and Charity Cannon Willard. Cambridge: D. S. Brewer, 2005.

Le livre de la cité des dames= La città delle dame. French edition by Earl Jeffrey Richards; Italian translation on facing pages by Patrizia Caraffi. Milan: Luni, 1997.

- *The Book of the City of Ladies.* Translated by Earl Jeffrey Richards. New York: Persea, 1982: 2nd revised edition, 1998.

Le livre de la mutacion de Fortune. Edited by Suzanne Solente. 4 vols. Paris: Picard, 1959–1966.

- Partial translation in Blumenfeld-Kosinski and Brownlee, *Selected Writings of Christine de Pizan*, 88–109.
- *The Book of the Mutability of Fortune.* Edited and translated by Geri L. Smith. Toronto: Iter Press; Tempe, AZ: Arizona Center for Medieval and Renaissance Studies, 2017.

The "Livre de la paix" of Christine de Pisan: A Critical Edition. Edited by Charity Cannon Willard. The Hague: Mouton, 1958.

- *The Book of Peace by Christine de Pizan.* Edited and translated by Karen Green, Constant J. Mews, and Janice Pinder. University Park: Pennsylvania State University Press, 2008.

Livre de la prod'hommie de l'homme. MS Vatican, Reg. lat. 1238.

Le livre des fais et bonnes meurs du sage roy Charles V. Edited by Suzanne Solente. 2 vols. Paris: Honoré Champion, 1936–1940. Reprint, Geneva: Slatkine, 1977.

- *Livre des faits et bonnes moeurs du sage roi Charles V.* Translated by Joël Blanchard and Michel Quereuil. Paris: Pocket, 2013.

Le livre des trois vertus. Edited by Eric Hicks. Introduction and notes by Charity Cannon Willard. Paris: Honoré Champion, 1989.

- *A Medieval Woman's Mirror of Honor: The Treasury of the City of Ladies.* Translated with an introduction by Charity Cannon Willard. Edited with an introduction by Madeleine Pelner Cosman. New York: Persea, 1989.
- *The Treasure of the City of Ladies, or the Book of the Three Virtues.* Revised edition. Translated with an introduction and notes by Sarah Lawson. New York: Penguin, 2003.

Le livre du corps de policie. Edited by Angus J. Kennedy. Paris: Champion, 1998.

- *The Book of the Body Politic.* Translated by Kate Langdon Forhan. Cambridge: Cambridge University Press, 1994.

Œuvres poétiques de Christine de Pisan. Edited by Maurice Roy. 3 vols. Paris: Firmin Didot, 1886–96. Reprint, New York: Johnson, 1965.

- A number of poems are translated in Blumenfeld-Kosinski and Brownlee, *Selected Writings of Christine de Pizan,* and Willard, *Writings of Christine de Pizan.*

The Selected Writings of Christine de Pizan. Edited by Renate Blumenfeld-Kosinski. Translated by Renate Blumenfeld-Kosinski and Kevin Brownlee. New York: W. W. Norton, 1997.

The Writings of Christine de Pizan. Edited by Charity Cannon Willard. New York: Persea, 1994.

Other Primary Sources

Ambrose, Saint. *Epistulae et acta.* Edited by Otto Faller. Vienna: Hoelder-Pinchler-Tempsky, 1968.

Arnulf of Orléans. *Allegorie super Ovidii Metamorphosin.* Edited by Fausto Ghisalberti. In "Arnolfo d'Orléans: Un cultore d'Ovidio nel secolo XII," *Memorie del reale istituto lombardo di scienze e lettere* 24 (1932): 157–234.

Augustine, Saint. *De moribus ecclesiae catholicae et de moribus Manichaeorum.* Edited by Johannes B. Bauer. Vienna: Hoelder-Pinchler-Tempsky, 1992.

Augustine of Dacia. *Augustini de Dacia O. P. "Rotulus pugillaris" examinatus atque editus.* Edited by Angelus Walz. Rome: Angelicum, 1929.

Benoît de Sainte-Maure. *Le roman de Troie.* Edited by Léopold Constans. 6 vols. Paris: Société des anciens textes français, 1904–1912.

Bersuire, Pierre [Petrus Berchorius]. "The 'Ovidius moralizatus' of Petrus Berchorius: An Introduction and Translation." Translated by William Donald Reynolds. PhD diss., University of Illinois at Urbana-Champaign, 1971.

Boccaccio, Giovanni. *Famous Women.* Edited and translated by Virginia Brown. Cambridge, MA: Harvard University Press, 2001.

Boethius. *The Consolation of Philosophy.* Trans. Victor Watts. Rev. ed. London: Penguin, 1999.

Deschamps, Eustace. *Œuvres complètes.* Edited by Auguste Queux de Saint-Hilaire and Gaston Raynaud. 11 vols. Paris: Firmin Didot, 1878–1903.

Dictys Cretensis and Dares Phrygius. *The Trojan War: The Chronicles of Dictys of Crete and Dares the Phrygian.* Translated by R. M. Frazer. Bloomington: Indiana University Press, 1966.

Évrart de Conty. *Le livre des eschez amoureux moralisés.* Edited by Françoise Guichard-Tesson and Bruno Roy. Montreal: CERES, 1993.

Fulgentius, Fabius Planciades. *The Mythologies.* In *Fulgentius the Mythographer,* edited and translated by Leslie G. Whitbread, 13–102. Columbus: Ohio State University Press, 1971.

Fulgentius metaforalis (John Ridewall). Edited by Hans Liebeschütz. Leipzig and Berlin: B. G. Teubner, 1926.

Les grandes chroniques de France. Edited by Jules Viard. 9 vols. Paris: Société de l'histoire de France, 1920–1937.

Gui de Cambrai (attributed). *Balaham und Josaphas.* Edited by Carl Appel. Halle: M. Niemeyer, 1907.

Guillaume de Tignonville. *Les dits moraux des philosophes.* Edited by Robert Eder. *Romanische Forschungen* 33 (1915): 851–1022.

Histoire ancienne jusqu'à César. Édition partielle. Edited by Marijke de Visser-van Terwiga. 2 vols. Orléans: Paradigme, 1995 and 1999. Does not include the Troy material.

Isidore of Seville. *Etymologiarium sive Originum Libri XX.* Edited by W. M. Lindsay. 2 vols. Oxford: Clarendon Press, 1911.

Jacobus de Voragine. *The Golden Legend.* Translated by William Granger Ryan. 2 vols. Princeton, NJ: Princeton University Press, 1995.

Mézières, Philippe de. *Une epistre lamentable et consolatoire adressée en 1397 à Philippe le Hardi, duc de Bourgogne, sur la défaite de Nicopolis, 1396.* Edited by Philippe Contamine and Jacques Paviot. Paris: Société de l'histoire de France, 2008.

———. *Letter to King Richard II: A Plea Made in 1395 for Peace between England and France.* Edited and translated by G. W. Coopland. Liverpool: Liverpool University Press, 1975. Includes text of Middle French *Epistre au roi Richart II.*

Ovide moralisé. Edited by Cornelis de Boer. *Verhandelingen der Koninklijke Akademie van Wetenschappen te Amsterdam: Afdeeling Letterkunde.* Vols. 15, 21, 30, 36–37, 43. Amsterdam, 1915–1938.

Paléologue, Théodore [Theodore Palaiologus]. *Les enseignements de Théodore Paléologue.* Translated by Jean de Vignay from Latin version into French. Edited by Christine Knowles. London: Modern Humanities Research Association, 1983.

Thomas, Aquinas, Saint. *In Psalmos reportatio.* Turnhout: Brepols Publishers, 2011. Based on ed. Parmensis, t. XIV (1863). <http://ezproxy.st-andrews.ac.uk/login?url=http://clt.brepolis.net/LLTA/pages/TextSearch.aspx?key=MTHAQRPS__>.

Thomas Hibernicus. *Manipulus florum.* Edited by Chris Nighman. *Digital Medievalist.* <http://web.wlu.ca/history/cnighman/>.

Secondary Sources

Adams, Tracy. *Christine de Pizan and the Fight for France.* University Park: Pennsylvania State University Press, 2014.

———. "Christine de Pizan, Isabeau of Bavaria, and Female Regency." *French Historical Studies* 32:1 (2009): 1–32.

Aitken, Marion Y. H. *Étude sur Le Miroir ou les Évangiles des domnées de Robert de Gretham.* Paris: Champion, 1922.

Altmann, Barbara K., and Deborah L. McGrady, eds. *Christine de Pizan: A Casebook.* New York and London: Routledge, 2003.

Anonymous [Wauchier de Denain?]. "La vraie histoire de Troye." Folios 48v°–58r°. In *Histoire ancienne jusqu'à César* [first redaction]. Manuscript Bibliothèque nationale de France, fonds français 246. Digitized in Gallica, the digital library of the Bibliothèque nationale de France, and cited here as *Histoire ancienne*: <http://gallica.bnf.fr/ark:/12148/btv1b8449715t/f120.image.r=Histoire%20ancienne%20246>.

Barton, David, Mary Hamilton, and Roz Ivanič, eds. *Situated Literacies: Theorising Reading and Writing in Context.* London: Routledge, 2000.

Beaune, Colette. *The Birth of an Ideology: Myths and Symbols of Nation in Late-Medieval France.* Translated by Susan Ross Huston. Edited by Fredric L. Cheyette. Berkeley and Los Angeles: University of California Press, 1991.

Becker, Philipp August. "Christine de Pizan." *Zeitschrift für französische Sprache und Literatur* 54 (1931): 129–64.

Bell, Susan Groag. *The Lost Tapestries of the* City of Ladies: *Christine de Pizan's Renaissance Legacy.* Berkeley and Los Angeles: University of California Press, 2004.

Blumenfeld-Kosinski, Renate. "Christine de Pizan and the Political Life in Late Medieval France." In *Christine de Pizan: A Casebook,* edited by Barbara K. Altmann and Deborah L. McGrady, 9–24. New York and London: Routledge, 2003.

———. "'Femme de corps et femme par sens': Christine de Pizan's Saintly Women." *Romanic Review* 87 (1996): 157–75.

———. "Overt and Covert : Amorous and Interpretive Strategies in the *Roman de la Rose.*" *Romania* 111 (1990): 432–53.

———. *Poets, Saints, and Visionaries of the Great Schism, 1378–1417.* University Park: Pennsylvania State University Press, 2006.

———. *Reading Myth: Classical Mythology and Its Interpretations in Medieval French Literature.* Stanford, CA: Stanford University Press, 1997.

———. "The Scandal of Pasiphaë: Narration and Interpretation in the 'Ovide moralisé.'" *Modern Philology* 93, no. 3 (1996), 307–26.

———. "Two Responses to Agincourt: Alain Chartier's *Livre des Quatre Dames* and Christine de Pizan's *Epistre de la Prison de la Vie Humaine.*" In *Contexts and Continuities: Proceedings of the IVth International Colloquium on Christine de Pizan, Glasgow 21–27 July 2000, Published in Honour of Liliane Dulac*, edited by Angus J. Kennedy et al., 3 vols., 1:75–85. Glasgow: University of Glasgow Press, 2002.

Brayer, Edith. "Contenu, structure et combinaisons du *Miroir du monde* et de la *Somme le roi.*" *Romania* 79 (1958): 1–38.

Brown-Grant, Rosalind. *Christine de Pizan and the Moral Defence of Women: Reading Beyond Gender.* Cambridge: Cambridge University Press, 1999.

Brownlee, Kevin. "Discourses of the Self: Christine de Pizan and the *Rose.*" *Romanic Review* 79 (1988): 199–221.

———. "Structures of Authority in Christine de Pizan's *Ditié de Jehanne d'Arc.* In Blumenfeld-Kosinski and Brownlee, *Selected Writings of Christine de Pizan*, 371–90.

———. "Widowhood, Sexuality, and Gender in Christine de Pizan." *Romanic Review* 86 (1995): 339–53.

Bühler, Curt F. "The Apostles and the Creed." *Speculum* 28 (1953): 335–39.

Campbell, P. G. C. *L'Épitre d'Othéa : Étude sur les sources de Christine de Pisan.* Paris: Champion, 1924.

Cerquiglini-Toulet, Jacqueline. "Christine de Pizan et le pouvoir du nom," *Le Moyen Français* 75 (2017): 3–17.

———. "Sexualité et politique: Le mythe d'Actéon chez Christine de Pizan." In *Une femme de lettres au Moyen Age: Etudes autour de Christine de Pizan*, edited by Liliane Dulac and Bernard Ribémont, 83–90. Orléans: Paradigme, 1995.

Chance, Jane. *Christine de Pizan's Letter of Othea to Hector.* Newburyport, MA: Focus, 1990.

———. "Franco-Italian Christine de Pizan's *Epistre Othea*, 1399–1401: A Feminized Commentary on Ovid." In Chance, *Medieval Mythography*, 3:206–71.

———. *Medieval Mythography.* Vol. 3, *The Emergence of Italian Humanism, 1321–1475.* Gainesville: University Press of Florida, 2015.

———, ed. *The Mythographic Art: Classical Fable and the Rise of the Vernacular in Early France and England.* Gainesville: University Press of Florida, 1990.

Chenu, Marie-Dominique. "'Involucrum': Le mythe selon les théologiens médiévaux." *Archives d'histoire doctrinale et littéraire du moyen âge* 22 (1955): 75–79.

Constable, Giles. "The Interpretation of Mary and Martha." In *Three Studies in Medieval Religious and Social Thought*, 1–141. Cambridge: Cambridge University Press, 1995.

Coulson, Frank T. "Ovid's *Metamorphoses* in the School Tradition of France, 1180–1400: Texts, Manuscript Tradition, Manuscript Settings." In *Ovid in the Middle Ages.* Edited by James C. Clark, Frank T. Coulson, and Kathryn L. McKinley, 48–82. Cambridge: Cambridge University Press, 2011.

Curry, Anne. *The Hundred Years War.* 2nd ed. New York: Palgrave Macmillan, 2003.

Curtius, Ernst Robert. *European Literature and the Latin Middle Ages.* Translated by Willard R. Trask. New York: Pantheon, 1953. Reprint, Princeton, NJ: Princeton University Press, 2013.

Demats, Paule. *Fabula: Trois études de mythographie antique et médiévale.* Geneva: Droz, 1973.

Dulac, Liliane, and Christine Reno. "L'humanisme vers 1400, essai d'exploration à partir d'un cas marginal: Christine de Pizan, traductrice de Thomas d'Aquin." In *Pratiques de la culture écrite en France au XVe siècle: Actes du Colloque international du CNRS, Paris, 16–18 mai 1992, organisé en l'honneur de Gilbert Ouy par l'unité de recherche "Culture écrite du Moyen Âge tardif,"* edited by Monique Ornato and Nicole Pons, 161–78. Louvain-la-Neuve: Fédération internationale des instituts d'études médiévales, 1995.

Ehrhart, Margaret J. *The Judgment of the Trojan Prince Paris in Medieval Literature.* Philadelphia: University of Pennsylvania Press, 1987.

Fenster, Thelma. "'Perdre son latin': Christine de Pizan and Vernacular Humanism." In *Christine de Pizan and the Categories of Difference,* edited by Marilynn Desmond, 91–107. Minneapolis: University of Minnesota Press, 1998.

Foulechat, Denis de. *Le Policratique de Jean de Salisbury, 1372, Livres I–III.* Edited by Charles Brucker. Geneva: Droz, 1994.

Gerson, Jean. *Canticordium.* In *La doctrine du chant du cœur de Jean Gerson. Édition critique, traduction et commentaire du 'Tractatus de canticis' et du 'Canticordum au pélerin,'* edited by Isabelle Fabre. Geneva: Droz, 2005.

———. *Œuvres françaises.* Vols. 7:1 and 7:2 (1966–68) of the *Œuvres complètes.* Edited by Palémon Glorieux. 10 vols. Paris: Desclée, 1960–1973.

Grandeau, Yann. "De quelques dames qui ont servi la reine Isabeau de Bavière." *Bulletin philologique et historique* (1975): 129–238.

Guenée, Bernard. *Un meurtre, une société: L'assassinat du duc d'Orléans, 23 novembre 1407.* Paris: Gallimard, 1992.

Guichard-Tesson, Françoise. "Évrart de Conty, auteur de la *Glose des echecs amoureux.*" *Le Moyen Français,* 8–9 (1982): 111–48.

Hindman, Sandra. *Christine de Pizan's "Epistre Othea": Painting and Politics at the Court of Charles VI.* Toronto: Pontifical Institute of Mediaeval Studies, 1986.

Hobbins, Daniel. "The Schoolman as Public Intellectual: Jean Gerson and the Late Medieval Tract." *American Historical Review* 108 (2003): 1308–1337.

Ignatius, Mary Ann. "Christine de Pizan's *Epistre Othea*: An Experiment in Literary Form." *Medievalia et Humanistica,* n.s. 9 (1979): 127–42.

Illich, Ivan. *In the Vineyard of the Text: A Commentary to Hugh's* Didascalion. Chicago: University of Chicago Press, 1993.

Jager, Eric. *Blood Royal: A True Tale of Crime and Detection in Medieval Paris.* New York: Little, Brown, 2014.

Jakobson, Roman. *Essais de linguistique générale.* Paris: Éditions de Minuit, 1963.

Kahn, Didier. "Recherches sur l'alchimie française des XVe, XVIe et XVIIe siècles." *Chrysopœia* 5 (1992–1996): 321–452.

———. "Un témoin précoce de la naissance du mythe de Flamel alchimiste: *Le Livre Flamel* (fin du XVe siècle)." In Kahn, "Recherches sur l'alchimie française des XVe, XVIe et XVIIe siècles," 387–429.

Kaminsky, Howard. "The Politics of France's Subtraction of Obedience from Pope Benedict XIII, 27 July 1398." *Proceedings of the American Philosophical Society* 115, no. 5 (1971): 366–97.

Kellogg, Judith L. "Christine de Pizan as Chivalric Mythographer: *L'Epistre d'Othea.*" In Chance, *The Mythographic Art,* 100–23.

Kennedy, Angus J. *Christine de Pizan: A Bibliographical Guide.* London: Grant and Cutler, 1984.

———. *Christine de Pizan: A Bibliographical Guide: Supplement 1.* London: Grant and Cutler, 1994.

———. *Christine de Pizan: A Bibliographical Guide: Supplement 2.* Rochester, NY: Tamesis, 2004.

Krynen, Jacques. *Idéal du prince et pouvoir royal en France à la fin du Moyen Âge, 1380-1440: Étude de la littérature politique du temps.* Paris: Picard, 1981.

Laidlaw, James L. "Christine de Pizan, the Earl of Salisbury, and Henry IV." *French Studies* 36, no. 2 (1982): 129–43.

Legrand, Jacques. *Archiloge Sophie et Livre des bonnes meurs.* Edited by Evencio Beltran. Paris: Champion, 1986.

Le Ninan, Claire. *Le sage roi et la clergesse: L'ecriture du politique dans l'œuvre de Christine de Pizan.* Paris: Honoré Champion, 2013.

Library of Latin Texts — Online. Brepols Publishers (2016). <http://www.brepols.net/Pages/BrowseBySeries.aspx?TreeSeries=LLT-O>.

Lorris, Guillaume de, and Jean de Meun. *Le Roman de la Rose.* Edited by Félix Lecoy. 3 vols. Paris: Champion, 1965–1970.

Machaut, Guillaume de. *La Fontaine amoureuse.* Edited by Jacqueline Cerquiglini-Toulet. Paris: Stock, 1993.

Maupeu, Philippe. *Pèlerins de vie humaine: Autobiographie et allégorie narrative de Guillaume de Deguileville à Octavien de Saint-Gelais.* Paris: Honoré Champion, 2009.

McGinn, Bernard. "*Teste David cum Sibylla:* The Significance of the Sibylline Tradition in the Middle Ages." In *Women of the Medieval World,* edited by Julius Kirshner and Suzanne F. Wemple, 7–35. Oxford: Basil Blackwell, 1985.

Mews, Constant J. "Latin Learning in Christine de Pizan's *Livre de paix.*" In *Healing the Body Politic: The Political Thought of Christine de Pizan,* edited by Karen Green and Constant J. Mews, 61–80. Turnhout: Brepols, 2005.

Newman, Barbara. *God and the Goddesses: Vision, Poetry, and Belief in the Middle Ages.* Philadelphia: University of Pennsylvania Press, 2003.

Oresme, Nicole. *Le livre de politiques d'Aristote.* Edited byAlbert Douglas Menut. Philadelphia: American Philosophical Society, 1970.

Ouy, Gilbert, Christine Reno, and Inès Villela-Petit. *Album Christine de Pizan.* Editeurs et collaborateurs, Olivier Delsaux and Tania van Hemelryck. Avec les conseils de James Laidlaw et Marie-Thérèse Gousset. Turnhout: Brepols, 2012.

Ovid. *Metamorphoses.* Edited and translated by Frank Justus Miller. Revised G. P. Goold. 2 vols. Cambridge, MA: Harvard University Press [Loeb Classical Library], 1916, 1982.

Pairet, Ana. *Les mutacions des fables: Figures de la métamorphose dans la littérature française du Moyen Age.* Paris: Champion, 2002.

Parussa, Gabriella. "Christine de Pizan: Une lectrice avide et une vulgarisatrice fidèle des *rumigacions du latin et des parleures des belles sciences.*" In *Traduction et adaptation en France à la fin du Moyen Âge et à la Renaissance: Actes du colloque organisé par l'Université de Nancy II, 23–25 mars 1995,* edited by Charles Brucker, 161–75. Paris: Champion, 1997.

Possamaï-Pérez, Marylène. *L'Ovide moralisé: Essai d'interprétation.* Paris: Champion, 2006.

Premierfait, Laurent de. *Livre de vieillesse.* Edited by Stefania Marzano. Turnhout: Brepols, 2009.

Richards, Earl Jeffrey. "*Les contraires choses*: Irony in Jean de Meun's Part of the *Roman de la Rose* and the Problem of Truth and Intelligibility in Thomas Aquinas." In *Nouvelles de la Rose: Actualité et perspectives du* Roman de la Rose, edited by Dulce María González Doreste and Maria del Pilar Mendoza-Ramos, 375–90. La Laguna: Servicio de Publicaciones, Universidad de La Laguna, 2011.

———. "*Glossa Aurelianensis est quae destruit textum*: Medieval Rhetoric, Thomism and Humanism in Christine de Pizan's Critique of the *Roman de la Rose.*" *Cahiers de recherches médiévales, XIIIe-XVe siècles* 5 (1998): 247–63.

———. "Introduction: Returning to a 'Gracious Debate': The Intellectual Context of the Epistolary Exchange of the Debate about the *Roman de la Rose.*" In McWebb and Richards, *Debating the* Roman de la Rose, xxi–xxxvi. New York: Routledge, 2007. Reprint, 2011.

——. "Political Thought as Improvisation: Female Regency and Mariology in Late Medieval French Thought." In *Virtue, Liberty, and Toleration: Political Ideas of European Women, 1400–1800*, edited by Jacqueline Broad and Karen Green, 1–22. Dordrecht: Springer, 2007.

——. "À la recherche du contexte perdu d'une ellipse chez Christine de Pizan: La 'coagulence regulee' et le pouvoir politique de la reine." In *Christine de Pizan, La scrittrice et la città / L'écrivaine et la ville / The Woman Writer and the City : Atti del VII Convegno Internazionale Christine de Pizan, Bologna, 22–26 settembre 2009*, edited by Patrizia Caraffi, 93–112. Florence: Alinea, 2013.

——. "In Search of a Feminist Patrology: Christine de Pizan and *les glorieux dotteurs*." In *Une femme de lettres au Moyen Âge: Études autour de Christine de Pizan*, edited by Liliane Dulac and Bernard Ribémont, 281–95. Orléans: Paradigme, 1995.

Rouse, Mary A., and Richard H. Rouse. "Prudence, Mother of Virtues: The *Chapelet des vertus* and Christine de Pizan." *Viator* 39 (2008): 185–228.

Seward, Desmond. *The Hundred Years War: The English in France, 1137–1453*. New York: Atheneum, 1978.

Seznec, Jean. *The Survival of the Pagan Gods: The Mythological Tradition and its Place in Renaissance Humanism and Art*. Translated by Barbara F. Sessions. New York: Pantheon, 1953. Reprint, Princeton, NJ: Princeton University Press, 1972.

Steadman, John M. "'Perseus upon Pegasus' and *Ovid Moralized*." *Review of English Studies* n.s. 9 (1958): 407–10.

Strubel, Armand. "*Grant senefiance a*": *Allégorie et littérature au Moyen Age*. Paris: Honoré Champion, 2002.

Tarnowski, Andrea. "Pallas Athena, la science et la chevalerie." In *Sur le chemin de longue étude…. Actes du colloque d'Orléans, juillet 1995*, edited by Bernard Ribémont, 149–58. Paris: Honoré Champion, 1998.

Tuve, Rosemond. *Allegorical Imagery: Some Mediaeval Books and Their Posterity*. Princeton, NJ: Princeton University Press, 1966.

Valois, Noël. *La France et le Grand Schisme d'Occident*. Vol. 3. Paris: Picard, 1901.

Wetherbee, Winthrop. *Platonism and Poetry in the Twelfth Century: The Literary Influence of the School of Chartres*. Princeton, NJ: Princeton University Press, 1972.

Wrisley, David J. "Modeling the Transmission of al-Mubashshir Ibn Fātik's *Mukhtār al-Ḥikam* in Medieval Europe: Some Initial Data-Driven Explorations." In "Digital Humanities in Jewish, Christian and Arabic/Islamic Ancient Traditions." Special issue, *Journal of Religion, Media, and Digital Culture* 5:1 (2016), 228–57.

Annotated Index of Proper Names and Places

This index aims to provide brief mythological explanations and to situate Christine's knowledge and use of myth within the context of her contemporaries' use of classical myths. With her mythological interpretations in *Othea*, Christine participated in a particular intellectual moment at the French court where mythological figures took on a political allegorical meaning, all in the context of a commentary on the dangers of civil strife. Equally striking here is how specific Christine's focus is on particular aspects of the mythographic tradition, and that her interpretations in their often arresting originality—not filtered through the sometimes more orthodox positions of such contemporary churchmen as Jacques Legrand, the confessor of King Charles VI, or of Jean Gerson—can now be more profitably read in light of their reception of classical mythology.

For this reason, this index has also tried to provide insights into Christine's sources in her selection of mythological figures which must be read alongside the sources of the allegories she supplies for them. Her allusions to classical mythology can be read, not only in terms of her primary sources, as indicated by Gabriella Parussa in her 1999 edition, namely the *Histoire ancienne jusqu'à César* and the *Ovide moralisé*, but also in comparison with references to classical mythology in Nicole Oresme's translations of Aristotle, Denis de Foulechat's translation of John of Salisbury's *Policraticus*, Évrart de Conty's *Livre des eschecs amoureux moralisés* and Jacques Legrand's *Archiloge Sophie* and *Livre de Bonnes Meurs*. Many of the mythological figures in the *Ovide moralisé* and *Histoire ancienne* were invoked in Dante's *Commedia*, which Christine knew quite well, so that sometimes the question of a single direct source for any particular mythological figure becomes moot. At the same time, one specific feature of the reception of classical mythology by Christine's contemporaries needs to be stressed: Évrart de Conty often offers extensive discussions of mythological figures followed by a "moral interpretation," and Jacques Legrand gives a list of various moral topics illustrated by mythological figures. In the gloss sections of the *Othea*, Christine has streamlined and systematized these two approaches. Moreover, as the cross-references given here, both to Christine's use of sapiential figures, inspired by Guillaume de Tignonville's *Dits moraux*, and to her subsequent mythological allusions in the *Mutacion de Fortune* and the *Cité des Dames* reveal, the *Othea* marks the beginning of an ongoing and profound reception of classical mythology on Christine's part which requires additional scrutiny in the future.

Earl Jeffrey Richards

Achilles, 31, 36, 40, 60, 68, 71, 81, 85, 92, 93. Hero of the Trojan War. Christine's source was the *Histoire ancienne, passim.*

Acis, 59. A young Sicilian shepherd, son of the god Faustus (Pan) and the nymph Symaethis, and the lover of Galatea. In Ovid's account (*Metamorphoses* 13:750–897; *Ovide moralisé*, 13:3726–4147), Galatea changes Acis into a river spirit to save him from the jealous Cyclops Polyphemus. Christine omits this detail. *See* Galatea.

Actaeon, 69, a famous hero of Thebes, who offended the goddess Artemis and was punished by being turned into a stag who was then torn apart by his own hunting dogs. The source here is the *Ovide moralisé*, 3:341–570, although Jean Gerson in his famous sermon from 1413 against Jean Petit's defense of the murder of Louis d'Orléans as tyrannicide—to whom the *Othea* was dedicated—alludes to the story as well (*Œuvres françaises*, vol. 7:2, p. 1020: Appliquons l'histoire Actheon qui fu devoré de ses chiens, "let us apply the story of Actheon devoured by his dogs").

Adonis, 65. A youth beloved of Venus. The classic version is found in Ovid, *Metamorphoses*, 10:298–518, and is commented upon. not only in the *Ovide moralisé*, 10:1960–2493, but also in Évrart de Conty's *Eschecs moralisés*, p. 403–422. Christine is the only author to spell his name as "Adonius."

Adrastus, 46, 50. King of Argos during the legendary Theban civil war (the topic of Aeschylus' *Seven Against Thebes*, 467 BCE). Adrastus is mentioned in the *Cité des Dames* (II.17) and the *Mutacion de Fortune* (vv. 12,479–13,339, always in the cautionary context of the dangers of civil disorder). Christine's source was the *Histoire ancienne.*

Aeolus, 79. The mythological god of the wind.

Aglauros, 18. Daughter of the mythic king of Athens Cecrops. The story of her jealousy is told by Ovid, *Metamorphoses* 2:708–832, and is otherwise only attested in the *Ovide moralisé*, 2:3974–4086, and the *Othea. See* Herse.

Ajax Telamonius, 66. Ajax, son of Telamon, was one of Greek generals during the siege of Troy.

Alcyone, 79. Legendary wife of Ceyx, and the two were a legendary couple of happy lovers who provoked the anger of Zeus in ancient mythology. Christine's account, while loosely based on Ovid, *Metamorphoses*, 11:410–748, via the *Ovide moralisé*, 11:3003–3787, is highly original, see the note on Chapter 79.

Alexander (the Great), 1, 28, 44, 75, 90. Alexander the Great (356–323 BCE).

Amazonia, 15, 57. The Kingdom of the Amazons, also mentioned in the *Cité des Dames*, 1:4 (*le royaume d'Amasonie*). *See also* Feminia.

Ambrose, Saint, 3, 10, 11, 79. 4th-century Bishop of Milan and one of the four (original) Doctors of the Church.

Amor, 22; [Cupid] 38, 47, 59, 84; [Love] 56. The god of love.

Amphiaraus, 50. In classical mythology, the brother-in-law of Adrastus, and with him, King of Argos, and famous as a seer. Christine's source is the *Histoire ancienne*. The spelling of the name as "Ampharos") is attested only there, in the *Othea* and the *Mutacion de Fortune* (vv. 12853–13053). The Latin form of the name is attested on in the *Roman d'Eneas*, a twelfth-century romance based on Virgil's *Aeneid*.

Andrew, Saint, 26. The Apostle Andrew, brother of Simon Peter.

Andromache, 88. The wife of Hector, attested in the *Histoire ancienne*, in Denis Foulechat, *Policratique* (pp. 158–159) and in Christine's *Cité des Dames*, 2:28, and *Mutacion de Fortune, passim*.

Andromeda, 5. In classical mythology, the daughter of Cepheus and Cassiopeia, rulers of Ethiopia. Cassiopeia boasted of her daughter's beauty and provoked the wrath of Poseidon who sent a sea monster to ravage the country. The oracle of Apollo said that Cepheus would have to sacrifice his daughter to stop this monster, whereupon she was chained to rock on the coast. The hero Perseus rescued her and killed the monster. Interestingly, Christine's orthography varies between "Andromada" and "Andromeda": the former is found in Oresme's translation of Aristotle's *Politics*, the latter is favored by Jacques Legrand (tutor and later confessor of Charles VI) in his *Archiloge Sophie*.

Antenor, 95. Counselor of Priam, King of Troy and proverbial traitor.

Apollo, 8, 9 (as "Phoebus or Apollo"), 40, 52, 53, 55, 81, 87 (as "Phoebus Apollo"). Pagan god associated with music, prophecy, light and wisdom. In chapter 40, Christine uses the rare variant "Appollin"

which she also uses seven times in the *Mutacion de Fortune*. The likely source for both chapters is the *Ovide moralisé*. See also Phoebus.

Apthalin, 22, a pagan sage whose name is only attested here and whose identity remains a mystery. There is no mention of this sapiential author in Tignonville's *Dits moraux* which would seem like the most likely source, and the citation attributed to him is remarkable because Christine uses the relatively rare word *impertinent/impartinent*, "impertinent."

Apulia, 68. The "heel" of the Italian boot in southeast Italy.

Arachne, 64. In classical mythology, Arachne was a mortal who challenged the goddess Athena to a weaving contest, and of course lost. Christine has taken the story from the *Ovide moralisé*, 6:1–318 (based on *Metamorphoses*, 6:1–145), but has dropped the story of the competition.

Argos, 46, 50. The city of Argos on the Peloponnese peninsula in Greece.

Argus, 30. In Greek mythology, Argus was the hundred-eyed giant who guarded the nymph Io, whom Zeus had transformed into a heifer to hide her from his wife. Christine's source was the *Ovide moralisé* (*see* Io), but the story is discussed by Évrart de Conty in a separate chapter in the *Eschecs moralisés* (pp. 256–258) and Jacques Legrand in his *Archiloge Sophie* (p. 333). *See* Io. The metaphor must have been common, for in his famous September 1413 sermon against Jean Petit after the assassination of Louis d'Orléans (*see* Louis d'Orléans), Gerson says that

University of Paris has more eyes than Argus, more than one hundred, nay a thousand views" (7:2, p. 1027, "l'Université a plus d'yeux que Argus, plus de cent regard, voir de mil").

Aristotle, 1, 4, 5, 24, 28, 44, 63, 75, 90, 94, 98, 99. The Greek philosopher Aristotle whom Christine frequently cites in her other works, including her earlier *Cent Balades*.

Asclepius, 39. Legendary god of medicine. Christine is the only medieval French writer to spell his name "Esculappion," closer to the Latin spelling "Aesculapius." Évrart de Conty devotes an entire chapter to him (*Eschecs moralisés*, pp. 340–345) and Jacques Legrand speaks of "Esculapius" three times (pp. 161, 162, 210). No classical source connects the medical knowledge of Asclepius to an antidote to Circe's potion.

Assaron, 79. An ancient philosopher cited as *Assoron* in Guillaume de Tignonville's *Dits moraux* (pp. 995–96), whose identity remains a mystery.

Assyria, 78. Assyria.

Atalanta, 72. A virgin huntress in ancient mythology. Christine's source was the *Ovide moralisé*. Christine's contemporary Jacques Legrand also mentions her in the *Archiloge Sophie*.

Athamas, 17. In ancient mythology, the king of Boetia in central Greece, whose capital was Thebes. Athamas is mentioned in both the *Ovide moralisé* 4:3835–3963, and Évrart de Conty's *Eschecs moralisés* (p. 392), but Christine has modified her source. *See* Ino, Madness, goddess of.

Athena, *see* Minerva, Pallas.

Athens, 18. The city of Athens.

Atropos, 24. One of the three Fates or *Moirai* of Greek mythology. Her sister Clotho spun the thread of a mortal's life, her other sister Lachesis measured its length, and Atropos finally cut the thread.

Augustine, Saint, 1, 2, 5, 17, 18, 20, 35, 36, 37, 38, 39, 41, 42, 43, 44, 46, 48, 62, 64, 66, 67, 69, 70, 72, 73, 80, 84, 89, 93, 94, 95, 96. Saint Augustine of Hippo (354–430), one of the Doctors of the Church, whom Christine cites from the *Manipulus Florum*.

Augustus, Caesar, 100. The Roman Emperor Augustus (63 BCE–14 CE).

Aurora, 44. The mythological goddess of the dawn. Christine's source seems to be the *Ovide moralisé*, 13:2321, but she has confused two warriors killed by Achilles during the Trojan War, Cygnus (who was not her son, but whose name means "swan" in Greek) and Memnon (who was, and whose ashes were changed into birds).

Babylon, 9. The city of Babylon.

Bacchus, 21. In Greek mythology Bacchus is the god of wine, associated with gluttony and debauchery. Following her regular euhemerist practice (that is, assuming myths had their origins in actual historical events or individuals), she has turned the mythological god Bacchus in her source, the *Ovide moralisé*, into a mortal.

Bartholomew, Saint, 29. The Apostle Bartholomew.

Basil of Caesarea, 72. Basil of Caesarea, or Saint Basil the Great, was a

subsequently believe her proph-
ecies. Cassandra was a common
mythological figure.

Cassiodorus, 7, 15, 60. Late Roman
statesman (ca. 485-ca. 585), who
retired from public life to found
a monastery called "Vivarium,"
as an island of literary culture in
a sea of barbarism. He wrote an
exposition of the Psalms during
this later period which Christine
cites from the *Manipulus florum*.
See Appendix on allegories for the
pertinent chapters.

Cecrops, 18. Mythological king of Ath-
ens. *See* Aglauros, Herse.

Cephalus, 76. A legendary hunter in
Greek mythology, whose involve-
ment with his wife Procris and his
lover, Eos, the goddess of dawn,
has been greatly abbreviated in
Christine's account. Upon recon-
ciling with Procris, she gave him a
javelin that never missed its mark.
While hunting, Cephalus hears
noise in the underbrush, threw
the javelin, and killed Procris. The
episode is mentioned once in the
Ovide moralisé, but six times in
Jacques Legrand's *Archiloge Sophie*
under the rubrics of "new love"
and "chastity" (p. 182–83).

Cerberus, 3, 21, 70. The mythological
(three-headed) dog who guarded
the gates of Hell. Christine had
already mentioned Cerberus in
Cent Ballades, 52, and he is men-
tioned twelve times by Évrart
de Conty in the *Eschecs morali-
sés*. Christine was aware of many
sources (including Dante) for the
story of Orpheus and Eurydice so
that her references to Cerberus
cannot be assigned to a single
source.

Ceres, 3, 24. The traditional Roman
goddess of agriculture. Besides
being mentioned frequently in
the *Ovide moralisé*, 7:2808–3271.
Ceres is discussed by Christine
in the *Cité des Dames*, by Évrart
de Conty in the *Eschecs moralisés*
and Jacques Legrand in the *Archi-
loge Sophie*.

Ceys, 79. A legendary king of the an-
cient Greek kingdom of Thessaly,
and husband of Alcyone. Chris-
tine's version is only loosely based
on the versions in the *Ovide mo-
ralisé*, 11:3003–3787, and in the
Fontaine amoureuse (vv. 692–97)
of Machaut.

Charles [V], Prologue. Charles V, King
of France from 1364 to 1380, who
was the patron of Christine's fa-
ther, Thomas de Pizan.

Charon, 70. The ferryman of Hades, a
name rarely attested in medieval
French sources, but found in Fou-
lechat's *Policratique*, III.

Christine [de Pizan], Prologue. Chris-
tine de Pizan herself, in subse-
quent works she will speak of her-
self much more frequently.

Chrysostom, Saint John, 9, 13, 55, 76.
Influential early Father of the
Church (ca. 349–407), famed for
his eloquence (his cognomen
means "golden-mouthed") whose
Greek writings circulated in Latin
translations throughout western
Europe.

Circe, 39, 98. Legendary enchantress
best known for turning Odysseus'
crew into swine. Christine alludes
only in passing in Chapter 39 to
this metamorphosis, and com-
ments on it much more extensive-
ly in Chapter 98.

Cleopatra, 45. The only medieval French source which attributes medicinal skills to Cleopatra (60–39 BCE), the last Ptolemaic ruler of Egypt, is Guillaume de Tignonville in his *Dits moraux* (ed. Eder, p. 1006, *Et [Galien] aprist medicine d'une femme, appellee Cleopatre, laquelle estoit moult sage et lui monstra moult de bonnes herbes*, "And [Galen] learned medicine from a woman named Cleopatra, who was very wise and showed him many good herbal remedies").

Colchis, 37, 80. An ancient Georgian kingdom on the eastern shore of the Black Sea.

Coronis, 48, 52. A mortal woman whom Apollo loved, mother of Asclepius. Based on a white raven's report to Apollo that Coronis had been unfaithful to him, Apollo had her killed. The story is reported in both the *Ovide moralisé*, 2:2143–2199, and Évrart de Conty's *Eschecs moralisés* (pp. 340, 345, 532, 621).

Crete, 4, 8. The island of Crete.

Cygnus, 44. A mythological figure from the Trojan War whose mother Christine mistakenly identifies as Aurora.

Cyprus, 7. The island of Cyprus in the Mediterranean. Christine speaks of a Queen of Cyprus named Venus, for which there is no historical corroboration, although Cyprus was the traditional birthplace of Venus.

Cyrus, 57. Cyrus the Great, King of Persia (ca. 600–530 BCE).

Daphne, 87. In classical mythology, a nymph, who, fleeing Apollo's advances, appealed for help to Diana, goddess of virginity, and was then turned into a laurel tree. Christine's spelling of the name ("Damné") is attested only in the *Othea*. Daphné's name itself is otherwise only attested in medieval French literature in the *Ovide moralisé*, 1:2737–3064, where it is spelled "Dané."

David, 7, 8, 44, 46, 51, 67, 87, 89, 96. David, King of Israel, who lived around the year 1000 BCE, whose psalms are a frequent source for Christine in all her writings.

Delphi, 81. The city of Delphi which housed the oracle of Apollo, and mentioned five times as well by Christine in the *Mutacion de Fortune*.

Democritus, 2. Pre-Socratic philosopher from the 5 century BCE. First attested in the translations of Aristotle's works by Oresme, Christine mentions him as well in the *Chemin de long estude*, the *Advision* and the *Livre de Policie*, and Gerson mentions him four times in his sermons.

Diana 23, 55, 63, 69, 87. In classical mythology, Diana was the virgin goddess of the hunt, of the moon and of childbirth.

Diogenes, 12, 26. An ancient Greek philosopher (410–323 [?] BCE) renowned for his refusal to flatter the ruling powers. Diogenes is frequently mentioned in the works of Christine's contemporaries, Philippe de Mézières, Évrart de Conty (*Eschecs moralisés*, pp. 503–508) and Jacques Legrand (*Archiloge Sophie*, p. 38), but hardly ever before them, which suggests he represented (as an anecdote recounted by Christine in her biography of Charles V, III.22) the figure of a wise counselor who spoke truth to power.

Diomedes, 84. King of Argos, hero of the Trojan War. *See* Argos.

Discord, goddess of, 60. In classical mythology, Discord (Latin, *Discordia*, Greek, *Eris*) is the goddess of discord and strife. Her most famous "appearance" in European literature was at the wedding of Peleus and Thetis, when, uninvited, she tossed a golden apple "for the fairest" among the invited guests. The earliest medieval French account of the Judgment of Paris itself is found at the opening of the *Roman d'Eneas*, which does not speak of the goddess of Discord. The first example of a "Goddess of Discord" in medieval French literature seems to turn up at vv. 1908–1910 of Guillaume de Machaut's *La fontaine amoureuse* from 1361 (p. 146), which was one of Christine's sources besides the *Ovide moralisé*, 11:1242–2131. Évrart de Conty, in turn, devotes an entire chapter of the *Eschecs moralisés* (pp. 348–370) to the Judgment of Paris and speaks as well of *la pomme de discorde* thrown into the wedding part by *Envie qui est deesse de discorde* (p. 360, "Envy, who is the goddess of discord").

Echo, 86. The legendary nymph who fell in love with Narcissus. Christine's direct source for her text is the *Ovide moralisé*, 3:1342–1463, but her allegorical explanation of Echo departs radically from her source.

Egypt, 47, 48. Egypt.

Envy, goddess of, 18. In classical mythology, Envy (Latin "Invidia," [feminine], Greek either "Nemesis" [feminine] or "Phthonos" [masculine]) the personified (but very minor) goddess of Envy. Christine's source here is the *Manipulus florum*. See the comments in the Appendix on Christine's sources for her allegories in Chapter 18.

Epicureans, 74. An ancient school of philosophy in which pleasure was held to be the highest good.

Eteocles, 46. The legendary King of Thebes, son of Oedipus and Jocasta, who fought a bitter civil war with his brother Polynices.

Eurydice, 70. A nymph beloved by Orpheus who tried to bring her back from Hades after her death. *See* Orpheus.

Feminia, 57. Another term for the Kingdom of the Amazons, also used in *Cité des Dames*, 2:12. (*ores est un nouvel royaume de Femenie encommencié*, "now the new kingdom of Feminia has begun").

Flamel, Nicolas. *See* Nicolas [Flamel].

Fortune, 74, 97. The goddess Fortune whose role in human history plays a central role in Christine's *Mutacion de Fortune*.

Galatea, 59. A sea-nymph, beloved of Acis.

Galathea, 1. A war-horse, given to Hector originally mentioned in the Roman de Troie and the "second redaction" of the *Histoire ancienne*, which are the only medieval sources to name this war-horse (no classical author does).

The latter seems to be Christine's source when she mentions this war horse again in the *Mutacion de Fortune*, vv. 16343–345.

Galen, 45. Famous 2nd-century Greek physician. Christine invokes indirectly his much disputed theory of female semen in the story of her birth in the *Mutacion de Fortune*. Her father, she explains, wanted a boy, "but he failed in this intent, for my mother, who had much greater power than he, so much wanted to have a female who resembled her that I was born a girl" (vv. 388–392: "Mais il failli a son entente, / Car ma mere, qui ot pouoir / Trop plus que lui, si voult avoir / Femelle a elle ressemblable, / Si fus nee fille").

Ganymede, 53. Cupbearer of the Olympian gods. Christine has confused the tale of Hyacinthus (*Ovide moralisé*, 10:852–878) with that of Ganymede (*Ovide moralisé*, 10:738–752). In classical mythology Hyacinthus was the mortal lover of Apollo and was killed when he tried to catch a discus thrown by Apollo.

Geber, 6. Jabir ibn Hayyan, 8th-century Persian-born Arabic alchemist.

Gorgon, 55. Gorgon (in this case, Medusa, whom Christine does not name). *See* Perseus.

Greece, 3, 19, 21, 43, 46, 54, 68, 77, 80, 83. Greece.

Greeks, 1, 15, 43, 61, 66, 71, 81, 84, 93, 95, 96. The Greeks.

Gregory, Saint, 8, 12, 21, 45, 50, 52, 53, 61, 68, 75, 82, 87, 88, 91, 98. Saint Gregory the Great, Pope from 590–694. Doctor of the Church and one of Christine's favorite patristic authors.

Hector, Prologue, 1, 3, 11, 13, 15, 36, 40, 77, 85, 88, 90, 91, 92, 93. In classical mythology the oldest son of King Priam and Queen Hecuba of Troy, killed in a duel with Achilles. For Christine Minerva is turned into the mother of Hector who represents the epitome of chivalry.

Hecuba, 13, 40, 93. Hecuba, Queen of Troy and wife of King Priam.

Helen, 43, 68, 73, 80. Helen, wife of King Menelaos of Sparta, whose abduction sparked the Trojan War.

Helenus, 77. Helenus, son of King Priam and Queen Hecuba of Troy, also mentioned several times.

Hercules, 3, 27, 37, 66. In traditional mythology, Hercules was the son of Zeus, renowned for his strength. Christine humanizes him and makes him a valorous Greek knight.

Hermaphroditus, 82. In traditional mythology, Hermaphroditus was a beautiful youth, the son of Hermes and Aphrodite (his name combines theirs). The nymph Salmacis fell in love with him, and while he was bathing in a pool, she accosted him, the only nymph rapist, wrapping her body around his and praying to the gods that the two be united forever. Her prayer was granted. Christine's immediate source was the *Ovide moralisé*, 4:1997–2223. For Christine the alchemist interpretation of the myth appears to be the most pertinent, according to which mercury is viewed as the prime matter or *prima materia* with hermaphroditic qualities.

kingdom in the west central part of Anatolia, and was legendary for two things: "his golden touch" and his donkey ears, which—according to the traditional tale which Christine had changed—he earned when he challenged Apollo to a trial of musical skill and lost. The tale of the donkey ears is told by Évrart de Conty, Jacques Legrand, and Gerson (in his *Canticordium*, ed. Fabre, p. 512: *fabulosus Midas cum auribus asininis*, "the legendary Midas with donkey ears").

Minerva, 1, 13, 14, 90, 96. In traditional mythology, Minerva (the Latin equivalent of the Greek goddess Athena) represented the goddess of wisdom. In the Greek tradition, *Athena Parthenos* ("Athena the Virgin") was also the goddess of arms and military strategy. The combination of these attributes is the fundamental subtext not only of the *Othea* but also of the later *Book of Feats of Arms and Chivalry*. See Pallas.

Minos, 4. Minos was the legendary King of Crete who demanded a tribute of seven young men and women to be fed to the Minotaur who resided in a labyrinth created by the legendary artist Daedalus. After his death he became the judge of the dead in hell, as in Dante's Inferno. While Minos and his labyrinth are mentioned by Machaut, Évrart de Conty and Jacques Legrand, they do not speak of his as the judge of the dead as does Dante. Significantly, Christine explains this role as judge as an example of allegorical covering (*couverture*), which she explains with the metaphor of a tree's bark or a fruit's peel in Chapter 82.

Minotaur, 45. The Minotaur was a half-human, half-bull monster, born of the union of Pasiphaë, the wife of Minos, with a bull, who resided in a maze-like labyrinth.

Morpheus, 78. Morpheus was the Greek god of dreams, the son of Hypnos, the god of sleep.

Myrmidons, 68. The collective noun for the soldiers who served under Achilles during the Trojan War.

Narcissus, 16, 86. In classical mythology Narcissus was a beautiful youth and known for his overweening pride which led him to reject all potential lovers. In the Ovidian version of the tale (which Christine could have read in the *Ovide moralisé* and most certainly knew from the *Roman de la Rose*) the nymph Echo falls in love with Narcissus who rebuffs her. Then Nemesis, the goddess of revenge, let Narcissus fall in love with his own image reflected in a pool. In some versions he commits suicide, in other versions he drowns when he tries to embrace his reflection. Christine focuses narrowly on the Narcissus' haughtiness.

Neptune, 33. The tradition god of the sea in classical mythology.

Nicolas [Flamel], 6. A contemporary alchemist, Nicolas Flamel (1330–1418), who was also a prominent Parisian scribe as well as alchemist. See Introduction.

Nimrod, 89. According to Genesis 10:10, Nimrod reigned over the cities of Babel, Erech, Akkad and

Calneh "in the land of Shinar [Mesopotamia]". He was traditionally considered the builder of the Tower of Babel. The form of the name used by Christine, *Nambrot*, is found only in her works—by contrast, in his *Epistre lamentable* (pp. 108–109), Philippe de Mézières speaks of "*Neuroch*, le premier roy tirant qui edifia la tour de Babel," ("Nimrod, the first tyrant kind who built the tower of Babel")—although Christine mentions him seven times in the *Mutacion de Fortune. See* Ninus.

Ninus, 89. The legendary founder of the city of Nineveh. Christine claims that he conquered Nimrod, and the only medieval French source which even connects these two figures was Philippe de Mézières' *Epistre lamentable* (pp. 108–109), which speaks of the decline of the virtues associated with chivalry in the times of Nimrod and Ninus. The decline of chivalry was a recurrent subtext of the *Othea. See* Nimrod.

Origen, 14, 16. Origen (ca. 184–ca. 254 CE) was an influential Father of the Church, based in Alexandria.

Orpheus, 67, 70. During the late Middle Ages, Orpheus was a frequently cited ancient Greek lyric poet, and his descent into Hades to retrieve Eurydice was often seen as a pagan allegory of the harrowing of Hell. In a work like the *Othea* so clearly intended to deliver a clear notion of allegory, it is striking that Christine ignores Orpheus as a "type" of Christ and instead focuses only on his qualities as a lyric poet.

Othea, *passim.* Christine invents the figure of Othea as a goddess of wisdom (a term she uses in the first chapter). See Introduction and notes.

Pallas, 14, 52, 60, 64, 73. Pallas Athena represented the sapiential aspects of this ancient goddess. *See* Minerva.

Pan, 26. In classical mythology Pan was the god of shepherds and of "rustic" music (the music of the "Pan flute" as opposed to the Apollo's lyre).

Paris, 40, 43, 60, 68, 73, 75, 77, 80. Paris was the youngest son of King Priam of Troy, whose first claim to fame was "the judgment of Paris" where he had to decide which of the three goddesses Hera, Athena and Aphrodite was the most beautiful. Promised the most beautiful mortal woman by Aphrodite, Paris decided in her favor, and then abducted Helen from Sparta, sparking the Trojan War. Later, during the war, he killed Achilles. Christine alludes to all these legends surrounding Paris. See note to Chapter 60.

Pasiphaë, 45. In Greek mythology, the daughter of Helios, the sun god, and wife of Minos, King of Crete. When Minos failed, as promised, to sacrifice a white bull to Poseidon, the sea god, Poseidon cursed Pasiphaë to fall in love with the bull, the "dissolute" passion of which Christine speaks. In order to copulate with him, Pasiphaë had the artist Daedalos (of labyrinth fame) construct an artificial cow that she could slip into. The fruit of this union was the

Christine's source for her allusion to him.

Pygamalion, 22. Pygmalion was a famous sculptor in Cyprus. Christine takes the details of the story from the *Ovide moralisé*.

Pyramus, 38. In the Ovidian tradition, Pyramus was the lover of his neighbor Thisbe, probably best known in the English-speaking world for its being a play within a play in Shakespeare's *A Midsummer Night's Dream*.

Pyrrhus, 31. Pyrrhus (usually called Neoptolemus) was the son of Achilles. Pyrrhus went to Troy to avenge his father. While Christine's likely source here may have been the *Ovide moralisé,* 13:1343–48, which mentions only this detail, she tells the story of Pyrrhus in much greater detail in the *Mutacion de Fortune* (vv. 19,135–19,336) and in the *Cité des Dames*, 1:19.

Pythagoras, 6, 16, 17, 34, 60. Ancient Greek philosopher and mathematician (ca. 570-ca. 495 BCE), to whom the "Pythagorean theorem" is attributed. Christine cites nearly verbatim various sayings attributed to Pythagoras in Guillaume de Tignonville's *Dits moraux*, (pp. 928–932), that is, she regarded him primarily as a sapiential author, although he was also particularly known for his theories on harmony in music. Besides Tignonville, Pythagoras is mentioned by other contemporaries of Christine at the royal court include Jacques Legrand (*Bonnes meurs*, p. 382), Laurent de Premierfait (*Livre de Vieillesse*, pp. 46, 79, 91, 145, 155), Gerson and Évrart de Conty (*Eschecs moralisés*, pp. 58, 140, 160, 208). Christine refers to Pythagoras in different contexts related to this broad contemporary reception of his work in the *Advision*, her biography of Charles V, the *Livre de Policie* and the *Livre de Paix*.

Salmacis, 92. The name of a legendary nymph and her fountain, where Hermaphroditus was bathing when she tried to rape him and the two were transformed into a single body with both male and female sexual characteristics.

Saturn, 6, 8, 51. In Latin mythology, Saturn was the father of the other Olympian gods and assumed many of the features of the Greek cult of Chronos.

Sedichias, 65. A sapiential author mentioned by Guillaume de Tignonville in the *Dits moraux*, (pp. 908–911) who has otherwise not yet been identified.

Semele, 62. Semele was one of the many mortal women who were Zeus' lovers. Christine's source was the *Ovide moralisé*. 2:701–810.

Sibyl of Cumae, 100. See note 80 to Chapter 100.

Sidon, 22. The eastern Mediterranean city of Sidon.

Simon, Saint, 32. Saint Simon the Zealot, one of the original Twelve Apostles, about whom very little is known, and not to be confused with the Apostle Simon Peter.

Socrates, 16, 18, 41, 74, 78. The ancient Green philosopher Socrates (ca. 470/469–399 BCE).

Solomon, 1. King Solomon, the epitome of the wise king.

Solon, 50, 70. Solon (640 BCE–558 BCE), reputed as one of the "Seven Sages of Greece," was a sapiential author whom Christine has cited from Guillaume de Tignonville's *Dits moraux* (pp. 923–924).

Temperance, 2. The virtue of temperance, whom Christine calls the sister of Othea, without in fact personifying her further.

Thamyris, 57. Christine speaks of Thamyris, one of the Queens of the Amazons, in the *Cité des Dames* (1:17) and the *Mutacion de Fortune* (vv. 9547–9765). She is previously mentioned in the *Histoire ancienne*.

Thebes, 28, 46, 50. The city of Thebes in central Greece.

Theseus, 3, 27. In classical mythology, a legendary hero of Athens.

Thetis, 60, 71. Thetis was a sea nymph, wife of the mortal Peleus, and mother of the hero of the Trojan War, Achilles.

Thisbe, 38. Thisbe was the young woman who was the lover of Pyramus. *See* Pyramus.

Thomas de Pizan, prologue. Christine's father, Thomas de Pizan, was the official court astrologer of King Charles V.

Thomas, Saint, 28. Saint Thomas the Apostle.

Tobias, 46. A biblical figure closely associated with Jewish sapiential literature.

Troilus, 40, 80, 84, 93. The son of King Priam of Troy.

Trojans, 1, 36, 40, 43, 53,77, 81, 93, 96. The inhabitants of ancient Troy.

Troy, prologue, 1, 13, 15, 19, 31, 37, 43, 44, 60, 66, 68, 73, 80, 81, 83, 84, 93, 95, 96, 97, 98. The ancient city of Troy, from which the French monarchy like to claim their descent.

Tydeus, 46. Tydeus was an early hero Greek mythological hero of the generation prior to the Trojan War. Christine's source for the episode here is the *Histoire ancienne*.

Ulysses, 19, 71, 83, 98. Ulysses was the legendary Greek hero of the Trojan War.

Venus, 7, 22, 56, 60, 65, 73. Venus was the mythological goddess of love.

Vesta, 71. In Latin mythology, Vesta was the virgin goddess of the hearth.

Vulcan, 56. In Latin mythology, Vulcan, the traditional god of fire, was often depicted as a skilled blacksmith who forged a very fine chain-link net to capture his wife Venus when she was cheating on him with Mars. The story is told both in the *Ovide moralisé*, 4:1283–1371, and by Évrart de Conty in his *Eschecs moralisés*.

Zaqualquin, 86. A sapiential author mentioned by Guillaume de Tignonville in the *Dits moraux*, (p. 921), who has otherwise not yet been identified.

Zeno, 36. An ancient Stoic philosopher and sapiential authority, Zeno of Citium (a city in Cyprus) taught in Athens around 300 BCE. Christine is citing him from Guillaume de Tignonville's *Dits moraux* ("Les ditz Rabion philosophe," pp. 924–925).